BAG
A LIFE IN
NOVA SCOTIA POLITICS
MAN

DONALD F. RIPLEY

KEY PORTER BOOKS

Canadian Cataloguing in Publication Data

Ripley, Don (Donald F.)
Bagman: a life in Nova Scotia politics

Includes index.
ISBN 1-55013-477-9

1. Ripley, Don (Donald F.). 2. Fund raisers (Persons) - Nova Scotia - Biography. 3.
Political corruption - Nova Scotia. 4. Nova Scotia - Politics and government - 1970-
1978.* 5. Nova Scotia - Politics and government - 1978-   .* I. Title.

FC2326.1.R56A3 1993   971.6'04   C93-094123-3
F1038.R56 1993

Key Porter Books Limited
70 The Esplanade
Toronto, Ontario
Canada M5E 1R2

The publisher gratefully acknowledges the assistance of the
Canada Council and the Government of Ontario.

Design and typesetting: Annabelle Stanley
Printed and bound in Canada

93 94 95 96 97 6 5 4 3 2 1

To Donald Marshall Jr., who spent eleven years in prison wrongfully convicted of a crime he did not commit and whose treatment the world now knows about, and to the many others whose stories have not been told.

The justice system that mistreated Donald Marshall Jr. and other socially disadvantaged people has not been corrected yet.

Some, who do not know the despair of suffering an injustice, may think rough talk or animosity too coarse, culturally unacceptable, or even unnecessary. But defiance is all the disadvantaged have to sustain their sanity lest the bitterness should consume them.

Author Harold Gloade, my Micmac Indian brother, observed that mistreatment in the name of justice is a disguise for prejudice whether it is administered in Selma, Alabama, at the Hanoi Hilton POW Camp in North Vietnam, or in Sydney, Nova Scotia. Of those who administer "injustice" he said: "Fuck 'em all save seven: six for pallbearers and one to kiss my ass goodbye."

I entered politics with the notion that I could change and improve the system. I accomplished neither.

CONTENTS

PROLOGUE

THE POLITICAL LIFE OF HUEY LONG, FORMER governor of the State of Louisiana, was the subject of books and movies. Politics in Nova Scotia is no less colourful and just as corrupt. Pork-barrelling and cronyism have prevailed. Students of the social, political, and legal systems of Canada and the United States carry on endless chicken-and-egg arguments about which system is worse. Having been able to study both systems firsthand, I suspect Nova Scotia's may look better superficially, but only because it escapes exposure by a press which doesn't have the same kind of protection as that afforded to the American media by the First Amendment of the U.S. Constitution.

Not long ago, judges, prosecutors, and even jailers were chosen in Nova Scotia on the basis of their political allegiance. Those selected were often fools appointed by bigger fools. Incompetence and injustice prevailed.

The most famous, but by no means the only case of injustice in Nova Scotia, and maybe one of the top one hundred injustices in North America, was the wrongful conviction of seventeen-year-old Donald Marshall Jr. in 1971 for murder in Sydney, Nova Scotia.

1

Eighteen years later, a royal commission reported the truth:

> *Shortly before midnight on May 28, 1971, Donald Marshall Jr., a 17 year old Micmac, and Sandy Seale, a 17 year old Black, met by chance and were walking through Wentworth Park in Sydney when they met two other men, Roy Ebsary, 59, a former ship's cook, and James (Jimmy) MacNeil, 25, an unemployed labourer.*
>
> *Following a brief conversation, Marshall and/or Seale tried to "pan-handle" Ebsary and MacNeil. That simple request — the kind most of us have encountered at one time or another — triggered a deadly over-reaction in the drunken and dangerous Ebsary. "This is for you, Black man," Ebsary said, and stabbed Seale in the stomach. He then lunged at Marshall, cutting him on the arm. Although Marshall's wound was superficial, Seale died less than a day later.*

The police at the crime site acted unprofessionally, not securing the crime scene, failing to collect evidence, and ignoring potential witnesses. Sergeant of Detectives John MacIntyre (later Chief of Police) decided quickly that Donald Marshall Jr. had stabbed Sandy Seale during the commission of a robbery. It appeared to the royal commission that looked into the case that the investigation was designed only to seek evidence to support MacIntyre's theory.

Two witnesses, one on probation and the other a sixteen-year-old with a history of instability whose doctor said was prone to inventing stories, gave contradictory statements to Sergeant MacIntyre. Those statements, which the royal commission later reported "occurred as a result of the witnesses accepting suggestions from the sergeant," led to Marshall being charged with murder in June 1971. A few friends and a silent witness knew that Marshall was a victim of white man's justice. Those who could have made a difference failed to act.

The Crown prosecutor, Donald C. MacNeil, a former Tory cabinet minister, may have acquired the position as prosecutor after the new Liberal government came into power because he was an in-law of a powerful Liberal. In the Marshall prosecution, MacNeil did not interview witnesses who gave opposing statements.

Marshall's defence lawyers, C.M. (Moe) Rosenblum and Simon Khattar, who were being paid and who had funds to conduct investigative legal work, interviewed no witnesses.

The judge, Justice Louis Dubinsky, made errors of law, according to the royal commission report: "The most serious of those was his misinterpretation of the Canada Evidence Act which prevented a thorough examination of a Crown witness dramatically recanting his statement against Marshall outside the court room."

Donald Marshall Jr. was convicted and sentenced to life in prison. Ten days later, a witness named Jimmy MacNeil (not a relative of the Crown prosecutor) reported he had seen a man named Roy Ebsary stab Seale. Ebsary's history should have led to his being interviewed by police, but no investigation was conducted. Eventually the Sydney Police notified the Department of the Attorney General of Jimmy MacNeil's claim, and the RCMP were called upon to investigate.

It was then that the first real chance to overturn Donald Marshall Jr.'s conviction was botched. RCMP Inspector Alan Marshall (not a relative of Donald Marshall Jr.) spoke briefly to Jimmy MacNeil, and then chose to accept Detective MacIntyre's version of events, without demanding to see the Sydney Police Department's complete file. The inspector did not interview Roy Ebsary, who was not considered a suspect despite being identified by an eyewitness.

Inspector Marshall's report claimed a thorough review occurred and concluded that Donald Jr. was guilty. The information about Jimmy MacNeil's accusation was not disclosed to Donald Marshall Jr.'s defence counsel.

Then Donna Ebsary, the daughter of the real killer, Roy Ebsary, reported to police that she had seen her father washing blood off a knife on the night of the murder. Sydney detective William Urquhart informed her the case was closed.

In keeping with the bizarre nature of the case, a chance encounter occurred between Donald Marshall Jr. and a witness who claimed that Roy Ebsary had confessed to the killing of Sandy Seale, for which Marshall had been convicted. On the basis of that information, Marshall's new lawyer, Stephen Aranson, reviewed the matter and asked police to reopen the case.

Finally, after ten years, an RCMP investigation was launched, and Staff Sergeant Harry Wheaton and Corporal James Carroll were assigned the case. They also believed Marshall was guilty, at first. But they conducted a professional investigation, and ironically one of the most convincing pieces of evidence turned out to be the knife Donna Ebsary had reported seeing her father washing the blood from, still in the possession of the Ebsary family. Forensic examination proved it was the murder weapon.

Sadly, and despite the competence with which the two RCMP officers conducted the new investigation, Marshall was made aware that he should create a reason for his being in the park the night Seale was killed. Wise to the system after eleven years in prison, Marshall understood the suggestion that he should admit his intent had been robbery, which clearly was not true.

The story did not end there, with Marshall riding off into the sunset, like in the movies. Instead, the forces of justice sought to cover their own trail of incompetence exposed by the professional investigation carried out by Wheaton and Carroll.

According to the royal commission, direct contact by Nova Scotia Chief Justice Ian MacKeigan with then federal justice minister Jean Chrétien influenced a decision by the federal minister which placed Marshall in the position of (still) having to prove his innocence. The system, it seemed, was determined to thwart Donald Marshall Jr.'s chances of being treated with fairness.

And the final insult, after Marshall was freed, was the statement of Mr. Justice Leonard Pace. (Pace had been Attorney General of Nova Scotia when the prosecution of Donald Marshall Jr. occurred, and was later appointed to the bench.) He said: "Any injustice was more apparent than real."

That report — running to five volumes, including studies of the justice system — was produced after the royal commission sifted through 16,390 pages of transcript evidence given by 113 witnesses during 93 days of public hearings in Halifax and Sydney, N.S., between 1987 and 1988.

The key line of the opening paragraph of that royal commission report is: "The criminal justice system failed Donald Marshall Jr. at virtually every turn. . . ."

It would be more accurate to say that the system did not merely fail him, but it shafted him by intent. The report continues: "The tragedy of the failure is compounded by the evidence that this miscarriage of justice could — and should — have been prevented or at least corrected quickly, if those involved in the system had carried out their duties in a professional and/or competent manner. That they did not is due, in part at least, to the fact that Donald Marshall Jr. is a Native."

Despite the royal commission's findings, not one person responsible for the atrocity was ever charged or disciplined. Two people were demoted, and one of them eventually received a golden-handshake settlement.

Anyone who believes that the Marshall case was an aberration is mistaken. The justice system in Nova Scotia has traditionally worked well for the white, rich, and well connected. The socially disadvantaged suffer under that system of the politically appointed old-boys cronyism.

I learned about justice Nova Scotia–style when I was still a child legally and physically. The experience resulted in my leaving Nova Scotia, armed with the total commitment to oppose all forms of injustice in every way I could. I never intended to live in Nova Scotia again.

One evening, when I was fifteen, I was walking along Kentville's Main Street with three pals. We were heading home from Sunday-night services at St. Paul and St. Stephen United Church. As we approached the drugstore on that warm May evening, a scuffle involving four military police (provost) from Camp Aldershot and a small Native soldier was taking place. It was obvious that the little guy was drunk, outnumbered, and overmatched by the four big meatheads trying to apprehend him. Fists, boots, and knees were applied to him without mercy. As we approached, I was overcome by the sight of his bleeding nose, cut lips, and inability to ward off the cruel blows. He was a drooling, senseless mass, almost unconscious and able to resist only in spirit, with the pride and stubbornness born of the Indian experience of mistreatment at the hands of white people. I was moved by my emotional response and the fact that no one else lifted a finger to help him.

I acted instinctively, without a plan, without hesitation, and without pausing to discuss the action with my pals. I commanded the approximately 700-plus pounds of sweating, cursing, brainless provost hulks to cease and desist or shoot him to end it quickly. Seeing my 170 pounds in a second-hand brown suit snapping at them was unlikely to have instilled much fear. Later it was said I inflicted a sting or two before I was badly beaten and dumped unceremoniously in the town jail. I was left for the night to fight off an old prisoner who had obviously acquired a fondness for young men in his years behind bars. His impending trip to the penitentiary for murder made him no less amorous. In the jail's bull-pen, a big local man, whom I knew, socked the old guy senseless as a not-so-subtle message to leave me alone. The civilian night constable threatened to beat me if I complained of the incident.

The next morning I was publicly paraded with other adult inmates up Cornwallis Street in plain view of dozens of my neighbours. The town's chief of police, John Brown, who was widely admired and deemed a "wonderful man," delivered me to the stern magistrate known by the street name of "Goat" because his white receding hairline made his head look a bit like that of a goat, both in shape and structure. Bail was set at an amazingly high $3,000, $100,000 or more in today's dollars. It took my father all day to raise the staggering sum from friends, to keep me from spending the week before my trial in the lousy Kentville jail. At my trial, held in Magistrate Goat Chase's personal law office, I was charged with everything but the Riel Rebellion. I was found guilty without being given an opportunity to speak, fined $60 that we didn't have, and given a stern lecture by the Goat. My father borrowed the $60, plus court costs of $9. The question then and now remains the same: "How come Mr. Chase prosecuted and was also the magistrate and the judge?" I told a lawyer about that incident forty years later, and he would not believe it had happened until the old papers were dug up to prove it.

Extensive observation of that old system of Nova Scotia justice, generally acknowledged to be rotten, has shown it to be like playing baseball with an umpire who is either a crony or a relative of the coach of the opposing team. The same chief of police and magistrate held a "scare" session in his Kentville office for the offspring of a prominent family, who was caught stealing from a car. It was deemed that he was a "good boy," and should not be charged — only scared "straight." They didn't scare me, but they inflicted a scar on both my lip and soul which has lasted over forty years.

Following my release from jail, a girl who worked at Maritime Telephone as an operator told me she overheard town policeman Sonny Smith laughing about my case, while spending his night tour of duty in the telephone operators' lounge. I had also been told that Smith's cousin, Crowell Rosco, who has since died, had beaten prisoners at the Kentville jail. My youthful idealism prompted me, one day, to tell those facts to the town mayor, who used to watch our baseball workouts at the town's ball field.

On the evening of the day I had enlightened the mayor, I was in my bedroom at the old Salvation Army duplex where we lived, listening to a major league ball game on a small radio. I heard the old-fashioned manual-twist door bell and started down to answer it. My mother, wiping her hands on her apron, said she'd look after the door. I sat at the top of the stairs, just out of sight of the front door, and was petrified to hear Chief of Police John Brown as he stepped into our living room. He made it clear, in spades, to my mother that any further mention of Constable Smith would result in jail for me. He said that I would "have troubles she couldn't imagine." I grew up fast, knowing that the system had the power that always screwed you. Native people in Canada all know that, and only cases like Donald Marshall Jr.'s will expose it.

I was born a Liberal. I became disillusioned with the party after Gerald Regan was elected Premier of Nova Scotia in 1970. I left politics, thinking I would never suffer that disease again.

But my mother's brother, George Brison, an aspiring Tory leader named John Buchanan, and a rich insurance broker named Ted Crease enticed me back into politics: I became a turncoat to Toryism, and worse, a fund raiser on their Finance Committee. I told them they were letting a born Liberal fox into their financial hen house.

At heart I am a revolutionary who believes in social justice: not socialism; but a fair deal for people who are socially disadvantaged. Not many people in public life really believe in social justice, not even the members of the people's party: the NDP. Nova Scotia's NDP leader, Alexa McDonough, proved that to me twice, once on a matter of patronage and once on a personal matter. On one occasion she kept quiet about a stinky real estate deal and another time she ignored an injustice because she did not like the persecuted person.

I returned to politics filled with idealistic ideas about changing the justice system, improving education and retraining programs, and making an impact on aboriginal or native rights issues.

Buchanan's trust in me provided me with twenty years of insight into his personality, his unbelievable political addiction, and his personal agony about his financial turmoil. Buchanan's head was never turned by power but in the end he was a disillusioned man. He was especially distressed by the new Tory Premier Donald Cameron's decision to call the RCMP in to investigate his embarrassing financial mess and the blind trust which had been set up for him.

The story is the players: the companies and the people who seek favours as well as the few idealists who fall by the wayside. The friends of the players are often as interesting as the game itself. This book reveals the dark side of partisan politics which never changes from party to party because human beings never change.

I helped create a community college system, a weak attempt at home nursing care, and a poor excuse for improvements in the justice system. I helped design the Nova Scotia Municipal Finance Corporation to help municipalities borrow funds in an efficient manner. I accomplished very little when these few victories are measured against the idealistic dreams I started with.

This book may help show the public that politicians are like those who elect them: imperfect, greedy, sad, sometimes even lovable, but never dull.

PART 1

THE STANFIELD AND REGAN YEARS

1956 – 1978

1

CHANGING THE GUARD

THE LIBERAL PARTY HAD GOVERNED NOVA SCOTIA FOR twenty-three years, from 1933 until 1956. Jobs on the roads, in the liquor stores, at provincial institutions were doled out to party supporters. Even apple inspectors were political appointees. If the Liberal party had not grown so greedy and callous they might have survived the death of their leader Angus L. Macdonald. But a party religious squabble and arrogance did them in.

Before the 1949 provincial election, the Tories, who held no seats in the Legislature, had chosen a sleepy-looking lawyer named Robert Lorne Stanfield from Truro, N.S., as party leader. While his family name was well known because they manufactured reliable under-wear, Bob was not considered a flashy guy, and certainly not a threat to the Grits. The Liberals said his chances of winning were like the "Chance Brothers": Slim and No.

I learned about party politics long before that. The power of office put bread on the table and could take it away. My grandfather had once failed to toe the party line while working on a government dyke project during a provincial election campaign. He dared to say that the government should be thrown out, and despite the fact that he was supporting seven children, they fired him.

After the election, the same bunch were back in office, and when election fever cooled they realized they needed him for his knowledge of how to build tide-proof dykes. A ward boss was dispatched to see him at the family house. He said to my grandfather, "Freddie, if you'd just say you were wrong and apologize, we'd take you back, and you need the work." Grandfather spat tobacco juice a hair's breadth from the man's foot and replied, "I never needed anything that gawd-damn bad."

Party allegiance in Nova Scotia was often predicated on bitter memories like my grandfather's. When they finally got in office, some sought revenge. They would not think twice about firing a political opponent, because long lines of supporters were waiting for their turn at the trough. Those were the rules.

It was that kind of partisanship which caused the Tories to be eager and the Grits to underestimate Bob Stanfield when times and population demographics were changing.

Bob Stanfield started with no seats in the Legislature. The premier, Angus L. Macdonald, had just returned from a wartime stint in Ottawa to reclaim the premier's chair. Mr. Macdonald had come along at the depth of the Depression in 1933; many people who were struggling for mere existence had voted for him, hoping for an improvement in their lives. Macdonald was a brilliant and cultured man who understood the frustration, suffering, and hopelessness in the hearts of Nova Scotians during the Depression. But by 1949 Macdonald was growing older, and some of his ministers had been around for too long. Burdened by a political party considered greedy and ministers who were unenthusiastic and spent, Macdonald died of heart failure in 1954.

Harold Connolly, a trusted cabinet minister, assumed temporary command of the premier's office until a leadership contest could be called. The party had an unwritten rule that the religion of leaders alternate. Macdonald had been a Roman Catholic, so it was expected a Protestant would be chosen as the new leader. Protestant Rhodes scholar Henry Hicks was a candidate, and so was the Catholic interim premier, Harold Connolly. The leadership race deteriorated into a religious battle on a scale that is hard to imagine in the 1990s. Hicks won, but the scars, and the subsequent conduct of his government, which grew more inept, arrogant, and unresponsive, set the stage for Stanfield to upset Hicks's Grits in 1956.

Stanfield built rural district high schools, paved roads, and attempted to attract industry to Nova Scotia by establishing a body of leading Nova Scotians in an agency called Industrial Estates Limited. His government's subsequent provision of medicare for Nova Scotia created a following for Stanfield that made it unpopular to bad-mouth him politically or personally. Industrial Estates had some notable successes in attracting industries to Nova Scotia. Among these were Michelin Tire of France, Canada Cement, Harding Carpets (later a problem), Huyck Canada, and Volvo from Sweden. Later, the failures, government waste, mistaken grants, gifts, tax concessions, and foolhardy investments would become better known than the good deals. The poor deals included a failed heavy-water plant in Cape Breton, Deuterium of Canada; a strawberry farm in Digby County; and one of the most controversial, Clairtone Sound. That company, headed by a man named Peter Munk, received investment funds from the province several times, even after its credibility had declined. The shares of the company traded on the stock exchange, and the Province of Nova Scotia got in deeper and heavier because it was hard to say no to the charming Munk, who was building television and stereo sound systems in Pictou County.

In the spring of 1967, the government of Robert Lorne Stanfield was still immensely popular. Nomination meetings in those years saw tougher fights than actual elections because Stanfield, and the right to be a "Stanfield man," gave an aspirant a better-than-even chance of winning a seat. The Liberal party was deeply in debt, despite a trust fund that had been built up over a period of years by people who knew that a party not in power would have trouble raising money. Old scars from the Hicks–Connolly fight and selfish interests still had not been erased or forgotten. The Progressive

Conservative Party, on the other hand, was rich, with more than $400,000 in savings and a financial organization which did not have to do much more than write letters on stationery bearing a picture of Stanfield to raise money.

In some ridings, the strength of the Stanfield image and the local "Stanfield man" kept scores of first-rate Liberal candidates away because it was almost certain that a drubbing awaited them.

Stanfield called the election for May 1967, and a smouldering rumour spread through Nova Scotia that Stanfield would run, win, and then resign to seek the Progressive Conservative federal leadership, which would be up for grabs in Ottawa in the near future. Stanfield remained quiet on the subject for some time, but then, looking his low-keyed, droll, and straight-faced best, he had to deal with the rumour. Stanfield issued a statement to the effect that he would "about as soon take up ski jumping as go to Ottawa"; he probably believed it at the time.

Stanfield's machine won big, despite the rumours. His lopsided victory might have been a potential danger to the career of the new Liberal leader, Gerald A. Regan, who managed to inspire the election of only six Liberal MLAs, including himself. But Stanfield was moving on.

2

THE CORPSE AT THE FUNERAL

DONALD (KEYHOLE) REID GREW UP NEAR GERRY Regan in Windsor, Nova Scotia, and told "Regan stories" even before Gerry became the Liberal leader. Keyhole, who got his name in a very unusual way, was a good hockey player and, although Gerry wasn't, he loved sports. Reid said Gerry was the only guy he knew who was so frugal he could start the week with a dollar and end up with a dollar-ten just by osmosis. Reid borrowed the old cliché and said to Gerry, "If you went to a funeral, you'd have to be the corpse to get all the attention." Gerry topped his line, and said, "No, I'd sooner be the undertaker and get all the money."

Gerald Regan broadcast sports events, and brought in professional teams to play exhibition games after they were eliminated in the regular NHL season. One year Regan lined up a team of National Hockey League players to play an exhibition game in Digby, Nova Scotia, on a natural-ice rink. Typically, he waited until the last minute to work out the details. According to his advance advertising the

NHLers would play a team of "Nova Scotia Senior Allstars." The promise of $10 and a borrowed hockey sweater was little enough according to Keyhole (who was one of the Allstars) but the discovery that all ten hockey players and all their gear would have to travel to Digby in only two cars was worse. Sadder yet, the so-called Senior Allstars, all boyhood pals of Regan's from Windsor, found out only at departure time that both cars had been borrowed from the two local used-car dealers on the pretext of being try-outs. Mo Smith, one of the most accomplished players, had been given an extra two dollars to drive the oldest klunker. Keyhole said, "Mo was more frugal than Gerry, who could live on a greased rag." Munro MacDonald, another player, said, "No, Gerry would rent the rag to somebody." The cramped drive to Digby was done on a strict conservation basis, as the two cars had to save gas by coasting down all the hills.

Gerald Regan is the son of the late Walter Regan, a frugal Windsor landlord and entrepreneur of Irish descent. Gerry's mother, Rose, a small princess of a lady, was the religious inspiration of the family. Gerry had always been destined for glory of some kind, and those who knew him, like car dealer Richard Taylor, realized early that Gerry would make a significant mark and be well known. In high school, he had a large circle of good friends; worked at making money; and was academically able, getting good marks with little apparent effort. Gerry came from a Tory family and in one election worked for the Progressive Conservative candidate. Once, when he was young, Premier Angus Macdonald visited Windsor and, in the course of meeting Air Cadets, he inspired young Gerald to announce that one day he, too, would be Premier of Nova Scotia. As the Liberal era of the 1930s and 1940s petered out, Gerald Regan ran in his first provincial election for the Liberals in 1956, losing in Hants West. When he married a beautiful Saskatchewan girl, Carole, whom he met at a political event in Ottawa, he found himself supported by a real political activist. She was the daughter of a federal Liberal MP and was well acquainted with the duties and demands of public life. Gerry left university at one time and worked as a radio sportscaster and sports promoter before putting himself through law school. He ran twice more provincially in the "down-swing Liberal era" and then twice federally, before successfully winning one of the dual-riding seats in Halifax in 1963.

The provincial Liberal party was at its lowest ebb then. Earl Urquhart, a lawyer and MLA from the Canso Strait area of Nova Scotia, had succeeded Henry Hicks as leader and had been steam-rolled by Stanfield. Urquhart was an honest man, but he lacked lustre, even compared with the dry but witty Stanfield. Once Urquhart, tripping over a mixed metaphor, threatened "to take his gloves off and give it to Stanfield with both barrels." Stanfield countered by saying, "I'd be more afraid if I understood the threat."

The Liberal party was always promoting and teaching young men, like a major league farm system, to ensure a future cadre of fresh new members in the party. Peter Green was only one of the young Halifax Grits involved in the Liberal party with lawyer David Mann, Michael Kirby (now a senator), and many others. The young man who would be most responsible for the Liberal party renewal was lawyer R. MacLeod Rogers. He was the son of a federal Liberal cabinet minister who had been killed in a plane crash. When young Rogers sought the party presidency in 1965, he set in motion events and people who would produce success at the polls in only five years; yet he would receive almost no credit for that remarkable turnaround.

In 1965, Mr. Urquhart decided to step down as leader. Halifax Liberal lawyer Robert Matheson announced that he would run. Matheson, a war hero and a respected family and community man, had a good chance to succeed. His credentials, ethics, and image presented Stanfield with a candidate much like himself, but a tad more charismatic. Matheson's campaign was promoted by his former partner Leonard Kitz of the legal firm Kitz, Matheson; Kitz was also a former Halifax mayor. Lawyer Peter Green, an ambitious and sulky young Turk of the same firm, managed Matheson's campaign.

Gerald probably already had provincial political ambitions when he went to Ottawa in 1963, but he concentrated on enhancing his image and reputation. He made connections, showed an ability to attract attention to himself, and was frequently found at the front of events — all of which amplified his popularity.

Regan arrived at a Liberal meeting, held at Saint Mary's University in 1965, with popular federal MP J.J. (Joe) Greene (called the sage of Renfrew, Ontario), and promptly set about asking "How would I do in the provincial leadership race and would you work for and support me?" The response must have satisfied him because, the following morning, at the general meeting of the provincial party, Regan, when introduced as the federal MP from Halifax, took the opportunity to announce, amid loud cheers, his candidacy. Regan, then thirty-seven years old, and his growing number of campaign workers spread out across Nova Scotia and absolutely outorganized Bob Matheson. Gerry's considerable ability and tireless efforts could be seen in every facet of the growing campaign. The teas, coffees, lobbies, travel, and arm twisting culminated in their arrival at the three-day convention, with Matheson's hopes of becoming leader fading fast.

Gerry Regan, unaffectionately known to the Tories as "Gabby Regan," outplayed the other leadership hopefuls and was elected leader. Matheson made the usual political request for a unanimous motion to support the new chief.

One of the strengths Regan displayed lay in healing the wounds of the past; he won over Matheson's campaign people, notably lawyer Peter Green. His childhood pal Gordon Hughes and Halifax stock-broker William (Bill) Ritchie were eventually absorbed into his organization. Gerry next brought Garnet Brown into the executive as president, and attracted A.I. (Irv) Barrow (later a senator who would have police troubles), Valley federal Liberal John E. Shaffner (later lieutenant-governor), and many wealthy Halifax people, including National Sea Products executive Charles MacFadden and fund-raiser Bill Simpson, who was known privately as "Suitcase Simpson" for his abilities to pry money out of less-than-enthusiastic donors.

Gerry had no seat in the provincial Legislature, and there was apparently no safe Liberal seat among the few the Grits held. For him to allow an MLA to resign for a by-election was too risky, so he managed the opposition from the gallery and continued to organize his forces. He resigned from his federal seat in Ottawa and moved into a house on Berlin Street in north-end Halifax. That seat was historically Liberal but was then held by popular Tory Jimmy Vaughan, who had managed to win the seat for the Conservatives by holding on to Robert L. Stanfield's coattails.

To get any candidate to run and face almost certain defeat was a test of Regan's powers of persuasion. He was equal to the task, as he recruited former university chums, ego-driven political aspirants, and even Bob Matheson.

Nova Scotia Grits faced a government that had been responsive and had done things. Liberal candidates did not stress Gerald Regan's leadership as a campaign asset because the Tories had been successful in depicting him as mouthy, erratic, and untried when compared with their steady man, Stanfield. It became obvious that the Liberal rural campaigns were fragmented, each seat featuring an almost independent Liberal. The leader's name and image might not have existed.

Victor Cleyle, a pal from Saint Mary's University, was a community leader in Kentville, Nova Scotia, whom Regan convinced to enter the fray. His prospective opponent in the constituency of Kings North was the powerful Tory member and former mayor of Kentville, Mrs. Gladys Porter. There was little doubt that she would win, even if she never left her home. She died suddenly, however, and the Tories had to scramble for a candidate. Mrs. Porter's constituency president, lawyer Victor N. Thorpe, known as a peacemaker and a very accommodating person, was chosen to be the Conservative candidate. It was against a 2000-plus Tory majority, in a small seat of slightly more than 7,000 voters that the two Vics, Cleyle and Thorpe, squared off. It was obvious that Cleyle was running uphill, but it was just as clear that he was making progress, and Thorpe started to run harder as he became aware of the danger. In that election, the Liberals picked small, local issues as the grounds on which to attack the government. One annoyance in Kings County was the Band-Aid-sized 1967 licence-plate sticker the provincial government sold that year instead of issuing new licence plates. At $48, the cost of the little sticker seemed an outrage. In Kentville, the Grits ran an ad, saying: "The 1967 license sticker is no bigger than a band-aid; for a better deal, vote Cleyle." When it was over, Thorpe won, but the Porter majority was cut to 764 votes. Cleyle had done well, and many believed he would win next time out.

Gerald Regan travelled night and day, campaigning door-to-door, in 1967 to get elected in Halifax Needham, while also preparing television, radio and newspaper material for the party in general. He could see his two problems clearly: he had to win in Needham, and he needed more depth in his organization. He recruited hundreds of people to campaign with him. He pounded on doors, on the theory that many door bells don't work and a knock is hard to ignore. His hands swelled badly. His wife, Carole, knocked on doors too, and did it in the toughest parts of a low- and medium-income district. Doubtless, she won his seventeen- or sixty-seven-vote majority (arguments continue about its size) in the contest in which he fought for his political life.

It was abundantly clear in the days and weeks following the election that Gerald Regan's leadership of the Liberal party had received a less-than-enthusiastic endorsement. There were rumbles of discontent and, despite his personal victory, Regan was in worse shape with the party than he had been before the election. Nevertheless, after the vote, Regan was up early every day, starting on a plan to reorganize. It was important to get all offices and positions in the party populated with his own people and to raise money for the party; however, he discovered it is not easy for the opposition to raise money. Those who make the big donations, those who need to stay in favour with a government, do not waste money on a half-dozen, ragtag members of the opposition.

Gerry's old tennis pal from Ottawa, maverick Tory MP Pat Nowlan, told Gerry not only that he couldn't play tennis but that he couldn't beat Bob Stanfield — ever! Regan also had known Pat's father, the Honourable George Nowlan, and appreciated their humour. Pat and Gerry both told stories on themselves. One Nowlan story was about an incident which took place in Kentville. According to Regan, Pat's father, George, was campaigning for the 1963 election, which everybody knew would be tight. Along the sidewalks of Kentville, at Lenihan's Corner, he saw a well-known Liberal supporter and town character, Earl Arenberg, rocking back and forth on the heels of his oversized work boots, with his thumbs stuck in the fireman's suspenders holding up his jumbo-sized Humphrey work pants. The trousers stood off his hips like a pair of big hockey pants. George thrust his hand out and Earl shook it politely. George said, "Listen, Earl, how 'bout help'n me out this time?" to which Earl, who was supposedly a little slow, gave the answer, "Damn sure, Mr. Nowlan, I'll help ya out, 'cause there's no damn way I'd help ya get in."

But Pat Nowlan's appraisal of Gerry's chances of winning was not accurate. Time, circumstance, and fate, aided by some crafty old Halifax Grits, were to cause a lot of changes.

Gerry Regan was not considered one of the better-dressed men in Canada, in Nova Scotia — or even in Scotts Bay. He had one or two shiny, depressing suits; several deadly tired or sick-looking neckties; shirts with paper-thin, dingy collars; and run-down dirty shoes; and he always seemed to need a haircut. Halifax accountant Irv Barrow, Bill Simpson, and Garnet Brown decided to spruce him up. They took him to Montreal, fitted him properly in dark, flattering suits that didn't shine or sag, bought ties that probably cost more than his old suits, and put good shoes on him. On top of that, they arranged for a Halifax barber to style and clip his almost unmanageable hair.

The "new Regan look" was launched, and he got his first break when Bob Stanfield announced that he would seek the federal Tory leadership.

3

THE SKIDS ARE GREASED

WHEN THE PRIVATE-SECTOR OWNERS announced that they would close Sydney Steel, the Nova Scotia government took it over and, in a desperate attempt to protect the economy of Cape Breton, bought the heavy-water plant there. The plant was a white elephant which had grown rusty and devoured public money without any production ever taking place. Federal Liberal MP and cabinet minister Joe Greene, a pal of Gerry Regan's, announced in Parliament that a sign should be placed at the rusting heavy-water plant, saying: "Bob Stanfield slept here." But by then Bob Stanfield was no longer the political boss in Nova Scotia, and in the public's opinion the new premier, G.I. Smith, had inherited the government's failures.

By 1969, Premier George Smith, who was affectionately called "G.I." or "Ike" by his friends, was tired, looked unhealthy, and was taking on more and more of the tasks his associates should have been carrying. Smith's assistant, Joe Clarke (later called "Pugwash Joe" to distinguish him from Ottawa's future Tory leader) was run ragged just collecting the problems brought to him from all over government and the province. Pugwash Joe Clarke has natural ability and a good personality for dealing with public matters, always showing courtesy and effectiveness. He was wise enough to know that the opinion given Regan by a Scotts Bay fisherman was correct: defeat loomed ahead of the Tories, and the "skids" were, in fact, "greased."

Not all Canadians know what Nova Scotians know about politics. Former Nova Scotia Liberal MLA Eric Balcom said that he once in the 1940s was in Ontario during a provincial election. He watched the local poll workers run an election-day centre for a Liberal candidate. Balcom marvelled at the lack of training and experience they exhibited, and told them so. He then showed them how to run a poll. First, he assigned two people to look up phone numbers of those on the voters' list. Then he made calls: "Hello, this is Eric Balcom, an election worker for Liberal Joe Doakes. Can we offer you a Liberal drive to the polls? . . ." Eric said that, in bigger Nova Scotia polls, if the person said "yes" to a Liberal drive to the poll, an appointment was made to pick him up. If the voter said "no," his name was circled and an hour later another Liberal worker would call the same negative voter back and pretend to be from the Tories and ask if the voter would accept a Conservative ride to the polls. If the voter said "yes," it was a fair bet that he supported the Tory candidate. An appointment would then be made to pick that doubtful voter up late in the day. The appointment would not be kept. The intention was to make the voter mad enough to stay home when his ride did not show up, or perhaps, just perhaps, mad enough to go on his own and vote the other way. Balcom claimed that in five out of ten cases the voters' list made available after elections would show that the person had stayed home. That is the politics of Nova Scotia.

In late 1967, in the Nova Scotia constituency of Kings North, the Tories and the Liberals met, after a record-setting spending spree on rum and money during the spring election, and agreed to stop vote buying. It appears that both sides kept the agreement, but as late as 1988, the authorities found evidence of vote buying in two other Nova Scotia constituencies.

After the 1967 election, Gerald Regan and his long-time pal Garnet Brown were off at once, canvassing to build a new organization. Regan found dissatisfaction in the constituencies about the government's industrial program and problems in agriculture and housing, with small scandals cropping up in government departments. Regan, now sporting navy blue suits, shined shoes, and newly trimmed hair, was starting to look like a premier. He made more responsible statements and offered solutions to problems. The Tory government obligingly did its best to shoot itself in the foot.

Several cabinet ministers were ineffective because of age and overwork; one man had a serious mental breakdown, while others were tired and out of enthusiasm gas. The Tory MLAs were bored because their party held so many seats that it was hard to get a time slot in the legislative roster in order to speak on problems. Regan got secret help from a civil servant who named a cabinet minister who had taken a government chair home. Regan exploited the incident as a joke, but the cabinet minister had to resign, and the exposure in the press was an embarrassment for the government. The chair had really been thrown out as waste, but the press ignored that. Another civil servant told Regan about a housing project in Sackville which raised real concerns about the fairness and propriety of the government's methods.

Liberals across Nova Scotia were heartened by the new Gerry Regan. Regan managed to delay a vote by the government on legislation to increase taxes by using an energetic overnight filibuster. Only the blind, the deaf, and those who thought with their hearts could fail to see that Regan would win the soon-to-be-called election. The period was not without its silliness. A Liberal supporter of Regan's named Sweet offered to bet $10,000 that Regan would be premier, saying he personally was helping to orchestrate the victory. One Tory in western Nova Scotia said, "They must be gonna win when their damn fools like that come out of the woodwork." The bet and the prediction were pretty safe. Regan paid no attention to the man, especially after the next federal election, when Sweet was caught putting sugar in federal Tory MP Pat Nowlan's gas tank.

Gerry Regan made two other small changes that helped to create a positive image, as the result of a suggestion given him by a Kentville man. He stopped referring to G.I. Smith as a friendly Uncle "Ike," and also dropped "G.I." Instead, he started calling Mr. Smith plain "Premier George Smith," making him sound very ordinary. The second thing he did was to forbid Liberal workers and all party advertising to call him Gerry. He was to be called Gerald, Mr. Regan, or the Leader; the use of "Gerry," according to Gerry, made him sound un-premierlike.

On the night that a Liberal candidate would be chosen in the provincial constituency of Kings North, Gerald Regan, his wife, Carole, and their new baby, Nancy, came to my house in Kentville for supper before the meeting. I was the constituency president. Regan was to be the guest speaker, and it soon became crystal clear that he wanted to prevent his university pal Vic Cleyle from winning the Liberal nomination again. Regan said, "Vic is Catholic and this is a very Protestant seat, and he's of Lebanese ancestry, which would be a liability in `Waspy' Kings North." (Regan is also Roman Catholic, so there was no bigotry in his opinion.) But his fickle political nature was revealed when he announced his support for a former classmate of mine, farmer Glen Ells. Ells was nicknamed "Elmer Fudd" by people who did not like him, after the innocuous Bugs Bunny cartoon character. He was lacklustre compared with Cleyle, but Cleyle and I had been friends since childhood, so my opinion was more biased.

Regan told me I had to prevent Cleyle from seeking the nomination to avoid a rift which would damage Ells's chances of winning the big election. The discussion became animated. I burned my political bridges with Regan when I refused to intercede against my friend Cleyle.

It is interesting to review Regan's opinion of Cleyle now that more than twenty years have passed. Vic Cleyle's first cousin is Joe Ghiz, who later became premier of "Waspy" P.E.I., with the same family background as Victor's. But Vic Cleyle was wise enough to see the cards were stacked against him and withdrew before a vote. Ells won the nomination.

Most Nova Scotians probably had their minds made up before the Tories called that provincial election. The campaign may have changed a few votes, but the tally on election night, October 30, 1970, gave Gerald A. Regan a sparse majority government. For the want of a couple of thousand more votes spread across the province, Regan would have won ten more seats. In Kings North, where Regan had engineered the Ells nomination over Vic Cleyle, the Tories hung on by a scant 242 votes. However, as the defeated candidate on the government side, Glen Ells would have more power than the elected Tory opposition member. In fact, Ells would be in charge of patronage, including the government's casual hiring for highways work, the purchasing for various agencies without tenders, and he would have a say in some government board appointments.

Regan's victory present was a trip to Baltimore for the World Series, but first he was to have a very important meeting at the Kings County retreat of defeated Liberal candidate and friend Dr. Clary Gosse. The original purpose of that meeting in the fall of 1970 was for economic and debt experts whose services I had arranged through my employers, Burns Bros. and Denton (now Burns Fry, an international investment dealer), to advise the new premier on financial planning for Nova Scotia. It was, in fact, the prelude to a patronage planning session between party president John Shaffner and the new premier. After I delivered the Burns people to the spacious country residence where Regan was relaxing, and made the introductions, John Shaffner not too subtly instructed me as to when I should return to pick them up. My associates would have no illusions about my role in the halls of power with the new government of Gerald A. Regan: I was a chauffeur.

Later that afternoon, Regan sheepishly phoned me to say that the obvious slight was a surprise to him and was entirely Shaffner's idea. That might have eased my embarrassment had not Shaffner also phoned me that evening from his Port Williams mansion to say that it was Regan's idea. Shaffner claimed that he was told just before we arrived to give me instructions about leaving the meeting.

Shaffner also told me the names of some who would organize the program for the new government and the financing of the Liberal party for Gerald A. Regan. They were: accountant A.I. (Irv) Barrow, known as the "grey eminence"; Shaffner; elected Legislature member A. Garnet Brown; and a famous old-time Liberal money collector J.G. (Bill) Simpson.

Barrow, Simpson, and National Sea Products executive C.R. MacFadden would become the object of national media attention about a dozen years hence, during an RCMP investigation of government and party fund-raising practices.

John Shaffner, who served as president of the Nova Scotia Liberal party in the lean years of Gerry Regan's stretch drive for the premiership, was to be remembered and rewarded by Regan. First, Mr. Shaffner was appointed Nova Scotia's agent general in London at a salary of about $100,000 a year with such perks as a free apartment, a limousine, and a chauffeur at his disposal. Then Shaffner was selected by Regan and federal cabinet minister Alan J. MacEachen for the prestigious position of Lieutenant-Governor of Nova Scotia. Mr. Shaffner's son-in-law William Lewis, who practised law briefly in Kingston, Nova Scotia, was appointed a judge by Gerald A. Regan.

I became a Tory.

4

TO A DIFFERENT DRUM

FORMER PRIME MINISTER JOHN G. DIEFENBAKER WAS A political hero to John M. Buchanan; his influence played a role in the decision and timing of Buchanan's search for his first political nomination. Mr. Diefenbaker had lusted after political office as a successful young lawyer in western Canada. He was defeated several times before finally winning office. The Chief's political ambitions drove him to success when lesser men would have quit. Buchanan recognized Mr. Diefenbaker's failures as Prime Minister of Canada, but he admired the man.

Buchanan came from a Cape Breton family of modest financial means, and as a young man in the late 1940s, he was compelled to respect work and money. One of his aunts was so religiously Liberal that long after he became premier he could never be sure that she voted for him. Although he had not shown any particular interest in public life, it was clear, to his sister Dorothy at least, that John marched to some distant drum and had a quiet, purposeful drive that would take him to the top of whatever career he chose. Buchanan had many friends, kept a dog, rode an old bike, sold newspapers, chased girls, and had many of the interests and concerns of other Cape Breton young people. He was handsome and popular; he walked firmly, leaning slightly forward, as if battling an invisible force while on the way to fame.

Prepared biographical sketches of public personalities seldom capture or do justice to the real person or to what drives them. An examination of John MacLennan Buchanan's life, especially his formative years, is vital to understanding him. A big man physically, he uses almost no alcohol, does not smoke, and is known to be strong willed and occasionally as downright stubborn as the legendary Scot. He is a one-woman man; even in private he has no use for vulgar talk, although he is far from being a prude. Early on, he recognized the value of academic attainments for success, and it was obvious, even during his high-school years in Sydney, Nova Scotia, that he was "going places." At Mount Allison University, he acquired a Bachelor of Science degree, then an Engineering Certificate at the Nova Scotia Technical College. Men like Purdy Crawford, now chief executive officer of the giant Canadian company Imasco, who knew him at university said that Buchanan had an obvious aura of success about him.

According to family, friends, and neighbours, some things stood out about John Buchanan in those early days. His ambition, academic success, and amazing ability to get along with people, even while working through potentially troublesome situations, were remarkable. He could keep negotiations cool and amiable.

He financed his early education by working in the steel mill in Cape Breton, raising the necessary funds for tuition, board, and his modest wardrobe. He once bought a $50 suit on sale and amazed his pals because, on him, it looked good and appeared expensive. He developed a strong sympathy for and understanding of the needs of Nova Scotians from his own experiences. He worked briefly in western Nova Scotia, in Digby, with a national finance company. This experience expanded his understanding of the plight of working people. His stay in that part of the province was most notable for his courtship of, and marriage to, Mavis Forsyth of Bear River. Mavis is blessed with a natural, sincere personality and has complemented and supported her husband's career with her strong people awareness and understanding.

Accepted for law school, Buchanan worked as a stevedore, and then as a timekeeper, for a waterfront company in Halifax. He also sold cars and encyclopedias, working almost every spare minute, mostly at night, to pay for their living and tuition. Mavis was an experienced telephone company employee, so she transferred to Maritime Tel and Tel in Halifax, and worked days to provide a supplement to their income. John joked about their only passing in the front porch for a fast kiss on the cheek as they were coming home from and going to work. Don Hall, an old legal pal who is now a judge, knew of their working and "only passing" in the front porch; he said, "Mavis and John obviously were not passing quickly enough" as Murdoch and Travis, the first two of five Buchanan children, were born to them during that period.

At law school, a delegation of classmates urged him to seek an office in the Student Liberal Party for the purpose of trying to convince Nova Scotia's federal Liberal cabinet great Robert H. Winters to keep the Dalhousie married quarters open. It was known that the government planned to close the apartments, which cost students and their wives a mere $20 a month. Buchanan won the office and, after nagging Winters almost to death, succeeded in keeping the married quarters open for two more years.

Buchanan's ability to listen and comprehend assisted his progress. He displayed little interest in or talent for administration, according to long-time friend Fred Dickson, a future legal and political adviser. Dickson said, "Buchanan has always doodled on paper, jotting down ideas and plans, of which he had a never-ending supply." Upon graduating, Buchanan worked briefly on a political (population) redistribution study. In the meantime, he practised law for a short time with Ralph M. Medjuck, the offspring of another Cape Breton family. Medjuck, Dickson, and Buchanan practised together briefly, however Medjuck was not really interested in the law, but in real estate development. Buchanan was more interested in people law and wanted only to dabble in small real estate deals, so he left Medjuck in order to open his own practice. At that time, other than his brief university exposure to the Liberal party, he had no political interests.

As a result of his work on the redistribution study, Buchanan was invited, by the Conservative party, to meet John Diefenbaker at the Lord Nelson Hotel. Buchanan went to the affair only to see Diefenbaker in person; political allegiance was not yet on his mind. When they were introduced, Buchanan blurted out that he admired him greatly. The Chief gripped his hand; discussed Buchanan's Scottish name, which was displayed on a nametag; and asked what he did for a living. Diefenbaker then took the time to preach a little sermon about the importance of the law and public service through politics. Several years later, during a federal election campaign, John Buchanan again bumped into Mr. Diefenbaker. When they shook hands, Buchanan started to tell the wily old Chief his name and where they had met. Dief said, "Wait — don't tell me —— you're a Scot, you're a lawyer and you should go into politics, your name is ah . . . ah . . . John Buchanan." That started a long friendship. One of Dief's last wishes, which was carried out, was that John M. Buchanan be an honorary pallbearer at his funeral.

Buchanan finally smelled the political flowers, and the perfume was overwhelmingly alluring. Shortly before the Tory nomination in the new seat of Halifax Atlantic, which was where he lived, Buchanan rushed home to tell his almost unflappable wife, Mavis, that he intended to be the Tory candidate. One of the people who made Buchanan's nomination possible was a powerful ward politician named Buddy Williams, who was a convert to Conservatism. Buddy's background and political life are typical of politics in Nova Scotia.

In Nova Scotia, daily decisions at school, in business, and even in social matters are often influenced by strong, inherited political loyalties. Buddy Williams had been born into a strongly Liberal family. Four or five years of participation in the Second World War softened his interest in politics, and he returned to Canada displeased with some public events and with his own lot in life. But that did not immediately change him politically. Buddy used to tell stories about the Liberal chairman in his district, a woman whom he came to call Mrs. Hitler, who dished out petty government jobs, favours, and appointments. She not only didn't do it fairly, but devoted the office to her own and her family's benefit. Buddy said, "I fought Hitler's army for four years, now I'm going to fight Mrs. Hitler," so he joined the Conservative party.

Years later, John Buchanan told, with visible emotion, of visiting Buddy when he was dying in the Victoria General Hospital. Buddy was so partisan that he wanted political people involved in his funeral arrangement. Williams asked his sister and John Buchanan to engage a Tory priest and he asked to be buried in a Tory blue suit with a blue carnation. His wishes were honoured.

Winning the Tory nomination, and later the election, with the help of people like Buddy Williams was not all there was to being a member of the Legislature. Buchanan had to learn protocol. He learned in his first session as a member that discipline in the party system did not include freedom of thought or action.

On one occasion there was a debate about Sydney Steel Corporation. Buchanan had worked in the steel plant as a metallurgical engineer and felt he could contribute to the debate. Unfortunately, he did not bother to clear his intended speech with Tory whip Pinky Gaum, who was also a Cape Bretoner with strong opinions. Buchanan nudged his seatmate, Tory Dr. Mike Laffin, an ex-POW who was so tough he once punched out a Liberal MLA on the floor of the Legislature for insulting his brother. Laffin told Buchanan to jump to his feet as soon as the person speaking was finished and ask for recognition from the Speaker. The MLA speaking sat down, and Buchanan bounced up. Before he could open his mouth, his irate whip Pinky Gaum turned and growled, "Sit down." Laffin pushed Buchanan and said, "Get up." Gaum, furious, again said, "Down." Buchanan was bouncing up and down in a tug of war between two strong-willed Cape Bretoners. Finally Laffin said, "Are you a man or a mouse? Don't sit down for him — on your feet."

Buchanan stood up once more only to meet the steel gaze of his premier who said, in a deadly cold voice, "Sit down and stay down." Buchanan whispered to Laffin, "Pass the cheese."

Buchanan was made Minister of Fisheries by Stanfield, and he used his appointment wisely, as a power base for his undeclared goal. The management of the fisheries portfolio proved Buchanan to be an able person. One of his assets was the ability to gain the loyalty of usually stern, dull, and often obstructionist civil servants. He was able to move projects along, and his staff were willing to pull with him. The public is not usually aware of the not-so-subtle tension that can exist between elected people and government employees, especially with civil servants who have long service under one political boss or who may have opposite political views to those of their elected bosses. They can obstruct and impede all proposed projects.

G.I. Smith once received a complaint from a constituent about a culvert that had been dislodged by a Department of Highways crew ditching in front of his farm. He wanted it repaired or replaced. Smith asked the deputy minister to get the work done, and the deputy nodded but said nothing. Weeks passed and the constituent called Mr. Smith again, complaining. Once more Smith spoke to the deputy minister and asked him if he understood where the problem was located. The deputy said he did. Four or five weeks passed, and the incensed voter called to tell Mr. Smith that nothing had been done and that he was very angry. Smith summoned his stubborn deputy and confronted him with neglecting the task, chewed him out for not acting, and instructed him to immediately write a memo, which Smith wanted to see, instructing the department to fix the culvert. Being shown the memo, Smith relaxed and assumed the matter was closed. Once again weeks passed and the almost incoherent constituent called Smith and dressed him down like a peon. Smith, red with rage, summoned the deputy minister, chastised him for five minutes, and then asked, "Did I not tell you to write the engineer a memo, and you showed me that memo?" The unflapped deputy minister said only "yes." Smith raved on, "Why, then, did nothing happen?" The civil servant looked blandly innocent and said, "Well, I haven't mailed the memo. You never told me to mail it." Eventually the wily deputy was given early retirement, but only after several more elected ministers of both political stripes suffered his obstructionism.

5

TWO NEW BROOMS

THE LIBERALS HAD THEIR NEW PREMIER AND THE handles of power; meanwhile, the Tories got set for a leadership convention to replace G.I. Smith, who had resigned. The new Tory "broom" would not be in place until the convention called for the winter of 1971. Around Christmas 1970, John Buchanan received a call at home from Nova Scotia MP Lloyd Crouse, who is currently Lieutenant-Governor of Nova Scotia. Crouse suggested that Buchanan consider seeking the provincial leadership, and promised his support. Buchanan had not thought of it until then, but he spoke to Mavis. She didn't think he would really consider it. As he talked to people about the party leadership, he soon learned that most people were split in their allegiance between Gerald Doucet, a member of the Legislature, and former cabinet colleague and Dartmouth alderman (and future mayor) Roland Thornhill.

Doucet was a young, highly intelligent Stanfield conscript in the Kennedy image. He had experience from a longer career in politics than either Buchanan's or Thornhill's. Doucet had already formed an organization, recruited campaign workers, and had even chosen his music for the convention — a song written by Gene MacLellan, called "Put Your Hand in the Hand of the Man Who Stills the Waters." Anne Murray had recorded the song, and it was a moving selection. To outsiders, Doucet appeared to be the odds-on favourite to win.

Roland Thornhill was the complete Tory, one who lived for politics. He was in the investment business with Eastern Securities (later Richardson's) and was as well known as Doucet in some areas. Thornhill had strong mainland support and appeared to be only a few votes behind Doucet. He was young, well-dressed, and handsome. Both men had engaging personalities and were very highly motivated.

Throughout his political career, Buchanan would surprise people. He was always being underestimated and, consequently, outperforming expectations. On this occasion, he surveyed his chances very carefully. He consulted his constituency people and received their support. Buchanan, who would not be forty until April 1971, had a thick, tough hide and was able to accept criticism without being crushed. He was willing to ask people for information and seemed to recognize good advice, which he took and acted upon. He was good-looking. But he was not as well off financially as the other aspirants. A shortage of money was always his political cross to bear. Buchanan asked former law partner Fred Dickson to be his campaign manager. Dickson, too busy, turned him down. A press conference had already been called in Buchanan's constituency and he was without a manager. At the conference, the CBC reporter asked about the important post of campaign manager. John blurted out, "Fred Dickson." Later in the day Dickson and his wife, Kay, were home, starting their evening meal, when Kay said, "Come quick! John is on TV announcing his candidacy for the Tory leadership." Dickson sat down just as Buchanan announced, "Fred Dickson is my campaign manager." Kay said, "I thought you turned him down." Fred said, "Jeez, I must've dreamed it." But he accepted.

It was a fortunate choice. Dickson speaks in fragmented, but thought-inspired phrases. He has a complex, first-class mind — it moves even faster than his tongue. Someone once said to Buchanan that Dickson was hard to understand, and Mrs. Buchanan, who was nearby, said, "Oh, you mean the Riddler," and for some people the nickname "Riddler" stuck. Dickson has an uncanny knack of being able to read public opinion and plan effective strategies. He can be evasive, has ants in his pants, and frequently walks off unexpectedly, muttering to himself while he formulates plans. He is bald and looks older than his years. He is a real Buchanan friend and was one of the key players, advisers, and planners for Buchanan from the day he was drafted into the campaign.

The Buchanan camp attracted another lawyer, Joe MacDonald (of McInnes Cooper Robertson), who was known as Little Joe. MacDonald is a perfect complement to Dickson by virtue of mind, personality, and intellect. Known to be frugal in all personal and business matters, he is a political spendthrift too. He and Dickson were pioneers in political polling in the Conservative party. Joe MacDonald was the tactician. They also could both shut Buchanan up, or off, and were not swayed by him when they thought him wrong. Dickson frequently broke pencils when frustrated or angry, and he broke many in his twenty years in politics. He would break a pencil, throw it in the air, turn red, and then cool off as if a lever had been pulled. Then he would make his point again.

One of the very first Buchanan addicts was powerful litigation lawyer David R. Chipman. Chipman was a supporter and loyalist from day one of Buchanan's candidacy. When I first met him in 1971, I wrote this of him in my diary: "I met David Chipman at the meeting too. He is very clever, austere, looks like a movie actor, Jack Nicholson, read us the law on influence peddling, is obviously squeaky clean and won't allow several things which are wrong; he just says they are not to be done. He has a sense of humour but is usually sombre and looks and acts like a damn judge." How true! Chipman ran the Finance Committee with a firm, dictatorial hand, both in opposition and later in the government in power. Chipman later relinquished the chairmanship and eventually fulfilled my diary prediction and was appointed to the Nova Scotia Appeal Court bench by Ottawa.

The leadership race was not very newsworthy in Nova Scotia. The public honeymoon with Gerald Regan's new government reinforced the general opinion that none of the Tory contenders was worth worrying about. As convention day neared, the camps got down to deal making and convention strategy. Doucet looked to have the best chance, and most people agreed that in experience he was number one. He had been a Stanfield cabinet minister at twenty-seven, and cabinet minister for G.I. Smith (in the difficult education portfolio). His masculine good looks and attire were Camelot-age charismatic. Thornhill was also attractive, sartorially splendid, and no slouch in his mental and speaking abilities. These characteristics complemented his strong public image. Buchanan was "one of the people." He was known for working his way through school, practising storefront law, and being well regarded as a person who understood the ordinary guys from the Legion. Conversely, he also was well educated and respected. The initial guess among the convention delegates and candidates was that, with Doucet, Thornhill, and Buchanan on the first ballot, Buchanan would come in third and, according to the rules, be first out. Fred Dickson, a natural political fox, went to Thornhill, knowing full well that the Dartmouth boys figured Rollie was number two. Dickson offered Thornhill a deal whereby Buchanan would go to Thornhill on the second ballot if Thornhill would come to Buchanan under the same circumstance. Rollie agreed.

A Buchanan friend, contractor Ben McCrea, helped set up another coup for Buchanan which would remain controversial for twenty years. The night before the convention, Ben McCrea moved a construction crew into the Forum and built a platform above the seats for Buchanan and his family so they could at all times be seen without straining. Some workers from Doucet's camp raised hell, condemning the platform as illegal and a form of trickery. One of Doucet's supporters came to blows with a Buchanan supporter who tried to protect the platform from opponents who tried to remove it. It played a very important role in the convention.

When Buchanan's men were on the floor with their two-way

radios, Joe MacDonald was in a trailer outside, coordinating them by using TV monitors. Buchanan's people would move within earshot of one of the other candidates' supporters and say, "We just got six from the Annapolis Valley," or "Seven from Cape Breton moved to us." The expressions of confidence (even though they were often just pretending) not only demoralized some opposition delegates and competitors, but also influenced a few to move to Buchanan.

Music and demonstration times were limited, but attention could be manipulated. Buchanan's pal Reg Allen, an elected municipal councillor, secretly arranged for a police escort to bring John Buchanan to the Forum to a great groundswell of horns, noise, sirens, and hoopla. Buchanan's speech went easy on bitter subjects, was strong on modern problems, and concentrated on demonstrating his sincerity. Thornhill made a thoughtful speech, but his subject-matter was too statesman-like and even a little dull. Doucet spoke too forcefully, perhaps overcompensating, because he is normally a soft-spoken, level-headed individual.

It is a matter of public record that on the first ballot on March 6, 1971, Gerald Doucet, as predicted, finished first. His votes numbered 282. To some people's surprise, but exactly as Dickson and Chipman had predicted, Buchanan came in second, with 242 votes, some of which were attracted by Buchanan's speech, the floor troops, and McCrea's platform exposure. The important 30 votes separating Thornhill and Buchanan appear to have been won at the convention and not by the pre-election campaigning. The Buchanan deal with Thornhill was the key factor before the second ballot. Being low man, Thornhill was off the ballot. Thornhill left his seat and walked to the Buchanan platform, shook hands with Buchanan, and raised his arm to demonstrate to all assembled whom he supported on the next ballot. It worked. Buchanan got 391 votes to Doucet's 346 and won the leadership of the Progressive Conservative Party.

The convention set the stage for future victories for Buchanan, as well as career changes, wounded feelings, days of triumph in the political sun, and nights of pain and sadness over the next nineteen years.

6

To the Victors Go the Plums

HEN GERALD REGAN TOOK OFFICE, HE was determined to change a lot of things that had received scant attention from the Tories. He planned to delegate authority without becoming bogged down in logistics, such as trying to draft his own legislation. He also seemed sincere in trying to avoid the petty, greedy patronage seekers who usurp government's time and effort.

As a placating gesture, Regan hired Halifax lawyer Peter Green, who had been a key man in Bob Matheson's leadership race, to write new legislation. Green is not without talent but seems to be a thin-skinned individual, and Regan was reported to handle him with kid gloves. Green did a good job but disliked it. Also his work as a government appointee kept his law firm, Kitz, Matheson, Green, and MacIsaac, from getting government legal business.

Green soon resigned and went back to his firm to practise law. That fact may have received little attention had it not been for a tough old socialist journalist, the late Frank Fillmore, who published a provocative paper called *The Journal*. Fillmore announced Green's departure from government and his re-employment at his law firm. As soon as the firm received its first government work, Fillmore, perhaps unfairly, renamed it "Kitz, Matheson, and Patronage," to draw attention to the allegedly shrewd Green move. Fillmore also printed a political gossip column called the "Ant-Hill," and political people were frequently surprised to see how accurate his gossip could be. He named the new premier "Loud Ant."

The new Liberal government of Gerald Regan had a number of non-elected assistants. He engaged Fred Drummie, a former special assistant to the defeated New Brunswick government. Mr. Drummie had political smarts, but people thought he had an arrogant manner that created votes for the Conservative party. I thought Mr. Drummie was a practitioner of equal treatment for the public: he infuriated everybody, not just those of opposing political faiths. Another Regan assistant, Michael Kirby, a snobbish Dalhousie academic with an obviously high IQ, seemed to display less warmth than Drummie. Kirby's demeanour conveyed the impression that he felt that he was a superior person. John Hickman, a Tory organizer, once said that Kirby had less humility than Muhammad Ali!

Regan had to deal with some political schizophrenia too. It is normal for supporters of political parties to question the political qualifications of other party supporters whom they envy or of whom they are jealous. The most common thought expressed to a party leader and any other supporter who will listen is "What did old So-and-so ever do for us all the years we were in opposition?" Answering their own rhetorical question, they almost always reply, "Not a damn thing." They then revel in relating their own commitment to, sacrifice for, and suffering on behalf of the party and the leader, planting a suggestion of honours due themselves.

Other problems, like ambitious elected members, are a nuisance too. Robert Lindsay, a popular mortician from Windsor, Nova Scotia, was elected MLA for Hants West, Gerry Regan's old home. Lindsay was both the cause and the victim of political paranoia. First, as a successful businessman, he felt that he should be a cabinet minister. Second, he felt that the Halifax bunch, as he called them, had shut him out, refusing to recognize either his ability or his power. Lindsay approached Senator A.I. Barrow, who was widely considered the power behind Gerald Regan. At a social event, Lindsay asked Barrow how he could get into the cabinet. To everybody's amusement, Barrow was reported to have walked over to a dining-room china cabinet, opened the door, and said to Lindsay, "This is your only chance." Ever after, Lindsay was suspicious, antagonistic, and subtly uncooperative. He fought with his own poll workers and highway foreman, and dealt with most issues on his own, not bothering with the niceties of democratic convention.

Lawyer Peter Green, who left government to go back to private practice, told me Michael Kirby upset him, and had similar opinions about Regan's right-hand man, Fred Drummie. Drummie was eventually replaced by Jim Robson, an ex-reporter. Robson was most useful to the Conservative party, who claimed he created a lot of Tories out of Liberals. Regan, in the meantime, conducted the premier's office in the style of the late federal Liberal Robert H. Winters, a Lunenburg native who was in the cabinet of Liberal prime minister Louis St. Laurent. Winters, like a Bay Street chief executive officer, had little time for political matters. He was a good person and businessman, but a lousy politician, and eventually he left politics because the pettiness of hand pumping bothered him.

Political criticisms Regan had made while in opposition were ignored by his own government. One thing he used to complain about was the old Tory government's expensive advertising float in the Parade of Roses, at the Rose Bowl game in California each New Year's Day. Despite the scorn he expressed during the election campaign, he accepted an invitation to be a dinner speaker during the Rose Bowl festivities. He had criticized government waste, but he took a bevy of political and civil-service types to California with him. When he addressed the public function, he glowingly and correctly spoke of that wonderful place which is Nova Scotia. He may, however, have exaggerated a tad as to how great the economy was doing, particularly when his remarks are compared with the gloom he'd described at home while trying to unseat the Tories.

A Tory in Regan's entourage, Ron MacDonald, recorded the "How Great Everything Is in Nova Scotia Speech," and upon returning to Halifax, gave the tape to the opposition. John Buchanan gleefully quoted the speech verbatim. The embarrassment to Mr. Regan and his government was clear, but it was overshadowed by the mad search for whoever had done the taping. Ron MacDonald was discovered and quite properly fired.

The majority of the public doesn't realize the many profitable opportunities that exist for doing business with the government. Loyal political party supporters are not the only people who seek those plums. Shrewd apolitical business people not only know of, but prospect those opportunities with the same care as a gold miner seeking the mother-lode. There are partisans of the party in office, called "The For-Its," and those in opposition who are called "The Agin-Its." Then there are those who try to benefit no matter which party governs (and who are despised by party people) called the "In-Its." No matter who's in, they're in.

I had worked for an investment dealer for about eight years and had been involved in politics for most of my life, but even I did not know what a cash cow it is for the investment dealer chosen to manage a provincial government's debt (bond selling) syndicate. When the Regan government came to power in October 1970, my employers exerted incredible pressure on me to curry favour on their behalf with the new premier. Their antics and weird strategies were ingratiating, demeaning, and nonsensical.

Bay Street men, who normally displayed reasonable judgement and manners, suddenly exhibited the same demeanour as a hyena in heat as they vied for the financial favours of the new politicians in power. A prominent Halifax lawyer, George MacDonald, later had occasion to do business with some Bay Street dealers and said, "I've been kidded about lawyers being greedy birds, but investment dealers are the hybrid of all vultures," to which my own father, who observed the mating dance of my employer, said, "The only difference between an investment dealer and a whore is a whore is honest and more sincere."

The dance of the investment dealer sugar-plum fairies was not limited to my employer. It went on from the night Regan won the election in 1970 until he announced his new bond sales list in about February 1971. That list of dealers, which is advertised in financial publications after each bond deal, is called a "tombstone." It displays the pecking order, from top to bottom, of dealer position with the government, and reflects the number of bonds a dealer is allotted to sell, and the profit earned. In debt syndicates, the dealer who appears at the top as manager also receives an override commission on what every other dealer sells; it is called a "step-up."

Regan floored some in the financial community by picking to be co-debt managers a small regional brokerage house, Scotia Bond Company, which was owned by J. William Ritchie and a Regan school friend from Windsor, Nova Scotia, Gordon Hughes. The Toronto-based firm chosen to work with the local firm was the very uppity, stuffy (and later bankrupt) A.E. Ames and Company. Ames and their officers, employees, and staff dressed and acted as if they got instructions from an 1890s English private school. Tweed suits and funereal neckties were the uniform of the day, as they drifted in and out of Halifax, making huge profits from the province while viewing their co-managing associates at Scotia Bond Company as financial plebeians. Burns, the firm I worked for, landed in a fair position, commensurate with its abilities at that time in its corporate life. The head-office pressure on me to improve that position eventually caused me to accept an offer from another firm: McLeod Young Weir.

Gerald Regan was confronted with the greed of those who aspired to the plums the Tories had enjoyed for fourteen years under Stanfield and Smith. Besides the bonds, there is a very profitable business in meeting the province's insurance requirements. Regan selected the firm of Simpson Hurst, headed by his fund-raiser Bill Simpson, to manage that business and parcel out small fees to various party supporters, some of whom deserved consideration, and some who did not.

The new government carried out the age-old Nova Scotia custom of firing the political employees of the defeated government. While the sanctimonious Tory opposition howled and the press complained, the Regan cabinet passed orders-in-council changing the guard and removing the Tories from the trough. Regan defended the practise by pointing to what happened when Tory leader John Diefenbaker eliminated patronage appointments in the Post Office — it became much less efficient. Regan defended patronage firings because it made it possible to get rid of deadwood.

Sadly, I was to find that all the successful brokerage firms had political departments. The people doing the "sucking up" did not call their job "political affairs," but "government finance." The guys who ran these departments had elastic expense accounts and used the best restaurants, limos, wines, and hotels. It was a Bay Street joke that financial hookers went to call on governments. Our chairman said that one European company provided a female companion who was listed in the trade as an adviser. She was extraordinary in appearance and a desirable companion. It was said she could straighten out even the dullest government person's psyche.

The chartered banks, at that time, did not control the investment dealers who did the lucrative financing for the provinces, in either domestic or foreign markets. It was different dealing with the banks for political donations. They were more discreet in their business pursuits. A bank officer, conveniently unconnected to either the political process or the personal-accounts side of business, always made a pitch for the desired government business at a dinner or social event or in a casual encounter. Once a senior Bank of Nova Scotia official pitched John Buchanan at the head table of a function where more polite people might have shown some restraint.

The U.S. syndicate for Nova Scotia bonds had once been headed by Bache (later Prudential Bache), but under Regan, Scotia Bond Company, which did not even have a New York office, was placed high in the management list of the province's U.S. syndicate. All political people and civil servants enjoy the New York Bond Market closing dinners and Broadway shows, which are part of the festivities following the settlement on a big deal. But the big question concerning the many U.S. bond deals from 1971 until 1978 is whether they were justified in terms of market savings on interest rates. At the time, they may have seemed good, but subsequent changes in the value of the U.S. dollar compared with the deteriorating Canadian dollar establish the possibility that millions of dollars were lost on foreign exchange. It does not take an MBA from Wharton or Harvard to figure that out. Money is lost if repayment costs more in U.S. dollars when the loans come due. Despite the recent improvements in the value of the Canadian dollar, the loss to Nova Scotia has been staggering. One example of a serious loss on foreign exchange is the Bridge Commission's borrowing to pay for the MacKay Bridge. The province, under successive governments, has done its financing in foreign currencies. It sounded good to say money was borrowed at between 2 3/4 and 8 per cent interest when these deals were done, but world currencies fluctuate. No one can guess what the German mark will be in comparison with Canadian or U.S. dollars five or ten years from now, when it's time to use Canadian dollars to pay the money back. The foreign currency may cost more to repay than the lower interest rate saved the province when the deal was done. To save money on interest rates, the province risked currency fluctuations, and these are recorded as a loss on the province's books; the book loss is awesome.

Foreign-exchange and capital markets are a complicated speciality, and elected people, even lawyers and civil servants who think they know and understand everything, are often not qualified to experiment in that area. Some of the much harped-on outstanding provincial debt came about as a result of foreign-exchange losses.

Trips to London or New York were not without some humour though. On one trip to close a U.S. bond deal, the usual cocktail party and dinner took place. During both events, the main topic of conversation was the serious pickpocket situation overrunning the city at that time. Every New Yorker had a story to tell about someone having his pocket picked. The boys from Nova Scotia listened, probably thinking to themselves how lucky they were not to have a pickpocket problem in Halifax. Filled with good drink and food, the provincial delegation returned to their expensive New York hotel for the night.

The next morning, still relishing the good time and alert to pickpockets, several of our Nova Scotian heroes were to ride on the subway from their hotel to Wall Street. Just as the delegation paid their tokens and went onto the busy, crowded subway platform, a tough-looking man in a loud, chequered suit bumped into one of the civil servants. The Canadian was immediately alert, felt his inside pocket, and discovered his wallet missing. He lunged quickly toward the man in the ugly suit, and managed to grab a lapel. The nabbed man, obviously frightened to death, pulled away from the provincial bond guy, and the lapel of his suit jacket tore and stayed in the Canadian's hand. The suspected pickpocket ran and escaped on a subway train. All day at the big New York broker's office the story of the visiting Canadian's pocket being picked was told and retold, with the coat lapel being shown as evidence of the event. That night, the boys travelled back to their hotel in the safety of a Bache limo. Upon reaching his hotel room, the weird piece of suit still in his hand, our hero almost croaked when he found his wallet on the bureau.

7

LET THERE BE LIGHT

EGAN AND HIS ASSOCIATES MADE A MOMENTOUS decision at that time and opened a can of worms which would eventually contribute to their own defeat. Regan's idea was intended to save householders money and was aimed at the elimination of duplication of effort in power generation and at giving the government control of a vital public utility. Regan's solution was to take over the publicly owned, well-managed, and profitable Nova Scotia Light and Power Company. He used the Nova Scotia government's Crown agency, Nova Scotia Power Corporation, as the takeover vehicle. A.E. Ames and Company, and Scotia Bond, the provincial bond managers, advised the provincial government on the takeover bid and set $13 per share as a fair price. A somewhat circular argument can be carried on forever by factions on the two sides of such an issue, but the $13 price could only have been chosen by Ouija, as no security analyst making use of mathematical precedents could have arrived at $13 a share. When Regan's decision to act was announced, Canada Permanent Trust was named as agent or depository for the shares solicited by the investment people, and for which they would receive a commission. Additionally, the managers of the province's "takeover" would get a managers' and advisers' fee.

The Nova Scotia Light and Power Company was a well-regarded organization. Some shareholders had been part of the firm since people such as Nova Scotia industrialist Roy A. Jodrey (now deceased), and other visionaries, like the MacKeen family, formed the company. The stock had been trading in the $9 range and shot up to $12–$13 very quickly. The Nova Scotia Light and Power people announced a fight to stave off the takeover and sought broker and public support to get the shareholders to vote against accepting the government's bid.

The Halifax brokerage community did business with the families and friends of the people who owned and ran Nova Scotia Light and Power. Many brokers opposed the takeover in deference to their clients and the belief that the government couldn't run it. It was an issue fraught with emotion. Roy Jodrey said, "The government couldn't run a gravity waterfall."

History proves he was correct.

The government could punish brokerage houses who took the company's side by knocking them down in the pecking order and reducing their percentage of the government bond syndicates. As a Halifax broker I was opposed to the takeover. I was walking south on Hollis Street one day, headed for the old Halifax Club. On the east side of the street, as I passed the arched door of the main branch of the Bank of Nova Scotia, I heard a "pssssst." It drew my attention to the big Liberal bagman standing in the archway, just out of the Halifax drizzle. I stepped into the doorway and he told me that I was on the wrong side of the power issue, that Regan was fuming, and that the managers would adjust my firm downward in the provincial bond syndicate after the takeover was complete. Further, he said, when or if my company complained, the government would tell them it was my fault. Angry beyond reason, I walked to the Halifax Club, swearing to devote my life to kicking Gerry Regan out of office.

These were exciting times. The Nova Scotia Light and Power officers made their shareholders' list available to the brokers, and so did the government through their agents, to facilitate solicitation of shares from the listed owners. The massive shareholders' lists were more thought-provoking and informative reading than a pulp novel about Bay Street. There were some strange coincidences in that list. One would not normally expect a staid, old, investor-owned public utility to have large blocks of stock owned by many people other than the founders of the company. The usual coterie of loyal friends and small investors could be expected to have held stock for years. The stock was, after all, a "thin" trading investment. Institutional investors and wise big investors usually avoid stocks unless they trade in big numbers, as they are hard to sell, except during a takeover. It would be unusual to find large blocks of that stock on the market. It would be difficult to acquire without a lot of luck, patience, and possibly inside information. Surprisingly, it turned out that some new shareholders owned fairly large numbers of shares. Some share registrations were reasonably new, which was of particular interest. Large blocks of the shares were held in trust-company numbered accounts, which did not tell the actual names of owners. Some of those accounts, at companies like International Trust in Toronto, had a large number of shares.

An accusation of insider trading would, of course, be a serious charge to make without proof, but the blind-trust accounts should have been looked into. A computer run of dates and participants might have been revealing. John Buchanan and a number of small shareholders called for an investigation. Nothing was done — no media, or regulators could be tempted to investigate the ownership of shares and the brokers who had handled the transactions.

Scotia Bond Company had a salesman at that time who was actively encouraging his clients, Ralph Medjuck and wheeler-dealer Charles MacCulloch, to buy Nova Scotia Light and Power shares. It appeared that he and his firm had been active in the stock. At the insistence of John Buchanan, the broker was called to appear before an official body of the Legislature to answer the kind of questions that flow from such a business matter. He appeared, but his reticence and arrogance shed little light on the benefits he may have caused some lucky shareholders in the stock of Nova Scotia Light and Power to enjoy.

The takeover of Nova Scotia Power Corporation was a *fait accompli!* All the investors did okay on their holdings, but some big, unknown investors made windfall fortunes. An average profit of $3 per share on 150,000 shares made an investor about $450,000, even after paying interest on the money borrowed to pay for the investment. John Hickman, a Mount Allison friend of John Buchanan's and a Progressive Conservative party employee, said that he was sickened by the takeover. John Buchanan said to him, "The case of Nova Scotia Power, and the real cost to the people and the government, will take years to become evident." The 1974 energy crisis and the subsequent rate increases, costs, and controversy came more quickly than Buchanan could have dreamed in 1972. Mr. Regan would be haunted by power and power rate increases, and his government would be blamed for poor judgement as oil prices drove the cost of electricity to householders out of sight in the 1970s.

Gerald Regan, still trying to do big deals for Nova Scotia, was exploiting contacts made with a New York financier named John Shaheen, who was supposed to be very wealthy and have many connections in the Middle East oil patch. Regan talked about building a great Shaheen Refinery in Nova Scotia. Like past Nova Scotia premiers of both political stripes, he had Cape Breton on the brain, so he talked of putting the billion-dollar refinery there. Mr. Shaheen flew in and out of Nova Scotia in grand style. He engaged a luxury liner, and made arrangements with the Regan government's protocol people to invite the social who's-who to a grand event on the vessel, which was to take them on an ocean cruise to the United States. The passenger list was a social register of Nova Scotians. Fortunately for Nova Scotia, a large refinery project in Newfoundland, in which Shaheen showed interest, ran into financial and structural problems.

Mr. Shaheen's attention was diverted to that, and eventually his interest in Nova Scotia waned. Buchanan said that Nova Scotia had enough natural problems in Cape Breton without importing outside troubles.

As an investment broker in the Buchanan camp during the early 1970s, I designed extensive plans for a new provincial body to be called the Nova Scotia Municipal Finance Corporation. Both Buchanan and his adviser, Pugwash Joe Clarke, were very impressed with the idea as a way to assist municipal units in Nova Scotia and save a great deal of money. The plan called for one government-run institution, which would require only two or three employees, to facilitate lending funds under the Province of Nova Scotia's banner to the province's many municipal institutions, counties, and towns. Those municipal institutions were cluttering the market with twenty-five to thirty bond issues a year, and it was obvious that, for example, Inverness County, with a limited tax base, would be required to pay more in interest than the City of Halifax, and would have more trouble selling their bonds. With the Nova Scotia Municipal Finance Corporation, it would be necessary to do only a few bond issues a year and then allow the counties and towns to borrow the money directly from the corporation. The obvious advantages were wider marketability under the province's sponsorship, lower interest rates, and a cleaner market. The Nova Scotia Municipal Affairs Department would still control the amount that a county could borrow, and the initial savings on computer-calculated interest looked to be about $10 million a year to Nova Scotia. Buchanan was so impressed that he told me to offer it to the Regan government's minister of finance. As a *former* Liberal, I had a very difficult time getting an appointment — it took four months and dozens of calls.

The day of the meeting, the deputy minister, stone-faced and sour, entered the small provincial board room probably expecting a scheme involving the omnipresent Arabs and tons of oil money. He refused to invite the minister of finance in to hear the proposal. To give him credit, he perked up when I outlined the idea but refused to listen to the meat of the plan. He said, "In 1972 or even 1982 I don't see any need to do that." The irony is that, in 1980, the same deputy minister was appointed chairman of the newly formed Nova Scotia Municipal Finance Corporation formed by the Buchanan government. His face got very red when he was reminded of his earlier reaction in 1982.

8
THE 1974 ELECTION

I N THE EARLY 1970s, THE MAJOR PROBLEM FACING THE Conservative party was its lack of funds. The situation was never to improve. The finances of the party were in disarray after the Nova Scotia Progressive Conservative Association had lent half a million dollars to the federal Conservative party, who did not pay it back. In 1970, the retiring finance people had no computerized lists, poor records, and no confidence that the party would be in power again in a hurry. The incoming chairmen, David Chipman and E.F. (Ted) Crease, inherited nothing but headaches from the former fund-raisers. The title "Finance Chairman" was the only usable tool they were given. Postage was not funded at party headquarters and the party apparatus was old, worn thin, and unable to provide assistance.

Ted Crease recruited me in July 1971 and assigned me a group of companies which had once been covered by a Halifax County businessman. That man, "Mr. Jones," would not give us his records or lists under any circumstances, even though we met with him several times. We had just about decided to make our own contacts, when Ted Crease asked me to make one last approach. I called Jones for an appointment and was invited to an apartment on South Park Street in Halifax. I was received there by a pleasant man and was served tea by his wife. When I asked for the lists, he was very nice, but refused. I went back to my office and called Ted Crease, who was very disappointed and a little angry. About half an hour passed and Mr. Jones phoned me. I could hardly hear him. He said he was calling from a public phone at the Lord Nelson Hotel. He had just received a call from a woman who informed him that the police were conducting an investigation into fund-raising by political parties and he wanted to dispose of his records at once. He asked me to meet him in the parking lot at the Lord Nelson Hotel and gave me a description of his car. I met him there later, expecting cartons of paper, but he handed over only one thick file before he ran to his car and drove away, leaving me standing, puzzled, in the middle of the lot. Back at the office, I found the file contained a poor list of companies; outdated phone numbers; and the names of executives, many of whom had retired. When I called Crease, he thought the whole thing riotously funny and I teased him about getting someone to call Jones to scare him into giving us his file.

In the past, the practice of political fund-raising in Nova Scotia was tainted by the charging of commissions, called tollgating, whereby liquor companies paid a political party a commission on each bottle or case they sold in the government stores. Chipman and Crease met with John Buchanan, and the three of them agreed that we would not indulge in the practice. We wrote to all liquor companies and promised, on PC Association stationery, that we would not collect a toll, either then or when we got in power. We thought companies would be sceptical, but we were believed. What we proposed to all individual and corporate donors was an annual donation to the democratic process and a special gift in election years. We built a list of contributors by writing letters, visiting corporate headquarters, and establishing a good personal relationship.

All fund-raising is a learning experience, but political fund-raising must head the nutty list. I once had an appointment to meet the treasurer of a major Canadian company in Toronto who was notoriously tough and difficult to deal with on donations. We met at the

Lobby Bar in the Royal York Hotel, and the gentleman was very nervous. I suggested we go to the restaurant next door, but he didn't want to be seen, so we stayed in the dark bar. He ordered Scotch and fumbled around in both his inside suit-coat pockets while mumbling to himself. Finally he slid a cheque for $2,000 across the table, payable to the Progressive Conservative Association of Nova Scotia. He then said, "Oh hell, I gave you the wrong cheque." I said, "No you didn't, it's payable to the Nova Scotia PC Association for $2,000." He looked like he was having a heart attack. He said, "I'm supposed to ask you to promise me that there won't be a toll if you guys get in. If you agreed, I was to give you the $2,000. If you did not agree, I was to give you this other cheque for $500." He was so upset he was almost crying. He said, "But now you've seen the bigger cheque, so I'll have to give it to you." I could hardly keep a straight face. I said, "The letter we wrote you would be a big embarrassment if we ever tried to go back on our word," but the poor man was still upset.

I called on one new account in the Toronto suburbs. He engaged in a long disquisition about how poor business was, how poor his profits were, and how he obviously couldn't give much to an opposition party. He talked on and on, and finally said okay but it would be small. He then asked a strange question: how much had he given my predecessor? I was surprised he couldn't look it up and I didn't know what to say, so I fudged: "How about eight?" I meant $800. He said, "Oh God no, I can only do half that." I said, "Okay." He went out and I heard a cheque machine being used in the outer office. He came back and gave me an envelope which I put in my inside pocket. When I got in the taxi, I looked at the cheque and it was for $4,000. I almost fainted, thinking I would have taken $800 gladly after his "hard times" message. I had the best laugh in Halifax when we looked up the amount donated the year before and found he had given Crease only $500.

One morning, the front page of the Halifax *Chronicle-Herald* carried a report of an NDP speech knocking the usurious rates charged by finance companies. I cut the article out and mailed it to finance companies operating in Nova Scotia and asked for a political donation. The response was so positive, we began to realize that we had not even scratched the surface in pinpointing potential donors. Beneficial Finance had an ad on the radio at about that same time which said, "Toot, toot — at Beneficial you'll get more" and "Toot, toot" became the rallying call for the PC Finance Committee. Chipman would phone and say "toot, toot" instead of "hello."

Gerald Regan's first three-and-one-half-year term passed very rapidly. In the late winter of 1974, he called a provincial election. It was a foregone conclusion that he would win, but the Conservative party helped him by doing everything possible to shoot themselves in the foot. Regan could have won if he had stayed at home.

The Regan campaign was simple and based on few platform promises. A proposal to give each property owner a $143 municipal tax refund was popular and effective. Meanwhile, in the Conservative party, the Advisory Board prepared a massive platform and manifesto. Reminiscing about it in 1990, strategist Joe MacDonald said, "It was a cannonball of confusing points which Regan's Liberals shot back at us, pellet by pellet, like buckshot." The advertising agency for the Conservative party in 1974 included a man named Neima, who has since died. Mr. Neima had an advertising tune prepared for Conservative leader John Buchanan saying, "Honest, it's John for Nova Scotia." It was catchy, cute, and a disaster; it was pumped out over the radio, at meetings, and on television.

One idea which made some sense, as the Conservative party drew close to the 1974 election and realized that there was almost no hope, was to have Buchanan make a helicopter tour of Nova Scotia. The party was broke, but the "Swamis," as a future Tory cabinet member called the Strategy Committee, were able to arrange a free chopper, but without pilot. We searched Canada and the United States and finally contacted a U.S. veteran who had been wounded in Vietnam and who did not know where Nova Scotia was. He quoted a fee of $5,000 because he thought Nova Scotia was a Latin American Banana Republic and he expected to be shot at while ferrying a politician around. The fee and his lack of knowledge about geography should have been fair warning. But a haggled discount in price, the short time left before polling day, and the lure of a free helicopter caused necessity to overrule good judgement, and we hired him. The guy was right out of a Rambo movie. Six feet tall, he was attired in pointed-toed, high-heeled cowboy boots; body-tight stretch jeans; a U.S. Army brass belt buckle; a fancy cowboy hat; combat leather flying jacket; and a Fu Manchu handlebar moustache which hung below his chin. He looked like Cheech the pilot. He flew the chopper like "Charlie" was still shooting at him from the rice paddies. His zigzag course, following highways with no regard for the map, was mind boggling. Buchanan's assistant, Pugwash Joe Clarke, is one of the classiest, most compassionate, and soft-hearted human beings in public life. When Buchanan and his wife climbed aboard the chopper with "Rambo," Joe looked at them with a distraught, almost hang-dog look, which implied, "God, I'll never see you alive again." Buchanan said later that he was so scared on the flight that he would have had a heart attack, but he had to keep Mavis, who was pregnant and air sick, in good cheer so he didn't dare die himself.

In Kings North, Tory MLA Vic Thorpe, whose health and age were taking their toll, had decided after a lifetime of public service to pack it in. There was no doubt that Liberal Glen Ells, a Kings County farmer who came close in 1970, would win the seat for the Liberals. The Tories searched and searched for a candidate to run against him. Lawyer David Waterbury won an uncontested nomination.

Glen Ells, as expected, won the seat and, like new politicians everywhere, in all parties, he had good motives and ideas. But no matter how sound, some plans cause trouble when unforeseen events occur. Ells was sincerely dedicated to ending patronage purchases of coal at the Nova Scotia Tuberculosis Sanatorium at Kentville in his constituency. Ells formed an advisory committee headed by Bill Townsend, a vague political thinker. Ells and the committee were besieged by greedy coal suppliers who wanted the profitable government contract. One big Liberal supporter had sold his business and was trying to land the contract with a mail-box agency. So Ells and his advisers decided to convert the sanatorium's big power-generation furnaces to oil-fired heat. Just as the construction of the new oil heaters started, the wild Arab oil-price rocket took off, and the government was trapped into buying oil. Sadly, not only was it an expensive conversion, but Ells discovered there were even more aspiring oil salesmen than coal dealers.

Following our loss in the 1974 election, there were disgruntled Tories who wanted to dump John Buchanan as party leader. The movement was led by a rotund Pictou County man named Joe Stewart from the constituency of PC Member of Parliament Elmer MacKay. Some people speculated that MacKay was programming Stewart, but that does not seem to be the case. Stewart was a backroom politician who craved power. He was to achieve success in the ownership of several pizza parlours. By nature, Stewart was abrasive and gave the impression that he was an authority on almost every subject. He obviously thought Buchanan was not the right man to lead the party, but this opinion was coloured by the fact that Stewart disliked Buchanan's wife, Mavis.

Joe Stewart plagued and complained about John Buchanan from the 1974 election defeat until 1991, when he was one of the people who gossiped to the press about Buchanan's financial troubles.

Just after our 1974 political disaster, the PC Planning Committee and the party fund-raisers were invited by Ted Crease to the Halifax Club's stodgy old upstairs private dining room for food and tears. We had a brief wake, but we pledged to win the next election. After an expensive brandy, tears were forgotten. We started the 1978 election campaign in all seriousness in 1974.

9

THE GIFT OF THE MAGI

R EGAN HAD VACATIONED AFTER THE ELECTION and had written up a number of flowing scenarios which were loose blueprints for action in possible government situations. For example, he theorized on the Nova Scotia Liquor Commission's being privatized, and the possibility of allowing the sale of beer and wine in grocery stores. That plan failed to take into account that a huge portion of the Nova Scotia government's revenue came from the Nova Scotia Liquor Commission and that political parties had also done well on liquor-industry donations. Regan talked about that idea but never tried to implement it. However, he correctly viewed Cape Breton labour unrest, unemployment, and troubles at Sydney Steel and in the coal-mining industry as problems needing attention. He proposed the name Cansteel for a major modern steel complex, based on what he had seen in West Germany, to improve the Cape Breton economy. He believed that a modern plant would operate world-wide, have competitive ability, and would burn Cape Breton coal; it would supply the miners and the steelworkers with long-term stable employment.

Regan had plans to promote and get help from his federal colleagues on the steel project. He hoped to fund an institution to promote industrial and manufacturing growth, using tax incentives and employment stimulants for the Halifax/Dartmouth metro area. Regan acted quickly to make contact with big companies, at the executive level, because he is a businessman at heart. His success in business while going through law school and the entrepreneurial spirit he displayed as a young man fuelled his hopes for the province. He saw himself as chief executive officer of a business-like government. He contacted Baron de Rothschild in order to exploit the banking firm's world-wide reputation in finance and merchant banking. Regan enjoyed that connection as it supported his hopes and endless talk about "Fundy Tidal Power," which would harness the fifty-foot-plus tides of Nova Scotia's Bay of Fundy and produce home-made, cheap power. He was reported to have more Japanese promoters going through his office than Japan's Second World War prime minister.

Derek Haysom was a South African professional manager, experienced in making steel, and he understood the mining industry. He was capable of dealing with officialdom and had a handle on the "system" — if there is a system in government. The Halifax *Chronicle-Herald*, obviously impressed with Mr. Haysom, often referred to him with a level of respect and admiration which probably had its origins in his social connections. A co-worker described Mr. Haysom in colourful language and said he was typical of many white South Africans in thinking that Canadians, among others, were inferior colonials. Years later, the media in the United States presented Mr. Haysom as the wealthy, retired husband of a Virginia socialite when they were both murdered in a shocking and brutal attack by their daughter and her callous, chemically deranged companion.

The Regan government inherited Mr. Haysom, who was protected by a contract given him by the previous Tory administration. The protective covenants had been created by the brilliant legal mind of the late Halifax lawyer Frank Covert. During the early part of his mandate, Gerald Regan sought to establish an organization, funded by Ottawa and Nova Scotia, to promote, stimulate, and create more prosperity in the metropolitan districts of Halifax and Dartmouth. The government named the resulting organization "Metropolitan Area Growth Investments," which became shortened to "MAGI" from its initials and its objective of lending money. Mr. Regan appointed Mr. Haysom as the president (CEO) and Scott MacNutt, a former cabinet colleague who had been defeated in Dartmouth (city) South during the 1974 election, as vice-president.

Mr. Haysom and Mr. MacNutt were incompatible. The objectives of MAGI were at once an issue between them: Haysom was satisfied to put the money in the bank, read the *Times*, and play bridge at the Halifax Club; MacNutt was an outgoing populist, determined to fulfil the Crown corporation's mandate — to invest money and promote jobs and growth in Halifax County. Mr. Haysom was critical of almost everyone and everything that was considered at MAGI, and because of both his judgement and his personality, several of his fellow workers found him difficult or impossible to deal with. Conflict was brewing from day one.

Robert D. Thomson, CA, a Dartmouth businessman, was selected to be the financial officer. Sponsored by David Hennigar, the local Burns Fry manager, Thomson was academically qualified and had a successful business record. Cast between Haysom, perpetually doubtful, and MacNutt, perpetually cheerful, Thomson was immediately out of sync with the two main MAGI officers, and represented yet a third frame of mind. The board, made up of good local business people, must soon have had doubts about the wisdom of having accepted their directorships.

Scott MacNutt had engaged his former political assistant, insurance executive Kevin Bayart, as investment manager. At MAGI, Bayart had shrewdly invested in various money-market instruments with staggered short-term maturities, and had established good liquidity and a strong cash flow. Mr. Haysom was not happy with Mr. Bayart, who was strong-willed, clever, and, although respectful, as blunt as a brick. With Bayart's improved cash flow on his side, MacNutt appeared at a board meeting and promoted the idea of having a cruise ship, like the "Love Boat" of TV fame, sail out of Halifax to various southward points on the Eastern Seaboard and to the Caribbean Islands. He had made contact with a person who knew of a European ship, the *Regina Maris*, which was described as a bargain and supposedly could be converted into a luxury liner. The objectives were to bring people back to Nova Scotia and to promote tourism, employment, and all the other motherhood ideas politicians adore. The proposal's potential for success or failure is a chicken-and-egg argument even in 1993.

Debate over the cruise ship proposal raged in the board room for a lengthy period. Haysom's volcanic temperament and contrarian personality were turning those who had strong doubts about the ship into supporters of the MacNutt deal. The board, at Bayart's suggestion, invited me to a meeting for the purpose of exploring the possibility of investing cash flow in German marks in case the purchase of the vessel took place. Several times, on cues from the directors, I attempted to explain sovereign risk (currency risk in foreign countries) to those assembled. Mr. Haysom interrupted constantly and, most likely assuming that I was there to make a deal or sell my own idea, was insulting. I closed my file and was about to depart the weird scene when Mr. MacNutt yelled at Haysom, who then rose and stomped out, muttering to himself.

MAGI had found a potential operator for the cruise line in Joseph Nugent, who was running a sea service company located in Dartmouth. Nugent was proposing to call the "yet-to-be-acquired ship" the *Mercator One* after his company, Mercator Enterprises. The funds were invested in marks and the ship was purchased, probably too quickly and without enough expert advice. Although the idea might have had merit, the buying price and the condition of the ship made it too expensive: it couldn't be run and so the initial outlay could not be recovered. What took place next turned it all into a media feeding frenzy. Haysom, furious at being defied by MacNutt, whom he considered an incompetent peon, told the story to a friend. That person made sure the story reached the right press people and also talked to Regan. Even though Regan probably realized that the major problem was Haysom, he responded with atypical vacillation, which amplified the MAGI personality conflict into a major event and seriously damaged the government's image. Scott MacNutt's expense accounts found their way into media hands. The *Mercator One* was nicknamed "Regan's Love Boat," and every political gnat was turned into a hornet by a hungry media.

Adding to the conflict was an internal argument that developed when director David Hennigar complained that all of the short-term investment funds were going to other brokers, while his firm, Burns Fry, was being ignored. Bayart, not one to be moved by hollow promises, maintained a very fair tender process, where only the safety of the instrument and the highest interest rate were considered; Burns Fry apparently did not present the best offers.

John Buchanan listened to, read about, and examined the saga of the *Mercator One*, and, like most of the public, found the deal inconceivable, even without its accompanying gaffs and mistakes. MAGI was spotlighting a government that not only repeatedly shot itself in the foot, but systematically did so in public. Haysom made it clear that privately he suspected MacNutt to be behind the publicity. Kevin Bayart asked, "Was it Shakespeare or John Buchanan who said, methinks Haysom protests too much?" The political lid was off, and subsequently even the most innocent remark about MAGI by the government became anathema; the exaggerated media attention hurt Regan.

10

WHEN YOU'RE HOT, YOU'RE HOT

A S THE SUMMER OF 1978 PROGRESSED, GERALD Regan's government was in trouble. He did not have to call an election, and yet he did so. Maybe public polling showed him a window of opportunity, but, in hindsight, Regan seems to have had plenty of advance notice that his government would be defeated. I was visiting Toronto and was taken to a public relations meeting with my firm's ad agency. At the social hour, I was pleased to find a Nova Scotia woman I knew in an important job with the agency. After some small talk, she told me that a survey her firm had conducted for the Liberal Party of Nova Scotia had shown very decisively that, "if an election was called in 1978, Gerald Regan's government would be defeated." Thanks to her indiscretion, the Conservative party received the poll results almost as early as did Mr. Regan's government.

There is a song which was peaking on the novelty charts about twenty years ago describing a gamblers' dice game in an alley — "When You're Hot, You're Hot (When You're Not, You're Not)." The

Conservative party in 1978 was hot (like Gerald Regan had been in 1970); everything Buchanan did in 1978 seemed blessed. Joe Nugent, the *Mercator One* promoter, bumped into Buchanan outside a meeting in Dartmouth and gave him an envelope containing a cheque payable to the Nova Scotia Progressive Conservative Party. Buchanan gave it to PCtreasurer Roy Busche and thought nothing more about it. During the election campaign, a TV reporter found Gerald Regan leaning against a fence and asked if Joe Nugent or his company, Mercator Enterprises, had made a sizable donation. Regan, quite within his rights, wouldn't comment. The reporter pushed for a reply and said he was entitled to an answer. Regan and the Liberal treasurer subsequently both refused to comment, as most political people have no desire to embarrass a donor. But, on television, Premier Regan looked harried and cornered by the fence and, because the company involved was controversial, the TV interview conveyed the appearance of stonewalling. Joe Nugent was not as reticent about his gift to the Liberal party as Regan was. Nugent, likely very angry at Regan's treatment of MAGI, the *Mercator One* project, and his friend MacNutt, publicly announced that he had given the Liberal party money and wondered why Regan would hide it. The amount was probably less than the vexed Nugent had bestowed upon the Tories, but his indignation left the silent Gerald Regan looking like he'd covered up the donation. Meanwhile, John Buchanan was mobbed by a bunch of media people who were fired up by the issue of Premier Regan and the *Mercator* question. Buchanan was asked if Nugent or his company had given any money to the PC party. Without a blink, Buchanan said, "Yes, two thousand dollars payable to the party, and it was handed to me." There was almost nothing more to ask.

John Buchanan set himself an unbelievable pace for criss-crossing the province. He virtually wore out PC party staff with his late-night visits to constituencies and early-morning starts for the next organizational or nominating visit. Buchanan was never an avid flyer, and a strange flying experience he had when travelling from Halifax to Sydney did little to change that. He boarded the early-morning flight at the wet, windy runway of Halifax Airport, where passengers for Eastern Provincial Air still had to go outside to board. Seated over the wing, he found the open airplane like a wind tunnel until the door closed for departure. The plane taxied out to take off, and the pilot revved the engines while waiting for tower instructions. Eventually the small plane awkwardly lurched forward on the bumpy, wind-blown runway, seemingly ready to rattle to pieces. Finally it lifted, but the wing on Buchanan's side jerked downward violently, stirring up a wet shower as it skimmed the runway. In a stomach-wrenching move, the plane then arched upward and banked abruptly so that the opposite window and wing pointed groundward while the labouring engines barely sucked the plane into the air. Just when the pale, speechless passengers and flight attendant were the most terrified, the pilot came on the intercom and announced in a bored, nasal twang: "Morninggg, this is yer captain speaking. There's a little turbulence today, no problems, enjoy your fliiight. Sydney arrival time is 9:05." Then there was a mechanical "click." But, at that point, Buchanan had not yet heard the end of the adventure. After leaving the plane in Sydney that morning, Buchanan ran into a pal who worked for Eastern Provincial. "You come in on EPA 6 from Halifax?" he asked. Buchanan answered, "Yup. It was a funny flight." His friend said, "Funny like a coffin. The pilot lost her on the runway in Halifax and all that saved it from crashing was his instinctive overcorrection and high throttle." Buchanan's terror returned: "I thought I must have overreacted. Until the pilot came on the intercom and was cool, I had almost lost my breakfast." His pal said, "The pilot may have been cool on the intercom, but he lost his composure and suffered shock, cause he crapped in his pants and didn't even realize it until about five minutes later."

During the campaign, there was often the threat of turbulence on the ground as well. Fred Dickson and Joe MacDonald borrowed a winning saying which I had used as coach of the 1974 Kings County Academy provincial hockey champions: "Just go up and down your wing and don't get any penalties." It sounds simple, but it's hot and confusing when you're performing out front, especially before a TV camera. Buchanan would say, "Sure, no penalties, but I hope I can keep my brain gear in sync with my tongue-fumble switch when the rat pack is trying to eat me alive." The Campaign Committee and Buchanan stressed positive alternatives instead of just harping about the Regan government's mistakes. Each time power rates were mentioned, Buchanan would outline his party's objectives for moving the province's electricity generation away from its large dependency on foreign oil.

Despite our lack of a bank balance, drumming up political donations and fund-raising got easier as the Conservative party's image improved. Political fund-raisers take pride in their abilities and engage in healthy competition with their colleagues. The competition in the PC party was intense, but always fun. If a party looks like a winner, it takes very little brain work to attract donations, especially from people with covert business ambitions; they flock like seagulls smelling dead fish and are always hungry. Ted Crease and David Chipman cautioned everybody about giving, promising, or accepting favours, and he had the relevant sections of the Criminal Code printed, to be given and explained to every fund-raiser. Every collector was quizzed to make sure that he or she understood the proprieties and what would not be tolerated.

The 1978 Liberal advertising campaign for their party's re-election bid was slick, expensive, and seemingly awesome. It was carefully reviewed by the PC Campaign Committee and their own advertising advisers. One ad in particular seemed to counter Buchanan's proposal to swing away from electricity produced by expensive oil. The Liberal ad said, "King Coal is back." Although environmental issues were not quite topical then, the ad was risky. Undoubtedly, masterminds of advertising had spent hours creating it, and Tory Swamis had spent as many hours attempting to debunk it, without being negative. In the end, though, one of John Buchanan's children invented an answer without much effort, asking innocently, "Where are the fiddlers three?" Coincidentally, there happened to be three main, well-known Liberal fund-raisers. And so, the game began. The Conservative party enjoyed the variations of puns and word-play that grew out of the King Coal advertisement. In speeches, the question was posed, "Where are those fund fiddlers fiddling, and with whom?" Another ad the Grits used, which appeared to hit the mark at first, was: "Check the record." The ad caused the public to think, and the follow-up could have been really effective, but the Liberal advisers "blinked." Ron Barkhouse, a mild, plain-speaking Tory from New Ross, said simply, "We have, and I wouldn't talk about it if I were you."

In Kings North, the street and byway opinion was that Kings County was basically Conservative, and if the PC party acted in a credible way, the seat could be Tory again. The only known Tory to have announced he would seek the Conservative banner against Liberal cabinet minister Glen Ells was Kentville lawyer Walter Newton. Nicknamed "Ironside," after actor Raymond Burr's character in the TV series, Walter favoured the performer slightly, including the wheelchair. Known as a man of iron will and dedication to overcoming difficulties, he looked like a winner. On the morning of the nomination, the rumour hit the airways that Kentville mayor R. Wendell Phinney was going to oppose Newton. Frank Nichols, a Tory broker in Kentville, had less than warm feelings for both candidates, but he especially disliked Phinney, whom he said would beat Newton. Phinney had spearheaded a town council movement which dumped popular police chief Alfred (Lefty) Graves, and some PC party people figured Phinney might win the nomination but lose the election against Ells; other candidates were sought.

The Twohigs are a strong Tory family who are well-liked residents of Kentville. Mrs. Twohig was a Christian worker and commanded respect and admiration, even among Liberal party members. Her husband, Edd Twohig, was a successful and respected businessman; their children were brilliant and had done well. Their oldest son, Edd, a chartered accountant, had just sold a fish business in Newfoundland and was in the process of resettling in Kings County. Mrs. Twohig was among the people who would work hard for any Tory, but she favoured Walter Newton. Edd was approached and, most likely on his mother's advice, said he would not run against Walter Newton. A poll of Tory workers showed that Phinney could beat Newton and win the first battle, but would never win the war against Ells. Finally, Edd Twohig was convinced to run, after the poll workers told Edd's mother that Newton would lose against Phinney, so Edd would really be beating Phinney and not Newton. Just before the deadline, Edd Twohig was dragged to the nomination altar.

Newton was nominated; Twohig was nominated; and Mayor Phinney was not, although he attended. Frank Nichols, a back-room Tory with clout, set the stage for the Conservative party in Kings North to have a split vote and shoot itself in the foot. Nichols said the mayor was afraid to run unless he was a sure bet. However, an old Tory worker, Bob Roberts, held the real power and was a popular peacemaker in the Conservative party in western Nova Scotia. Generous beyond his own well-being and active in Junior Hockey and a devout churchman, Roberts held the constituency together and kept the likeable Newton's goodwill after he lost the nomination to Twohig. Roberts also orchestrated the campaign for Twohig, and extracted Tory votes from polls where tradition was tough to overcome. Baxter's Harbour, for example, a poll which had voted Conservative only a few times since Confederation, went Tory. Roberts worked the hell out of the poll, and Ells was wild. When he met Roberts on the street long after the election, Ells still couldn't overcome his anger. Glen said, "Damn you, Roberts, I'll bet you gave every SOB in Baxter's Harbour rum or money." Roberts, with a cigarette dangling from his mouth, only mumbled, "Naw, Glen, I just showed 'em your picture."

On election night in Kings North, the PC party celebrated winning the seat with a rave up at a social club on West Main Street. A poll chairman from a rural polling station, "Joe Oaks," filled with enthusiasm and rum, drove a half-mile against traffic on Kentville's one-way Main Street and was stopped by the town's finest. Taking into account that it was election night, the officer was inclined to give Joe a ticket for the street infraction, make him park his car, and call it square. Joe was quiet, polite, and charming, and everything was going well until his wife, in the passenger's seat, suddenly opened up with a verbal blitz-krieg against the cop. The police officer, remarkably, was unfazed and stuck to the original plan. Joe, who needed his driver's licence to keep his job as a school-bus driver, asked the officer what would happen if the chief of police found out. The officer said, "I am the Chief. Married to her, you've got enough trouble — even a judge would understand."

PART 2

BUCHANAN ASCENDANT

1978 – 1984

11

I'VE ALWAYS LOVED YOU

THE CONSERVATIVE PARTY, LED BY JOHN BUCHANAN, won a majority of the seats and formed the government in September 1978. Gerry Regan, speaking from experience, said, "Tomorrow everybody will be a Tory, and anyone meeting John Buchanan will want to get on his bandwagon. Buchanan will hear that so many people loved him that the published percentage of votes should look like PC 90 per cent, Liberal 8 per cent, NDP 2 per cent." Regan continued, "People will walk up to the new premier, smile, and profess their allegiance. Even civil servants will 'ooze' up to him, and out of the corner of their mouths will whisper, 'Pssst, I've always voted PC and think you're the greatest.'" Regan was a perceptive man; Buchanan got more support "lines" than there are on a backyard spinner clothes-dryer. One known Liberal supporter, a broker named Lonnie Holland, had the best line of all, spoken in truth. He bumped into Buchanan on Hollis Street and said, "Congratulations, Premier. I didn't vote for you and I really don't expect or want anything, but could you just keep the vindictiveness in check and leave me alone."

Everybody involved in Buchanan's win had at least one dream or objective. I had two. I wanted to quit; so I told all concerned that, if we won, I was retiring, but, if we lost, I'd stay on, only because volunteers would be tough to find and I couldn't desert. The second thing I wanted was to attend Buchanan's swearing-in ceremony. The second objective was easy. Mary MacKinnon, the seasoned assistant to seven premiers, including Buchanan, stood with me beneath the picture of famous Liberal premier Angus Macdonald, who had been revered in both our families. Mary winked at me and said, "Angus Macdonald is spinning in his grave tonight, seeing us at a Tory premier's function."

The next morning Buchanan called and wanted me to meet him at eleven o'clock near the Legislature building. Buchanan was known to run thirty minutes late for everything because he gets into long, unexpected conversations with people and never looks at a watch (if he bothered to wear one). I am usually on time, but allowed for a thirty-minute delay, and arrived to find him deep in conversation with a Salvation Army officer about home health care. Trying to talk outdoors while walking was next to impossible because we kept meeting people, some of whom fit into Gerry Regan's "I've always loved you" group. Finally, as we turned onto busy Spring Garden Road, I stopped him between well-wishers and said, "I'm not staying on." He did what he always did, and always will do to anybody who tells him something he doesn't want to hear: he ignored completely what was said and kept right on talking. Knowing that it is almost impossible to stop him or to restate what he wants to ignore, I pressed hard. He said only, "Later," as he hugged an older lady he knew outside a dress shop. "Later" didn't come for twelve years.

On that day in September 1978, I found that my important assignment for the new premier was to use my imagination and help him pick an election present for his wife. My input in that capacity was ignored too, as he dragged me into a ladies' shop and, after what seemed like an hour, picked out a pretty blue dress. Realizing how difficult it is for any man to buy clothes for a woman, I told him his idea wouldn't fly and suggested jewellery. He said, "Mavis is not really a jewellery buff, and if I buy her the dress she would never say that it didn't please her." He borrowed a cheque from me, crossed out my name and account number and inserted his, and paid for the dress with the messy-looking result. His bank was forever complaining about his made-over cheques. Usually he carried no money, and almost never a wallet, credit card, or piece of identification, but he always seemed to manage without them. Once, after a meeting in Montreal, we went to see the Canadiens play at the Forum. We took a taxi to the rink and after we got inside, realized that, although we already had tickets, we had only $20. I panicked as the nearest people from whom I could borrow money lived too far outside the city. Just then Buchanan noticed a neighbour from Spryfield standing not three feet from him, and the nice man cashed a $100 cheque for us.

On the day he bought Mavis the dress, we walked for miles, and he talked of power rates and converting power plants to coal use. He also discussed a private mutual-fund company operating in the province, Service Investments, which the Nova Scotia Securities Registrar, Slim Chisholm, had warned him was in bad shape and posed a threat to its investors. The last thing I had expected on that day was an outline of the things he was planning to do, but he had a list and had obviously spent a long time thinking about the items on it. One of the government organizations that really bugged him was the Workman's Compensation Board (later renamed "Workers Compensation" to remove gender bias). Buchanan felt the board was not good at dealing with people. He planned to undertake a brief study of the board's governing act and its organization and structure. Eventually he would appoint an old friend, Reg Allen, to head the board, and his family physician, Dr. Ernie Johnson, as the board's medical consultant.

On our long walk, it was obvious that Buchanan was also wrestling mentally with some personal concern. Finally, he told me he would initially keep the finance portfolio as well as being premier. I didn't ask who else was in cabinet; I knew he would tell me in his own good time. He did say that a meeting was scheduled with Dickson and MacDonald for that very night to go over some thoughts he had about various projects. One of them was to modernize the Department of Finance. Buchanan suspected, correctly, that the department was outdated as no new ideas had been implemented since Lorne Goodfellow had been brought in by Bob Stanfield as the deputy minister of finance. Before Mr. Goodfellow died, he made a few progressive changes to the growing department, but almost all record-keeping at Finance was still manual, and there was no will to computerize. Management of the investments, for both the substantial and growing sinking funds and the pension funds, was frustrating and amateur, according to investment officers who tried to speed up the department's investment-decision process. Keith Shaw, the investment officer on the debt side, said that getting a decision from department directors Leo Lacusta and Harvey Matthews was so time-consuming and tear-inducing that he often did nothing rather than suffer two or three days of mind-bending indecisiveness. Buchanan said professional investment counsellors should be hired. The department would not only increase its productivity, but people like Shaw would be able to act in a timely fashion. Most investment dealers and finance staff recognized that need long before the counsellors were in place.

Buchanan spoke to me about making a special trip to Toronto to canvas national companies for PC donations. We were almost broke, having been elected in September 1978 with only $130,000. Conversely, reliable sources told us that the Liberal party had spent about $1 million and been defeated. It seemed to prove that parties can't always spend their way into office. Despite that comfort, I found the financial area of politics filled with unusual and almost shadowy people. Some lawyers, liquor executives, and others in that world had elastic ethics, although still lacking the hubris of the Canadian Investment Dealers. My own employers had so many diverse political connections, I couldn't guess how they managed to remember all their opinions.

In visiting my head office I made a casual remark about removing myself from politics. My boss almost bounced off the ceiling. Contemptuous of my stupidity in being ready to give up powerful connections, he delivered a long lecture on how he had ingratiated himself with various political people, including the premier of one province, and how he commanded power by wining, dining, and courting various strongly connected people of both political parties. His political activities seemed to include his blatant patronizing of civil servants at any useful level.

As it happens, I stayed in politics for several more years.

12

POWER, PATRONAGE, AND PROBLEMS

HE CIVIL SERVICE, MOST OF WHOM HAVE ONLY THEIR jobs at heart, presented a few troubles for the new government. During the Christmas recess in 1978, the premier took off for a few days, his first rest since 1974. He went to visit his sister in a small community outside Boston, incorrectly assuming that everybody knew what was expected of them back at the "Store."

Back in Kentville, Nova Scotia, my mother was listening to my son's two-way radio in the kitchen, while she baked to pass the time on a snowy day. She heard a government snowplough operator receive instructions from the local Highways garage dispatcher, telling him not to clear a road near the village of Port Williams, Kings County. The instructions had been issued by the Halifax chief engineer at the Department of Highways. The plough operator voiced concern for the people living on the road in question, including an older woman who was sick. The dispatcher grew serious and animated as he made it clear that not following the instructions from the Halifax-based civil servant would result in the operator's immediate dismissal. The plough operator was very upset and said that the road had been regularly cleared of snow for ages, and, even though it was a narrow road and did not meet the department's specifications for new roads or subdivision ploughing, it was very thickly populated. The dispatcher told the operator not even to contemplate sneaking in to plough the road in question. The dispatcher next called the heavy-equipment operator and told him he had received exact instructions from the deputy's office that no operator was to accept instructions contrary to those coming from the engineers, or from elected members of the Nova Scotia Legislature. Kings North rookie MLA Edd Twohig was drawn into the argument, and the dispatcher refused his instructions. Furious, Twohig called Tom McInnes, Minister of Transportation. McInnes first avoided his call and then reluctantly listened to Twohig's complaint. McInnes said the same problem existed all over Nova Scotia and that the department official would not respond to McInnes's request. Twohig told McInnes what should be done with the pig-headed civil servant, and said McInnes should show guts and serve the public; Twohig then contacted Buchanan at his sister's and told the premier exactly what was not occurring on many storm-stayed Nova Scotia byways. The usually placid John Buchanan ascended to ever-higher grades of anger as he listened to the enraged Twohig.

Buchanan hung up and tried to reach McInnes, the deputy, the chief engineer, and even the executive assistant to Minister McInnes. Finally, in a rare tantrum, he called several homes until he at last got a senior, non-elected person. He told the man that a firm instruction was to be issued to all Highways garages in Nova Scotia to resume ploughing unapproved but populated byways. The man said that the deputy would fire him. Buchanan asked, "Who's your boss?" The man said, "The deputy." Then Buchanan demanded, "Who's his boss?" The quivering senior servant, obviously not used to being called by the premier, said, "The minister is his boss." Buchanan continued, "And who is the minister's boss?" Once again the stammering man spoke, "You are." Buchanan said, "If you don't issue the order, I'll fire you on the floor of the Legislature by majority vote." The man said, "Yes, sir."

My mother heard the various plough operators' arguments over the two-way radio throughout that long winter day. She said that, at about four o'clock, she heard the following conversation between the dispatcher and the plough operator:

> Dispatcher: "You are now to plough the byways you were previously told not to plough! Is that clear?"
>
> Plough Operator: "Negative, the engineer told me he would fire me!"
>
> Dispatcher: "Ignore previous and plough byways!"
>
> Plough Operator: "Negative, it means my job!"
>
> Dispatcher: "God-dammit, plough the fuckin' byways at once!"
>
> Plough Operator: "But I thought the deputy said he'd fire anyone who —"
>
> Dispatcher: "Listen shithead, the Premier of Nova Scotia just ordered us to plough, so you damn well better plough — copy?"
>
> Plough Operator: "Heh, Heh, Heh, Ha! Ah that's a ten four!"

John Buchanan was determined to run Nova Scotia, right down to the plough operators, with no red tape or obstructionism from the civil service.

Buchanan had time for everybody, and sometimes saw, without an appointment, people whom he bumped into in the hall outside his office. As a result, he usually ran late and off schedule. He was accessible and cheerful, but his optimistic nature often gave the impression of acquiesence or of offering a simplistic solution to complicated problems. Unlike Gerry Regan, who frequently stated contrary positions to problems for the sake of eliciting the opinions of others, Buchanan seldom tipped his hand and almost never argued offensively. While he hid his feelings behind a cheerful countenance, he was still as stubborn as a deaf Scot when it came to doing a thing wished it to be done. He was not, however, the same Scot when it came to his own finances, especially when family or friends were involved. He had almost no ability to refuse anybody's request, and constantly had money problems because of that trait.

In dealing with people who sought help, favours, or outright patronage, Buchanan was very nice and never directly said "no"; he was repeatedly lobbied for things he could have refused or dismissed in two seconds, but he hated to hurt people. Such was the case of lawyer John Grant and his incessant lobby for the legal business of the Nova Scotia Power Corporation.

Grant's firm, Cox, Downie, had legal work of the Nova Scotia Power Corporation through lawyer David Mann, who was an adviser to former premier Gerald Regan, and they wished to retain the account when the Buchanan government was elected. Grant was president of the Progressive Conservative Party of Nova Scotia and said his partners placed personal pressure on him to exploit that position to retain their legal plum. Grant could have been excused for acting under pressure, but he also lobbied with the intensity of a hungry woodpecker for any or all government legal work that became available. Scores of Tory lawyers like Fred Dickson coveted the same lucrative legal business, and there was tension among the political lawyers hoping to settle the Nova Scotia Power Corporation account. David Chipman, who is now a justice of the Appeal Court of Nova Scotia, grew tired of Grant and his law firm. Chipman is time-frugal and does not waste or mince words in cutting to the centre of problems or discussions. He also has an author's uncanny ability to describe people, but he uses nicknames to do so with laser-beam accuracy.

Buchanan asked Chipman for an opinion on the Grant situation. Chipman's one-word answer was "Jaws." Buchanan said, "Do you mean the movie?" and Chipman replied, "Not the movie, the shark." The name was to stick, but Buchanan initially gave the Power Corporation account to John Grant. He later gave some of the legal work to Fred Dickson.

Dickson had once practised law with developer Ralph Medjuck but had left that firm to join a Truro, Nova Scotia, firm in which former Tory premier G.I. Smith had been a law partner. Dickson later engineered a union of that firm with Halifax Liberal lawyer Peter Green of Kitz, Matheson, Green, and MacIsaac to form Patterson, Kitz.

For a short period while John Buchanan was premier of Nova Scotia, the Tories, under Prime Minister Joe Clark, formed a minority government in Ottawa. The expectation of cooperative, mutual action on social and political problems was overshadowed by the federal government's inexperience and naïvety. Clarke was treated badly by the media, who may not have intended to be, but certainly were, cruel in dubbing him "Joe Who." Even the hand gestures he used when speaking were critically presented by the media. When Clark's luggage went missing on one of his official trips, the press made it sound like a matter of personal incompetence. The federal Tory backbenchers, some with years of Ottawa experience, were constantly taken to task by constituents about the new government's insensitive and amateur conduct of political affairs. Some cabinet ministers, who should have known better, didn't return calls, answer mail, or carry out basic tasks. Some government appointments went to competent Canadians, but many went to people who were academically, socially, and even politically inept.

Some provincial Tories were disappointed, not only with the Clark Tory government, but especially with Nova Scotia's senior cabinet minister in that government, Elmer MacKay. In opposition, MacKay had presented himself as a tough, fearless, investigative MP bent on correcting injustice and exposing corruption in government. After the Tories formed the government, MacKay had the power of his cabinet office, but he seemed to be timid, quiet, and perhaps hesitant to act on the simplest problem. He appeared to be indecisive and was often reported not to respond to phone calls or letters, including those from Premier Buchanan. Privately, MacKay told me that he had not expected Buchanan to win the premiership of Nova Scotia, and he had planned to run for the Tory leadership himself if Buchanan failed in 1978; however, Buchanan surprised MacKay and won. MacKay's disappointment turned to obvious depression, and he looked like he had lost interest in the problems of Nova Scotia and was hiding out. MacKay's state of mind was to turn him against Joe Clark. Openly hostile and angry about Clark, he later spearheaded the movement to dump him.

Fred Dickson was a strong federal Tory and often sought to smooth over their mediocre performance; he quoted MacKay as saying, "They're trying to help." Buchanan's reply was, "Yes, they are very trying." I was reminded of an old hockey coach who chastised a young defenceman after he inadvertently scored two goals in his own net and offered the lame excuse that he was "only trying to help." The wild-tempered French-Canadian coach yelled back, "Help us — help us — Jeezas — Christ. If you keep helping us, we be ruined." MacKay's mood swings took a toll on his personal life. Getting along with him on a regular basis took a lot of understanding, according to his second wife, Laura, who was to leave him during his future second stint as a cabinet minister.

Finally a shrewd old House of Commons tiger, Allan J. MacEachen, of the Liberal party, sandbagged the sleeping Tory caucus who often missed routine House of Commons sessions; he called a surprise non-confidence motion. MacEachen was called by those who admired him "Allan J." and less affectionate names by others. But, in the case of the Clark government, he outclassed them tactically and they were thrown out of office. Many Tories were angry at Clark, as the subsequent federal election proved.

Political power begets problems, and decisions are often a "Hobson's choice" for the person charged with making them. That is why political people mimic the tried and tested method used by the Second World War Liberal prime minister Mackenzie King. He often took no action. Unattended, the problem sometimes disappeared or resolved itself, making a decision unnecessary in the end. Buchanan was a definite devotee of that tack, which frustrated his staff and party people, but was as interesting as a chess game to observers endowed with patience. Tory MLA Pat Hunt was just such a problem to Buchanan.

Hunt was elected in the constituency of Hants East, which is populated by hearty rural people who have no time for fools. Hunt was elected on Buchanan's coattails and because of the failing support for the Regan government; however, he was barely acceptable to his constituents because he was "from away." Surpassing even the most idealistic vision of clean government, Hunt was not only non-partisan but inactively neutral, but he saw himself as a statesman. Once he responded to an old lady who accused him of inactivity by saying, "I work like a horse." The tiger-tongued senior citizen replied, "Yes, sir, but the only part of that horse I've seen is the south end."

The constant parade of Pat Hunt's detractors to Buchanan's office produced a soap-opera campaign for his dismissal. Hunt would not deal with highway problems or snow-removal complaints, and ignored the democratic advice of the constituency organization. His attitude was that he was elected on his own abilities, made his own decisions, and did not have to listen to the petty gripes of party people. His ego, according to his executive, would test the mellow nature of Gandhi. The complaints grew more bitter, and the Tory constituency organization in Hants East was about to resign, but Buchanan stalled and played the Mackenzie King waiting game. Time did solve the problem as the people and democracy took care of the unique Mr. Hunt before the next provincial election.

13

CHARIOTS OF FIRE

N 1981, THE MEMBERS OF THE LEGISLATURE SMELLED AN approaching election. The intense jockeying for position, in anticipation of the vote, was so hot one Tory tried to convince Buchanan's Campaign Committee to use the theme from *Chariots of Fire* as the PC campaign music. As the Liberal opposition applied verbal flamethrowers in the House in an attempt to embarrass the government, the stage was being set for a political tragedy which would run until 1992. It was the matter of Tory cabinet minister Roland Thornhill and what became known as the Thornhill affair.

Former Liberal premier Gerald A. Regan had resigned provincially and returned to federal politics on the Trudeau promise of a cabinet post if he defeated incumbent Halifax MP George Cooper. Cooper, whose credentials as a Rhodes scholar and lawyer were impressive, had the most inept political organization many of us had ever seen. Regan's victory cleared the way for a provincial Liberal leadership convention.

Two main aspirants emerged; they were to dominate their own party, as well as provincial politics, for a considerable period — including three provincial elections.

Vincent MacLean, a teacher by profession, had been a cabinet minister and Speaker of the House during his time in the Regan government. He was bombastic, severe, and tough in the House, and came across like a pit bull. A.M. (Sandy) Cameron, a third-generation MLA who had also been a minister in the Regan government, was amiable, friendly, and witty. His natural ability and personality reminded many of Robert L. Stanfield, although Cameron was handsomer, according to female observers.

Cameron won the Liberal race, but two circumstances almost at once set his course for failure. The first was the bitterness harboured by Vince MacLean, and the second was the group of people who would advise Cameron. One of them, lawyer Ted Danielson from the old firm of Kitz, Matheson, couldn't seem to identify issues, and focused instead on human frailties and personalities. Cameron's own personal appeal was soon clouded by attempts to remake him into a leader who would appear as tough as defeated MLA Vince MacLean. It was to cost Cameron the premier's office, not once, but twice.

Just after Cameron's victory, the Liberal party seemed to suffer internal strife as Vincent MacLean was obviously bitter about losing the leadership race to Cameron. At one point Vince MacLean had the gall to ask Premier Buchanan for a government appointment, but Fred Dickson quickly shot down that idea. Buchanan told me he would have given Vince the job to shut him up.

Perhaps Vince MacLean was misunderstood because of his nature and the impression his efforts created, but he raised matters in the Legislature in such an aggressive way that it reflected poorly on the new leader and on the Liberal party. Some of the subjects MacLean raised were pretty close to the bone. One matter produced a dozen years of grief not only for Tory cabinet minister Roland Thornhill, but also for his family and scores of others, including one RCMP officer who resigned from the force in anger.

The Roland Thornhill story starts in 1974 and ends in 1992. Thornhill had been mayor of Dartmouth, Nova Scotia, and had run against Buchanan for the Tory leadership in 1971. Thornhill then sought and won the Tory nomination in Dartmouth South in the

1974 provincial election and was elected to the Legislature. Thornhill was having domestic problems and had also lost money investing in the stock market. He was in debt and had a series of loans with several chartered banks. After a long period of trying to manage the debt, he engaged an accountant and a lawyer who represented him in negotiating a settlement with the lending institutions for $0.25 on the dollar. Shortly after Thornhill was elected for the second time, in 1978, he entered into the negotiated agreement and paid the $0.25 on every dollar he owed.

Arrangements of that nature are not unusual, and ordinary citizens sometimes settle debts that way without difficulty. But, apparently, under Section 121(1)c of the Criminal Code it could be deemed that a government official or employee who accepted such a settlement had received a benefit if he or she made the arrangement without the consent, in writing, of his or her superior.

There is no way to assess the intent of lending institutions, but they make such arrangements frequently. Furthermore, since Thornhill was acting on the advice of professional advisers, and therefore within the law, the event, while it might be embarrassing, could not be considered wrongdoing, especially by people who have had to deal with debt themselves.

There is an old expression that claims that "the truth, even if it's as thick as molasses, will eventually leak through the staves of the tightest barrel." In the case of Rollie Thornhill, the truth leaked out as if the barrel had been strafed by machinegun fire.

The Tories blamed the leak on a Liberal party adviser, lawyer Ted Danielson. The firm where he practised apparently represented one of the banks, and speculation was that some confidential documents were seen or gossiped about by Danielson. Accusations would have been much less damaging except Danielson, for some undisclosed reason, was suddenly separated from the law firm and subsequently was convicted of an offence in British Columbia involving a real estate débâcle. However, the opposition and the media found out about the debt settlement, and it became a millstone to Thornhill and the Tory party.

Almost weekly, Liberal Vince MacLean raised the issue of Thornhill's problem, demanding an investigation of his conduct or his resignation. The result was panic and fear in the Tory caucus, cabinet, and party. Every act was examined so meticulously and methodically to forestall future criticism that the government was, in effect, paralysed. Meanwhile, two-faced MLAs and party people slithered into Buchanan's office, trying to convince him to turf Thornhill.

But Buchanan refused to budge, because Thornhill had thrown his 1971 leadership support to Buchanan at the PC party convention, ensuring the premier's victory. Privately, Buchanan said he'd quit himself before he'd fire anyone for being in debt, because half the people in the world were in debt— including Buchanan himself.

The tirades in the Legislature eventually led to an RCMP investigation of Roland Thornhill's debt settlement. Despite the ongoing investigation, and contrary to custom, Vince MacLean's invective against Thornhill continued to arouse passionate feelings. His attacks were so unreasonable he may, in fact, have saved Thornhill from being forced to resign by creating sympathy for him. In 1980, the case was suddenly abandoned without public explanation. But, like the molasses in the barrel, the truth would eventually leak out. In the meantime, MacLean was relentless, never dropping the so-called Thornhill affair, and some Liberal party supporters printed $0.25 Thornhill dollars and distributed them in his constituency.

Sandy Cameron, the Liberal leader, ran two elections and then resigned as leader. At the next convention, Vincent MacLean was successful, and his leadership put a new stamp on the Legislature, according to Buchanan, who called it "Senator Joe McCarthy's Nova Scotia Funny Farm."

Fate then handed the Liberals a boon. The royal commission report on the prosecution of Donald Marshall Jr. also studied the justice system in Nova Scotia. The report, released in 1989, presented a concise description of the facts surrounding the decision not to prosecute Roland Thornhill nine years earlier for his bank debt agreement.

The report stated:

*An initial RCMP "investigation" into whether Thornhill could be charged
as a result of this agreement was abandoned in early 1980 after some preliminary inquiries. The officers apparently decided that they could not proceed because they did not know if Thornhill was a member of the Government
at the time the offence was committed. The RCMP's apparent disinterest in
pursuing an investigation against a prominent politician caused us concern.*

*When the RCMP did take up the case again in April 1980, the investigating
officers quickly concluded that in their view, there was a prima facie case
against Thornhill. After a preliminary report was forwarded to the
Department of the Attorney General, Deputy Attorney General Gordon Coles
instructed that a directive be issued forbidding the RCMP to have any contact
with local prosecutors on the case until the investigation was completed and
a report filed with the Attorney General. Despite Coles' claims to the contrary, this was a clear divergence from normal Department practice.*

*The RCMP filed a final report in September 1980 in which they recom-
mended that at least one charge be laid, and in which they requested a Crown
prosecutor be appointed to offer advice regarding existing and additional
evidence, questions of law and court procedures.*

*However, Attorney General Harry How — without further consultation
with the RCMP — announced on October 29, 1980 that there had been no
criminal wrongdoing by Thornhill. Although this announcement was made
by Attorney General How, he testified that he himself did not consider the
merits of the case because of its sensitive nature, but simply relied upon and
accepted the recommendation of his Deputy, Gordon Coles.*

*Although Coles admitted he was not an expert in criminal law, he pre-
pared a woefully inadequate and misleading legal opinion for the Attorney
General — without consulting either his senior officials or the RCMP — that
claimed there was no basis for the charge against Thornhill.*

*While we accept that How genuinely and properly wished to distance
himself from the decision in the Thornhill matter, we believe once the matter was brought to his attention he had a duty to satisfy himself that normal reviews and procedures had been followed, as well as to determine what
the RCMP had recommended.*

Although the RCMP did consider laying charges on its own — as was its right and responsibility — Coles pointedly suggested to RCMP officials that such a course of action might jeopardize working relationships between the Province and the RCMP. Eventually the RCMP agreed not to lay charges "in contradiction to the wishes of the Attorney General."

We found that this matter was not handled in the "normal" way, either by the Department or the RCMP. We believe this was because of Thornhill's high profile within Government. The RCMP failed in its obligation to be independent and impartial. The Department of the Attorney General failed to follow normal procedures.

Thornhill was not aware of the steps that were taken which constituted a preferred handling of his case. However, the result was that Thornhill — although he neither requested nor encouraged it — appeared to have received preferential treatment.

It was apparently then that RCMP corporal Cyril House resigned, citing his disappointment that the force did not proceed with a prosecution without the support of the Department of the Attorney General.

Vincent MacLean went on the attack, and his invective resulted in the RCMP's reopening of the Thornhill case. While the new RCMP investigation was going on, an unrelated political event caused John Buchanan to resign and accept a Senate seat, which led to the PC party calling a leadership convention for February 1991. One of the candidates was Roland Thornhill; however, rumour and innuendo suggesting that criminal charges would drive Thornhill from office definitely cost him the leadership of the PC party.

Not long after that convention, the new premier, Donald Cameron, selected a cabinet which did not include Rollie Thornhill. And the RCMP finally, after a dozen bitter years, filed multiple charges against Thornhill. Thornhill kept his seat in the Legislature but did not attend caucus meetings. He also hired famous Toronto trial lawyer Eddie Greenspan to defend him.

In the first court appearance, Greenspan had all but three of the charges dropped. He was quoted as saying, "I tried to hit a home run, but I only hit a triple." However, in the next engagement, the judge dismissed the remaining charges, and Greenspan had his home run.

Fate wasn't through with the political players yet — especially Vincent MacLean. The new premier, Don Cameron, nicknamed "King Donnie" by Dartmouth Tories, had only a bare majority of seats in the Legislature and faced a potential non-confidence vote and an election he wasn't yet ready for. Vincent MacLean, according to public-opinion polls, real or invented, was close to becoming Premier of Nova Scotia. All he needed was a non-confidence vote in the Legislature to force an election.

Roland Thornhill had not so quietly decided to leave the government side of the House and to sit as an independent MLA. He said he would not necessarily support the PC government in a legislative vote. Next, Tory MLA Dr. Colin Stewart, supposedly angry about being excluded from cabinet, suddenly became ill and was hospitalized, cutting the Tory majority again. Defeat was a strong possibility.

While the political drama was unfolding, Vince MacLean once again blundered. He made an unfortunate remark about Thornhill, obviously forgetting that Rollie was the potential key to defeating the new Cameron government. MacLean's former adviser Al Hollingsworth recalled that no amount of pressure could shut MacLean up, despite the fact that Thornhill's support was all they needed to force an election. And Thornhill was known to regard Premier Cameron as a political undesirable.

Before the vote was taken, Thornhill kept his own counsel, despite media attempts to get an advance hint. The tension mounted as the first vote was called in the House.

According to friends, Thornhill had wrestled with himself about the decision. It was a dilemma because neither leader had endeared himself to Thornhill. In the end, he voted for the Conservative party, out of loyalty, despite the fact that it included Donald Cameron.

After more than a decade of abuse by MacLean over his bank settlement, and two police investigations, it was a fitting irony that Roland Thornhill denied him power.

Thornhill is too much of a gentleman to say much about it publicly, but one prominent Liberal said, "We should have stepped on Vince's tongue years ago. Vince sat on his own sword and it will cost him his job." And, within a short time, that prediction came true.

14

THE 1981 NON-EVENT

BUCHANAN'S INABILITY TO SAY "NO" AND HIS SINCERE concern for people were the main weaknesses in his political makeup, and Ted Crease frequently said that Buchanan's friends would be the cause of his undoing. He was dead right. In one instance, his compassion created a media and opposition circus.

G.H. (Paddy) Fitzgerald had once been a Tory MLA in the Stanfield government, as well as the Speaker of the House. He left politics and established a successful law practice, but a female client accused him of rape. The Barristers' Society disbarred him for the condition of his accounts, and he was convicted of the sexual offence and went to prison. He served his time, but when he got out he was down on his luck, had few friends who would help, and had lost his house. Buchanan ignored Dickson's warnings, giving Fitzgerald a job at home rewriting the "legalese" of the Liquor Control Act. It was a quiet job which harmed no one. Buchanan said that even former premier Gerry Regan, who was by that time back in Ottawa, expressed compassion for Fitzgerald. Regan had once, under similar circumstances, given a job to a disbarred lawyer who had been a compulsive gambler. The fact that Paddy was once an elected Tory caused the opposition to crucify Buchanan, but he refused to fire Fitzgerald. However, Fitzgerald had political smarts and resigned on his own to save Buchanan the agony. Then Buchanan appointed Paddy Fitzgerald's wife an inspector at the Nova Scotia Liquor Commission, saying only, "They have to eat, no matter what Paddy did."

The 1981 election campaign was, in many ways, a non-event. The federal Liberals and Trudeau's controversial position on off-shore mineral and energy ownership hurt the provincial Liberals. Buchanan subtly married the Cameron provincial Grits to Trudeau's Ottawa has-beens; the people of Nova Scotia, who never totally trusted Trudeau, got the message.

The party in power has inherent strength and the ability to announce needed and desired projects during an election campaign, which, in theory, pleases voters. Older politicians claimed that the former great Liberal premier Angus L. Macdonald used to say new-project announcements at election time were vote bribes and were more hindrance than help. Road paving was one example. Macdonald said it was important, but it killed votes because people who worked on the road were often greedy; the people not working were jealous; and those living along the road were upset with dust and dirt in their homes, on their curtains, and on their clean laundry. He added, "The motoring public hates highway delays." Macdonald did not condone election-time paving.

Liberal leader Sandy Cameron had been in office as a cabinet minister in the Regan government and understood the power available to the governing party. He said that Buchanan had paved so many roads that his political scouts couldn't find anything more to black-top. Meanwhile, Buchanan said that the government would further reduce the province's dependency on oil-generated electricity from 65 to 10 per cent by 1986. The monthly electric power bills to home owners still showed a modest government subsidy credit, and public opinion seemed to be that Buchanan was slowing the rise of electricity costs by realistic means.

Guided by public-opinion polls, Tory strategists Fred Dickson and Joe MacDonald made a blueprint for the Buchanan election and insisted that the premier stick to it. When Buchanan strayed from the appointed path, he knew what to expect: Dickson would scream in half-sentences and phrases, implying dozens of possible negative results; MacDonald would yell at the premier; then Dickson would break and throw pencils, and turn scarlet all the way from his chin to his retreating hairline. MacDonald said that Fred Dickson was a world-class pencil breaker. Buchanan, always easy going, would try to placate Fred, saying, "We won't stray from the plan again," to which Fred would shout in reply, "*We*! Who the hell is *we*? Are you pregnant? Do you have someone in your pocket? It's not *we*, it's *you*!" Dickson is an unusual, complex, and sensitive person who has trouble getting his tongue to move as fast as his brain does; he can sense a political mistake in the making and acted as Buchanan's battery and restraining mechanism.

Liberal Sandy Cameron had a big load to carry in the 1981 election too. His own party was divided, he was overshadowed by a federal Liberal government which had grown unpopular, and he faced a new provincial government whose members were still public favourites. Cameron referred to the coming contest as the "Buchanan energy election," and refused to be lured into the energy debate, thinking that he could win the next election, in 1984. However, Cameron's advisers did not recognize his natural assets, and their bad advice would cost him two elections.

Cameron said that energy speculators would be attracted to the province, like carpetbaggers to the South after the Civil War. Oil and gas expectations and a bigger majority only added to Buchanan's burdens as it seemed everyone had an energy idea or a supply company and wanted to "get rich in Nova Scotia." Everyone — from the mighty Mobil Oil Company to the guy next door — tried to court the government. Sandy Cameron, with a natural wit that served him better than his advisers did, said that the movie *On Golden Pond* was being remade without Henry Fonda and with a new script; it was to star John Buchanan and be set on the Nova Scotia shore, an area the oil and gas patronage prospectors thought of as "Golden Pond."

Cameron handled himself and his defeat in a statesman-like way, while some of his colleagues undermined his personal strength. But the Tories were not long in helping Cameron and causing Buchanan to suffer through their own stupid conduct. One of those mistakes was the cabinet decision that the province needed an airplane for use as an air ambulance and by cabinet ministers on government business. Former Liberal MLA Eric Balcom's sage political advice had been ignored by Buchanan. Balcom said, "You can do the right thing, and get killed, but if you 'do things right,' it will cause no trouble." In terms of the airplane, Tories didn't do it right. Several provinces effectively utilized their own aircraft for similar purposes and claimed success with them; New Brunswick at one time had two airplanes. However, the decision to buy the plane was a surprise to some Tory MLAs, and the rumour of the purchase met mixed reactions, ranging from disbelief to suspicion of a joke. But the plane was leased, with an option to buy, in the province's favour. Liberal leader Cameron started out criticizing the plane's acquisition in a very effective way: he made it into an issue without rhetoric, using his natural wit, charm, and personality, and caught the government completely off balance. In exploiting the plane as emblematic of government wastefulness, Cameron turned it into an issue that went against the grain of frugal Nova Scotians. Even strong PC party people were embarrassed and upset. In cabinet, some members panicked, and all useful discussion was clouded by the plane furore, which the press stirred up like mad. The comments on the street ranged from the Liberal-inspired "King John and the Royal Air Farce" to the "Expensive Toy" and "Buchanan Air." No subject of political conversation was as controversial as the aircraft, but politicians hate to admit to having made a mistake — especially when it involves a political wound they have inflicted upon themselves. To satisfy his political colleagues and silence the opposition, Buchanan tried unsuccessfully for three years to sell the plane. The incident revealed how easily intimidated the Tory MLAs were on any subject, good or bad, when the opposition howled loudly enough.

For the first few years of the Buchanan government, only one or two ministers had the courage to make a decision and stick to it, or, even more importantly, to admit a real mistake and then "can it."

Sandy Cameron spoke of the poor quality of his own party's performance in opposition following their defeat, saying that he had inherited too many individual stars and advisers to run an effective opposition. He accepted the blame, but it was clear that the Liberals had learned nothing after being thrown out, and were not ready to gain the people's confidence. It looked like a poor opposition was keeping the popular Buchanan, whom the press nicknamed "Teflon Man," in office. Cameron considered the PC caucus weak, but he felt that his own party was insuring the PC re-election because major Tory blunders were missed! Even when Buchanan blundered, the Grits eased up too quickly.

Before the 1981 election, Buchanan hired a former CBC reporter as press secretary. John O'Brien was an investigative reporter with above-average skill who once did a lengthy, provocative film report on the Portland Estates land development, which was not particularly flattering to Buchanan's government, even though O'Brien did point out the Liberal involvement in it. The Buchanan press release announced O'Brien's appointment in August 1981. The Liberal leader wanted one of his strong backbenchers to attack the appointment as a media patronage pay-off aimed at shutting O'Brien up. But Cameron's advisers did not agree; he raised the subject a few times himself and then let it fade. On one occasion, O'Brien chuckled and said, "I would have beat the government to death on an appointment like mine," but Cameron dropped it. Later Cameron said he could get no support from his own caucus on issues that he knew were topical or that offended the public. Some of Cameron's Liberals were too busy searching for a big Watergate-type scandal to pay attention to seemingly minor things like "Air Buchanan" or the appointment of John O'Brien as press secretary.

Another potentially interesting issue was created by the Halifax Board of Trade. James Radford, a Halifax businessman who was CEO of the old Nova Scotia Savings and Loan Company, was very active in the Halifax Board of Trade. Obviously unimpressed by the Buchanan government's financial abilities, he established a base at the executive level of the Halifax Board of Trade from which to attack the provincial government's growing debt. All members seemed to agree that criticizing the government is fair, logical, and the right of citizens, but the use of a non-political organization to do it upset some members of the community, both inside and outside the Board of Trade. Membership in the board obviously included people of all political beliefs, and there was considerable anger about the Radford attack. The Grits missed the importance of the board's claims, and the board itself eventually suffered from a spate of resignations and the resulting financial distress. One of the factors contributing to decreased membership was the 1980s partisanship of certain board members. One Tory member resigned over the board's political activities, announcing, "If I had wanted to join the Liberal party it would not have been through the Board of Trade." This sort of reaction proves that Nova Scotians take their political loyalties very seriously, even when they know criticism is warranted, and some of the Tory members indeed warranted it. Malcolm MacKay was one of them.

Tory MLA Malcolm MacKay, from Sackville, Nova Scotia, looked like an advertising photo for a perfect head of hair. Plump and usually dressed in colourful suspenders and loud bow ties, he was, in appearance, closer to a movie version of an Arkansas senator than an urban member from Nova Scotia. He was known to meet the opposition and the media with the same forceful manner as the Liberal party's Vincent MacLean. It was natural that he and MacLean would cross paths, and their political clash would be inevitable, like a fight between Muhammad Ali and George Foreman. MacLean accused MacKay of incorrectly filing expense chits for mileage from his residence to the Legislature, claiming that although Malcolm had moved, and his new residence was closer to the capital, the mileage reimbursments were the same as they had been from his former house.

As the winter session of the Legislature unfolded, the climate was one of mud-slinging, rhetoric, and scandal-mongering. Liberal leader Sandy Cameron was not displaying his Stanfield-like stability as his advisers and Vince MacLean went after the government, bent on uncovering embarrassments. The NDP and the Tories were dragged into the same muck-raking, and while Buchanan hated that type of politics, the Tory members were as determined to get something on the opposition as Vince MacLean was to question Malcolm MacKay's expense account. Vince MacLean called for RCMP investigators so often that David Chipman called him "Inspector Clouseau," after Peter Sellers's character in the *Pink Panther* movies.

But Malcolm MacKay had troubles that Vince MacLean did not know about. MacKay came to my office early one morning and informed me that he needed $10,000 to avoid going bankrupt and embarrassing the government. He said that he was to do a political survey for the "Chairman," and I assumed that he meant Nova Scotia Power chairman, "Little Joe" MacDonald. Malcolm seemed surprised that the Finance Committee had no signing authority and could not pay or give him money. I told him to go to party treasurer Roy Busche and, if Joe MacDonald had authorized it, he would get paid. Out of curiosity, I phoned Dickson and asked if he and Joe were doing a survey, and Dickson, who was one of the most influential and powerful people in the party, knew nothing about it.

I couldn't contact MacDonald, and while it was really none of my business, I called Roy Busche the same day. Busche said he was authorized to pay Malcolm $10,000 and had done so. In the course of the conversation, I sensed that Roy did not like the idea, and when I suggested that a payment to Malcolm could be front-page news, he was appalled. MacKay still went bankrupt.

In the meantime, Buchanan told me that he was leaving politics and hoped to move to the small community in the Boston area where his sister lived. I sensed that he wanted to get away from his financial mess and was comforting himself with the idea of getting out and living a normal life. But Buchanan was serious, as Dickson confirmed when I bumped into him in the bank a few days later. Dickson urged me to recruit everybody to help talk the premier out of leaving until after a provincial election. I refused. I thought that he should be allowed to retire undefeated.

I could understand Dickson's concern, as the polls showed that party support was down, even though Buchanan's personal popularity was still remarkably high. We had been in office for only five years and already the symptoms of politician's disease were evident. The common affliction of elected people the world over is alcohol. After the Legislature is closed each night, some elected people are bored; they are a long distance from their real homes and are temporarily housed in apartments or hotels, so they play around the bars nightly to kill time.

Cabinet fever is another disease that sets in as governments grow stale. Some of the MLAs suddenly develop a not-so-subtle urge to become cabinet ministers. One of those was Donald Cameron, who had been in cabinet after the 1978 election, but became unhappy and left voluntarily. He mounted a lobby through friends and associates, but Buchanan would not take him back as the cabinet was already large and the opposition were complaining about cost and waste.

Finally Buchanan gave in and brought Donald Cameron back into cabinet despite the fact that Mavis had warned the Premier not to.

Mrs. Buchanan had outstanding political judgement. Cameron was not only troublesome to Premier Buchanan in cabinet, but he eventually caused an RCMP investigation into Buchanan's troubled finances and the blind trust. Cameron did his best to separate himself from Buchanan and in the end his actions damaged both their political careers.

15

THE BUCHANAN BLIND TRUST

BEFORE ENTERING POLITICS, JOHN BUCHANAN HAD developed and acquired various business interests and real estate in partnership with his friend and family doctor Ernie Johnson. From 1967, when Buchanan first ran for office, until 1978, when he became premier, his political addiction caused him to almost ignore his own business ventures, and Dr. Johnson was either too busy or thought Buchanan was managing them.

Being a political junkie, Buchanan devoted little attention to his household expenses and never paid anything, including his telephone bill, until it could no longer be ignored. I had never heard him discuss his business affairs outside his former law practice, but I assumed his household budget was strained because he had a big family and, as leader of the opposition, his pay was poor. But when he became premier, I was sure the increase in salary would remedy that situation.

In fact, I doubt anyone on the Finance Committee was aware of the new premier's money problems, as in that seven years I never heard a whisper of it. But, in 1979, Fred Dickson, at least, knew that the new premier was deeply in debt and that his business affairs were a mess. Mushrooming interest rates and lack of attention to those matters were producing a crisis. Dickson realized the magnitude of the scandal that would break if the media or opposition found out. Dickson and another close friend of the premier's, lawyer Joe MacDonald, had tried to deal with the personal side of the premier's debts, but neither had the time or information necessary to manage his business. Reluctantly, MacDonald advised Dickson that they had to bring in help, but MacDonald feared that the more people who became involved, the greater the chance of a leak. It is amazing to realize now that the secret was kept for thirteen years, until a new premier took office.

Joe MacDonald is one of the original Buchanan political regulars and, with David Chipman and Fred Dickson, was among his closest advisers and friends. MacDonald, known as "Little Joe" by everybody but David Chipman, who gave him the nickname "Back-room Joe," had fuzzy, receding, Einstein-like hair; wore hideous bow ties; smoked cheap cigars; worshipped baseball; and wore suits that looked second-hand. However, there was nothing fuzzy about his brain, and his pipe-cleaner physique bore no relation to the strength of his intelligence and political smarts. Buchanan made him chairman of the Nova Scotia Power Corporation.

Dickson and MacDonald initially decided to call a secret meeting without disclosing the full nature of the premier's problems. Discussion was to be restricted to his personal debts and the inadequacy of his government salary in relation to the financial demands he faced. The following were invited to attend: PC Finance Committee Chairman David Chipman, QC (now a justice of the Appeal Court of Nova Scotia); Kenneth Matthew, QC (now a justice of the Appeal Court of Nova Scotia); party treasurer Roy Busche, CA (now a retired partner of Peat Marwick Thorne); PC Finance Committee co-chairman, insurance magnate E.F. (Ted) Crease (now deceased); Bruce Nickerson, QC (later of the Public Utilities Board); John Grant, QC, then PC party president (now deceased under tragic circumstances); and me, Chipman and Crease's appointed fund-raiser.

Joe MacDonald's summer cottage was selected as the gathering place, and its unwinterized construction caused initial shivers as the midwinter meeting convened. While the fireplace and stove were being cranked up, Grant produced big steaks, and Crease delivered an adequate supply of Seagram's finest brands.

Ken Matthews's conclusion at the end of a long and not unpleasant evening was like a childhood rhyme most of us were old enough to remember, which said: "You can't make a dollar out of ninety-nine cents." Matthews pointed out the premier had a large family, must dress in a presentable fashion, and couldn't be expected to survive on the $60,000–70,000 a year that the government was paying him. Roy Busche and John Grant were asked to approach the party executive for permission to pay Buchanan a monthly allowance to supplement his income. John Grant told us that his Liberal partners had informed him that Gerry Regan had received such a supplement from his party when he was premier. Grant was a good party president and a hard worker, and he managed to convince his executive to pay the money we requested for the premier.

That was how the trouble was to start for the PC party, and like many good intentions, that decision was the first paving stone on the road to hell. Dickson referred to political people who received an appointment as "Gone to Glory." Of those who attended that meeting, most had taken up residence there or had died a dozen or so years later, and I was left, almost alone, to answer RCMP questions and to learn the real depressing story of the premier's financial mess almost by accident.

In the winter, I lived at the Lord Nelson Hotel in Halifax, to avoid the questionable driving conditions of the 130-mile route to my home in Kentville. I had gone to my grandmother's funeral on a cold December day, not too long after the meeting at Joe MacDonald's cottage. I was feeling blue that night and went across Spring Garden Road to Pepes Restaurant, more for company than from hunger. I saw Fred Dickson and Ted Crease huddled at a table near the huge fireplace, and they insisted that I join them. I was cheered by them, and after a long dinner we walked outside and, despite the cold, stood on the windy corner of Spring Garden Road and South Park Street. Dickson said he wanted to tell us about a most confidential problem Buchanan was facing. Dickson is difficult to understand because his mind works faster than his mouth. He speaks in riddles, delivering vague half-sentences and interspersing them with frequent pauses and gestures. Crease was not a young man, and the cold was obviously bothering him as he held a slim riverboat-gambler cigar between his teeth and kept his hands jammed deep into the patch pockets of his military-style camel-coloured coat while trying to turtle his neck and ears into its upturned collar. I was also growing numb and impatient with Dickson's verbal meanderings, when Crease said, "For God's sake, Freddie, get to the point!" Dickson said, "Boys, Buchanan owes almost $1 million personally, and he can't pay it." Crease almost sucked the foul-smelling cigar down his throat in shock. According to Crease's later version, I was just as jolted. As Dickson droned on, the Buchanan financial picture looked bleaker. Crease instructed Dickson to call an emergency meeting of the same people who had attended the secret session at Joe MacDonald's cottage. There were, in fact, to be many meetings. One of the impediments to solving the problem was apparently a legal hitch. The other was Dr. Ernie Johnson, Buchanan's business partner.

Johnson is fairly tall and extroverted; women found him handsome, and his obvious need for approval and attention made it clear he was ego-driven. He relished being viewed as a confidant of the premier, and he consistently manoeuvred himself into photos and TV tapings, where he appeared, standing just behind the premier with his smiling face showing over Buchanan's shoulder. David Chipman called him the "Prince," after Prince Philip, whose pleasant face always appears just behind Queen Elizabeth in media coverage. Ken Matthews had an amusing version which mirrored his opinion of Johnson, involving John Buchanan sitting on the toilet and Ernie Johnson's smiling face visible over the premier's shoulder — denying him even that moment of privacy.

Matthews, silver-haired with a matching Clark Gable moustache, is a brilliant lawyer, and is widely respected for his legal and political track record. He was one of the scarred Tory veterans dating back to the Great Stanfield Organization but had no equal in his loyalty to Buchanan. Matthews would eventually go to "Glory" as an Appeal Court justice.

Meetings about the Buchanan financial mess were held at John Grant's summer home in Chester, at David Chipman's summer cottage, and at the Citadel Inn, where owner Ralph Medjuck provided free meeting space to Dickson. Chipman was particularly uneasy at the Citadel Inn meetings, and he frequently walked about, looking out into the hall and checking the bathrooms. This behaviour was attributable in part to his nervous energy, but was more directly caused by his suspicion about the surroundings. Good food and wine did not reduce the growing worries about solving the problem as the 1981 election loomed ahead.

Buchanan and Johnson were partnered in companies, on bank notes, and in the ownership of various properties, plus a small potentially lucrative enterprise called "Action Delivery." In addition, the premier was involved, without Johnson, in several motels. One ninety-unit low-rental apartment complex had a federally subsidized 8 per cent mortgage which was fixed for life, even though the normal mortgage rate at the time was 16 per cent. Even that project was behind in its payments as a result of management neglect and poor supervision. As matters got worse, Johnson became more aggressive and volatile, dreaming up new get-rich schemes to try to solve the growing demands of several banks. Johnson's wife, a sensible lady from the family of the late, beloved Liberal MLA from the Eastern Shore, Dr. Duncan MacMillan, tried to curb Ernie's business involvement and urged him to stick to medicine, but he ignored her wise counsel.

Initially Crease and Matthews had mulled over the idea of a blind trust at Grant's cottage, and while I was convinced of their expertise, I also decided to ask Harry Rhude, who once practised law in the same firm as Chipman. I teased Rhude, saying that it was unusual to discuss the Tory premier's problems with a staunch Liberal, but he did advise me. Rhude said that giving money directly to a political figure like Buchanan might be considered "bestowing a benefit," which could be an offence. He suggested a blind trust, but said that he had done no research on the subject, and recommended competent legal advice. He also suggested that a first-class accountant should be involved, and gave me the name of Bob Bruce, a partner at Coopers and Lybrand, whom I knew slightly.

I called Crease and told him what I had learned, and then I broached the subject of the premier's problems with Bob Bruce, who would later inform me that he knew about Buchanan's financial crisis since the Bank of Montreal had once tried to get Buchanan to place his affairs in Mr. Bruce's hands. Harry Rhude had also told me to stay out of the blind trust, and not to act as the trustee — especially if I was going to raise funds. There were more complications to come, and some of us would regret that we had ever heard of a blind trust.

Meanwhile, interest rates were going through the roof, and Buchanan's bankers were getting nervous. He was falling behind and they were pushing him. The pressure on Buchanan from his creditors was enormous, but worse was his fear that his growing debt would be exposed. A widening circle of people knew of the status of his business and personal money problems. PC president John Grant often made indiscreet comments, which exemplified the potential danger, and calls from numerous bank employees, and secretaries typing reports, presented another potential source of leaks. Buchanan could imagine bank employees at social affairs, or standing around the coffee urn at the office, gossiping about the premier's financial mess. He became depressed, and so fearful that, to those of us who knew him best, his ability to function was obviously impaired.

The major purpose of the blind trust, according to Crease and Matthews, was to relieve the premier of pressure and eliminate the possibility of creating a bad impression. The blind trust would allow creditors to be dealt with in a manner that avoided the appearance of fear or favour. And the donors would be unknown to each other and to Buchanan, a potential arms'-length arrangement that apparently was confirmed as desirable by legal opinions about propriety.

Dr. Johnson was a financial concern because of his interest in expanding his already troubled business empire and its connection to the premier's debt burden. Johnson and a lawyer arranged to buy the charter of an old inactive investment company called Atlantic Securities. Johnson told me that, if Atlantic Securities could duplicate the success of Scotia Bond Company under the former Liberal government, he would be able to recoup his business losses.

Despite my warning that the investment business was capital intensive, Johnson proceeded and, worse, followed his usual practice of not participating in the firm's management. Money was borrowed from the Bank of Nova Scotia.

At first Atlantic Securities could not become a member of the Investment Dealers Association (IDA) and, without that membership, could not participate in the Province of Nova Scotia's bond-selling syndicate. That was a serious setback as it deprived the firm of a lucrative area of profit potential.

The national investment dealer McLeod Young Weir, where I worked, managed the provincial debt syndicate and backed Atlantic Securities' next application for IDA membership. That bid was successful, which led the late Frank Guptill of Atlantic Securities to say McLeod had clout with the IDA. Some local investment dealer, who had tried, in the public interest, to keep the financially weak company out of the IDA, agreed with Guptill.

Atlantic Securities did not prosper. In the end, it turned out to be a good thing for Dr. Johnson that he was not involved in the management of the firm as an RCMP investigation of the firm's activities led to two people being charged and convicted, and the firm declared bankruptcy.

As a result, a suit was filed by the Investment Dealers Association against the Bank of Nova Scotia. The IDA, which had allowed cash-strapped Atlantic Securities to be a member, alleged that the bank had made temporary loans to Atlantic, before IDA audits, to enhance the appearance of Atlantic's books. As part of its successful defence, the Bank of Nova Scotia testified in public court that Atlantic Securities personnel entertained the IDA auditor at long pleasant lunches during audits, thereby pre-empting the intense accounting practices required to understand the firm's true financial position.

As the time for the 1981 election drew near, the Atlantic vice-president of the Bank of Montreal, J.R. (Pat) Ellis, not satisfied that Buchanan was responding to the crisis, made frequent telephone calls to the premier. Finally exasperated, Ellis demanded that Buchanan take action; aware of the premier's tendency to vacillate, he issued an ultimatum: "Start reducing the debt, stop living off your MasterCard, at once, or we shall take action which can only result in widespread public knowledge of this situation." (Buchanan's MasterCard account was badly overdrawn.) Ellis, a small, white-haired man with a boyish expression, is no pushover, despite his pleasantness. Widely admired, he is a competent banker who rose to a responsible position from a modest background much like Buchanan's. Active in Christian endeavours, Ellis is a clean-living man with strong faith and character, which were his salvation when his son drowned in British Columbia. There was no question that he wanted action on Buchanan's bank debt. He called Roy Busche and asked for a meeting for the purpose of applying pressure to the premier.

Spiralling interest rates had tied up Buchanan's finances so tightly that his monthly income, including the amount he was being paid by the PC party, was almost completely swallowed up by debt. As he had no disposable income, he resorted to his MasterCard to meet personal and household demands. The card debt became unmanageable as interest on the outstanding balance grew at an unbelievable rate. Ellis correctly brought the crisis to a head.

Mr. Ellis and Roy Busche phoned and asked me to accompany them to see Buchanan. I was fond of the premier and I was reputed to be more direct and blunt with him about my opinions on the debt than some people with alternative agendas, who obviously didn't want to offend him. I refused at first, but eventually did attend the meeting in the premier's office. Mr. Ellis had discussed the problem with Bob Bruce, and it was decided that the premier should engage a professional to budget and manage his personal income in order to reduce expenditures and debt.

Buchanan sat in the old chair behind the desk of power, one foot propped on an open drawer as he stared out of the massive window overlooking Hollis Street and the Provincial Building. Behind him, the garden and the statue of Joseph Howe could be seen against the wrought-iron fence and the Hollis building, gleaming in the afternoon light. On that occasion, that light was the only bright spot in the office. Ellis said that Bruce was too busy to manage the business affairs and the personal finances, so they suggested a competent, soon-to-retire accountant, Douglas Cherry, who had agreed to take on the gargantuan task for no fees or costs.

Buchanan vigorously resisted the idea of what he deemed a "purse-keeper," but it was obvious that he had no choice as Mr. Ellis was adamant. Busche pointed out that the premier's income tax liability was growing because of the payments from the PC party, and that despite the tax deduction of interest expense on business, he was falling behind at an alarming rate. His personal expenses, such as insurance, heating oil, and clothing, were being paid on his MasterCard account. Finally, almost as if he were talking to himself, the premier said, "Okay, if it's Cherry, then let's get on with it."

Despite his acquiescence, born of panic, I knew that he would not go through with the repugnant plan to have Mr. Cherry straighten up his finances; he would avoid facing that solution with every ounce of his endless determination. The fact that this complicated mess, with numerous outside people involved, had avoided the light of publicity was nothing short of a miracle. Then I almost ruined the progress made by Ellis and Busche when I suggested that Mrs. Buchanan be enlisted to assist in budgeting for and managing the family's needs and expenditures. Mavis Buchanan is a typical, unpretentious rural Nova Scotian; she is sometimes blunt, and has a keen ability to recognize patronizing self-serving individuals, long before the limits of John's gullible nature are reached. A no-nonsense individual, Mavis was a powerhouse of service in the premier's constituency and never had her head turned by being the premier's wife. She smoked excessively, and had high blood pressure and a bad heart. Buchanan adored her with a school-boy's puppy love and fascination; he saw it as his duty to reward her for years of frugality in their marriage by being unnecessarily generous with her and the children. He absolutely forbade me to involve Mavis, saying that the shock and stress would tax her already fragile health.

Consistent with the nature of his problems, Buchanan suffered personal depression, withdrawal, unnatural anxiety, and personal physical complaints and ailments, which were quite obviously stress-related. His ability to function was impaired, and his staff, especially Dickson and Joe MacDonald, were forced to be more deeply involved, with implied authority, in the functions of his office.

As I privately predicted, the Douglas Cherry plan was not implemented. The delaying tactics used by the Russians in the winter of the 1942 battle against the mighty German army were no stronger than Buchanan's stubborn ability to wait out pressure, despite the bad effect on his own health. In 1982 a miracle materialized through the wizardry of Bob Bruce. Buchanan owned several motels, and Bruce managed an almost impossible financing for a buyer who took one of them out from the debt umbrella and produced cash for the bank and for the premier's personal account to ease the immediate demands. Bruce had also arranged for Buchanan's sister Dorothy to manage one of the motels, the Sea King located on the Bedford Highway, just outside Halifax. Her management acumen, frugal nature, and obvious ability to resist John's powers of persuasion were traits which Bruce wished he could rely on in other family members in dealing with such expenditures as cars and business enterprises involving the children. While the premier drove a ramshackle, bald-tired station wagon, several of his children had been encouraged by his generosity to own sporty, expensive autos.

Buchanan's mood and personal worries had usurped his attention at a key time, and the premier's office and political affairs of the party were not in the most desirable condition. The PC party's bank account was depleted, and the monthly payments to the premier put pressure on the party and the fund-raisers. The Royal Bank was in touch with party treasurer Roy Busche, as they were concerned about the party's loans and overdraft. Busche would receive a dunning call from the Royal and then scurry about, trying to stimulate the overworked Finance Committee. Busche often called when he needed me to round up donations for his overdraft, and would use the famous English highwayman's expression "Stand and deliver." Busche was under terrible pressure, and his dedication and frugal management were the salvation of the PC party and the premier throughout the Buchanan years.

Finally, Busche called a meeting of the people who usually advised and helped, to alleviate the crisis situation he lived with constantly. The familiar group of Tories gathered again at Medjuck's Citadel Inn, as arranged by Dickson. Chipman again found the setting particularly upsetting. His complaints and his frequent trips to surveille the hall and the bathroom presented an amusing distraction. Chipman's straight-arrow nature is sometimes carried to ridiculous lengths, but he is an honest man. He is a straight-laced, right-wing Conservative whom some of my Tory colleagues considered a political iceman. His running in and out of the room caused someone to mumble, audibly, "David can certainly swear that he didn't hear everything that was said here, in the event anything goes wrong, and because of his spastic roaming around." Everybody roared.

Busche and Crease announced to the meeting that they had a source of money that would relieve the party problems if we could bring their idea to fruition. The idea was actually born in the late 1960s when Crease was a key adviser to federal Tory leader Robert Stanfield. Crease had then convinced the provincial PC party to lend the broke federal Tories the provincial war chest, of about a half a million dollars, for the support of Stanfield's federal leadership. No political loan has much legal protection, and the loan to the Feds was considered a dead loss. However, Crease and Busche, and later the rest of us, were so worried that we decided to try to realize funds from the repayment of that loan. Busche was asked to seek the

PC party executives' blessing to approach the federal Tories about our money.

Crease had also completed the formation of the Buchanan blind trust. After a series of meetings, he and Bob Bruce engaged Patterson, Kitz lawyer Richard Rafuse, and the necessary legal research and administrative details were accomplished with care. Crease next took Rafuse's legal work to have it reviewed by Kenneth Matthews, who practised law in Truro, Nova Scotia, and had agreed to act as "devil's advocate" in researching the blueprint for the trust fund. The plan passed the "smell test," as Mr. Rhude called such examinations, but Crease was so cautious that he applied one more test. He had a friend who was a judge.

A prominent Liberal lawyer, the late Leonard "Lum" Pace, had been elected with the Regan government and had become attorney general. After leaving politics, he was made a judge. Crease had a cordial relationship with Mr. Pace, which possibly originated from their younger days. He met secretly and unofficially with Pace and had him review the planned blind trust, using a judge's critical approach, with a view to telling Crease how other judges might decide if the matter were ever to receive official review or judgement.

Satisfied with all the opinions, Crease and Bob Bruce engaged the Toronto law firm of Fraser, Beatty to do the final work and to act as custodians of the funds, which Crease would attempt to collect. Bob Bruce arranged for two men of outstanding reputation to serve as trustees. Richard Murphy, a Roman Catholic monsignor, and Dr. Earle Reid, both of whom were capable, impartial, discreet, and honest, years later would be pilloried by the media for acting as trustees.

As Buchanan grew tired and haggard from worry, Bob Bruce used a holding company he had formed for the protection of Buchanan's assets to sell real estate to an associate of Ralph Medjuck's in Toronto, and to other people who were connected with Medjuck. A son-in-law of a Medjuck employee bought a motel, with Ralph's backing; the sale involved a leveraged double-mortgage deal that was more magic than substance.

Crease reported to Bruce regularly. Some of the trust money he raised was first paid to the trust's lawyers, Fraser, Beatty in Toronto, and then dispersed by Bruce out of Halifax. But, Crease said, as they tried to keep up with Buchanan's banks, "There is too much blister and too little bandage."

16

THE HOUNDS

RUMOURS CIRCULATED THAT THE RCMP WERE investigating political party fund-raising in Nova Scotia. The Tory party in New Brunswick had gone through that reputation-breaking process during the 1970s. Several charges relating to party activities had been laid, and while they had not resulted in convictions, several people's personal careers and finances had been wiped out, leaving lifelong scars.

Political fund-raising in the corporate sector is fraught with opportunities for misconduct. On one side is a party in power, which the law apparently takes for granted as having influence, and on the other are firms doing or trying to do business with the government. Even if a company legally acquires a government contract without a hint of tollgating, the appearance of misconduct remains if that company has donated money. The result is that some companies who do large amounts of business in a province do not make donations to any political party. The democratic process does not run on good wishes. Some people advocate a form of public disclosure as a way to make the process totally clean. That practice might help, but it, too, offers several loopholes. Some companies use disassociated, yet connected, corporate entities through which they funnel donations so as not to have their own name disclosed. There are any number of scams in use, including donation of cash, goods, or credits, which could circumvent the law of disclosure. If the present system is corrupt, and that seems to be the perception, the answer would be to cut out corporate gifts and limit individual political donations. The best policy could be to expand the current government policy of paying political parties a pre-arranged expense per voter from the public purse, making sure that the parties are scrupulously audited.

A second government option could be to make a yearly grant to each of the three major parties, with which they could operate a party headquarters and information service with a reasonable staff of government-paid workers. Those who would deride this scheme as an unnecessary public expense should consider that it would be far more accessible to public scrutiny and, in the end, cheaper than the old ways of raising funds with a toll or commission.

The investigation by the RCMP became widely known in the early 1980s. Interviews and documents were sought and, in the case of the PC party, the RCMP phoned various people and asked questions. Most of us had not been involved in the previous PC government of the 1956–70 era. My own political involvement for that period had been with the Liberal party, for whom I did not raise funds.

The RCMP fund-raising investigator who called on me was Corporal Bishop; he asked me a seemingly simple question, which I did not answer until I called PC fund-raising chairman David Chipman. In essence the question I relayed to Chipman was, "Did the PC party retain the old collection records from the Stanfield years?" Chipman said approximately this: "The old collectors gave us nothing, not even cooperation, so maybe they burned the stuff like they did everything else." I turned to Bishop and repeated Chipman's remarks and, with tongue in cheek, added, "Maybe President Nixon should have followed that plan and burned the

White House tapes." Even then I could not leave well enough alone and added, "I would have had no place for the 1960s records except the fireplace." Those careless words would later come back to haunt me.

Apparently the RCMP had many documents and PC records, but time had dimmed the connections to the people involved. Thus the RCMP charged only three Liberal fund-raisers: Senator A.I. Barrow, C.R. MacFadden, and Bill Simpson. Apparently the law takes the influence of political people for granted, whether or not they can, in fact, sway or control decisions.

A national media circus attracted attention to our backward methods of raising funds. It amazed me that no mention was made of, and no charges were laid in regard to the Canadian board-room executives who admitted to paying the bribe-like gifts, called commissions, to political parties. It seemed inconsistent to me that law officers would, in effect, charge the prostitute but not the people seeking the prostitute's service. There was never any hint that the men who were charged had kept or received any benefits for themselves, but the businessmen who paid the commissions and camouflaged their method of "buying business" for their firms were let alone.

Bill Simpson was retired, enjoying matrimonial bliss, and travelling. Perhaps wisely, in light of the future suffering and expense to the others involved, Mr. Simpson pleaded guilty and was fined $75,000. He then walked away, free of the mess, while scarcely interrupting his good-time years. The others involved quite correctly pleaded not guilty. Two of the best trial lawyers in Canada, J.J. Robinette and Austin Cooper, both of Toronto, were engaged by the two accused Liberal fund-raisers. Mr. Robinette's impressive court performances were legendary, and Mr. Cooper had defended Toronto nurse Susan Nelles, who had been incorrectly accused in the deaths of children at a Toronto hospital. In Nova Scotia, the legal fees were speculated to be $500,000 for these two fund-raisers' defence.

The witnesses paraded through the court by the Crown comprised a "Who's Who" of Nova Scotia politics, and also of the Toronto business community who were paying the political commissions. Gerald Regan and Senator Henry Hicks, former premiers of Nova Scotia, were named as witnesses. Dr. Hicks had not been premier since 1956 but was still called in the court-room drama that was becoming like a TV soap opera. Former Liberal Liquor Control Act cabinet ministers Fraser Mooney and Bill Gillis were the centre of attention for the Crown, who tried to link the politicians' management to fund-raisers' receipts and requests.

Defence lawyer Cooper did not call Corporal Bishop, the RCMP officer who had interviewed me, but did put another RCMP member who had acquired Bishop's information second-hand on the stand. Cooper asked him why the PC party was not charged, then he prodded the Mountie, who answered, "Because Ripley, the Tory fund-raiser, burned the records." The resulting coast-to-coast publicity caused relatives, business associates, and my son's school chums to tease us without mercy. When I met Bob Stanfield at a social occasion, he held out his hand and said in a voice that he obviously wanted overheard, "Mr. Ripley — awfully pleased to hear about your fire."

Meanwhile, the painful trial of the Liberal fund-raisers was not to be concluded until 1983 when A.I. Barrow and C.R. MacFadden were found guilty of influence peddling and fined $25,000 each by the court, which ignored the Crown's request for fines of $75,000. Eventually MacFadden, who found the matter painful, paid the fine and did not appeal the conviction; he gave in for the sake of peace, privacy, and the hope that his life would return to normal. Barrow chose to appeal and, after a long period of time and much money spent, was acquitted; speculation about the cost of his legal fees, time lost, suffering, and the reported illness of his wife made his life difficult, and people paid little attention to his winning the appeal. The charges, the trial, and the press had done their damage, and the appeal verdict was hardly noticed.

But a better story existed and was never reported. The Liberal party had acquired substantial trust funds, allegedly growing from

126

their fund-raising activities. It would be many years before that fact was revealed by a Liberal party insider, but it raises a question about news reporting or investigative journalism in Canada. Since no charges are levelled against the media for not uncovering or reporting a story, does media chill exist in Canada under our laws? It certainly does not exist to any large degree in the United States.

The late U.S. senator Joe McCarthy kept his communist witch hunts in the public eye and caused the word "McCarthyism" to become part of the English language. McCarthy claimed, "Reporters are like hounds: they follow the scent, but they don't always catch the fox unless you keep the smell right under their noses."

Zsa Zsa Gabor had more luck with a bored media than she did with the courts after she had a run-in with police. Her quip, which illustrates how the publicity put her name back in public consciousness was: "Spare me from bored policemen but not from bored reporters."

In Halifax, the Liberal party fund-raisers' trial for influence peddling was an easy headline grabber. The facts exposed in the court room were neither actionable nor costly in fees for pre-release lawyer laundering, so it was easier to report court-room pap than to chase chance investigative news. It was evident from the testimony that the Liberals had raised a ton of money by charging business people a commission on government supplies and contracts — in other words, "tollgating." Millions of tainted dollars were squirrelled away, and only a few superficial questions were asked of Liberal party leader Sandy Cameron, but no cigars were awarded when the questions missed the mark.

In fairness to media people, it is sometimes an editor or news director who does not recognize a potentially important story, or develops cold feet over possible legal action. After the Watergate affair in the United States, reporters Bernstein and Woodward were heralded as "the real thing," but, without the guts and determination of their editors, the paper, and Ben Bradlee, their story might have been spiked. After all, they were trifling with the White House, and that's a gutsy undertaking. So the difference between a journalist and a reporter is "the facts." Anybody can report news, but only he who can ferret out the facts is a real journalist. In Canada, according to numerous media people, the lack of the United States–type First Amendment protection of free speech turns some editors into fear-impaired news eunuchs.

17

THE ATLANTIC SEA BUBBLE

I N 1981, THE ENERGY BUBBLE, THE ELECTION CAMPAIGN, AND PLAIN good luck diverted attention from John Buchanan and his crumbling real estate business. The nation, and particularly Nova Scotia, was gripped with energy fever as novice investors pursued Mobil options, Gulf Oil Canada, and wild oil stocks in the hope of striking it rich. Similar ambitions were to lead to the creation of a politically sponsored energy company.

Just after the 1981 election, former Tory cabinet minister lawyer Gerald Doucet, and his brother Dr. J. Alfred (Fred) Doucet, who had been a public relations fund-raiser for St. Francis Xavier University, went into business. The Doucet brothers were hardly the Hunts of Texas, but their speculation was to have similar results. They had no oil-patch experience and no drilling rights to acreage offshore, but Gerald Doucet could walk in and out of Premier Buchanan's office almost at will. Gerry Doucet knew Buchanan would help him because it was no secret that the premier wanted to make up for Doucet's 1971 defeat.

Gerald Doucet, a soft-spoken Acadian who was the youngest minister in the Stanfield government, is brilliant. The young MLA had won his spurs when he knocked off Liberal leader Earl Urquhart on his first election attempt. He went on to run for the Tory party leadership against Buchanan and Thornhill in 1971. Victory had been snatched from Doucet's hand, and he never recovered from Thornhill's throwing second-ballot support to John Buchanan. Silent, but obviously bitter, Doucet would not run in the 1974 provincial election. He was known to have developed a friendship with Liberal Gerry Regan, and his law practice prospered during the Liberal government years. Buchanan is unable to stand anyone being upset with him, and had worried about Doucet's feelings for years, going out of his way to make amends. To start their energy company, the Doucets needed an offshore drilling licence and acreage. Buchanan's kind nature and wish to please them produced the miraculous piece of paper that gave them drilling rights off Nova Scotia's coast. Suddenly the Doucets had the sizzle that would allow them to attract investors and money to form a company they called East Coast Energy.

Buchanan's good nature would allow an act of kindness to become a financial disaster. What saved the government of John Buchanan after the Doucet-promoted East Coast Energy fiasco can only be described as exceptional luck. Sandy Cameron later said it was a miracle in the order of what would have been necessary for Custer to have survived Little Big Horn. The timing, the opposition, and the media contributed — mostly by inaction — to a national story slipping away with little attention directed to facts and details. Sandy Cameron blamed the media, but the opposition's failure to support his instincts is the real reason that the story died.

Cameron wanted to fight against the East Coast Energy getting government preference, and possibly a determined fight would have stopped the deal. But Dr. J. Alfred Doucet was a determined man too — more so than his brother Gerry — a driving force who could move mountains, and the opposition did not embarrass him or stop his ambitious plan. Dr. J. Alfred Doucet is a banty rooster-like individual, slightly overweight, temperamental and more extroverted than his quiet, mannerly brother. He has a Ph.D, but it's certainly not in business, if the performance of East Coast Energy is any indication. To Doucet's credit, his humble start in life did not deter him from eventually reaching the halls of power, as a special adviser to Prime Minister Brian Mulroney. Various opinions of his people skills, advice, and political management seem to compare his effectiveness in those areas with his performance in managing East Coast Energy. But Dr. Doucet seemed capable of recognizing those who are stars, and those who would be, and then hitching his wagon to them.

Buchanan wanted the energy company to succeed because he was obsessed with reducing Nova Scotia's dependence on foreign oil. He correctly believed that the cost of electricity had to be controlled, because spiralling power bills had put Regan out of office. But Buchanan was equally devoted to making his government and himself responsive and popular. It was that combination of factors which readied the traces for the Doucets' energy wagon.

The job of being premier, or of holding elected office, was not a badge or symbol of social position to Buchanan. It was a way of life, a personal compulsion which he understood and enjoyed in every way. Simply signing his name, participating in party meetings or functions, attending social events — from an employee's wedding to the Queen Mother's reception — he enjoyed them all, and it was apparent that he loved the job. He liked cabinet, the big junk-food lunches, the banter, and the process. While he loved bestowing benefits and favours, and helping people, it was not just having the power which pleased him. It was being able to make a difference.

I knew him intimately, and saw him daily for twenty years, and his head never swelled, his attitude never deteriorated. He liked the heat of the political process. He liked the taxi driver and the guy on the corner as much as he did the members of his Campaign Committee. He often talked for half an hour at a time with my long-time assistant, Charlene Titus, who was a shy Liberal, but genuinely respected and liked "JMB," as she called him; she was not without good sense and practical advice for him too.

Buchanan could take so long picking up his dry-cleaning that his chauffeur, Jack Wheatly, would sooner pick it up than waste two hours following Buchanan around while he talked with anyone who smiled at him. While his wardrobe was sharp and professional, Buchanan could wear a pair of $250 Dack triple-soled brogues down to a dilapidated, shabby, running-shoe state in six months. (My mother, who worked in our family shoe business for forty-two years, would get my father to order him new shoes and make Buchanan discard the old ones.)

Buchanan's sense of humour was not without uniqueness too. He once convinced a visiting English nobleman that the world's largest inkwell, and major natural source of ink, were located outside Windsor, Nova Scotia.

It was a political weakness of John Buchanan's management that he needed to be liked and wanted to help people. He never seemed to be able to say "no" to anyone. That fact set the stage for Gerald and Fred Doucet to form their energy company and raise just enough money to get themselves, and a lot of innocent investors, into trouble. Unfortunately Buchanan's approach to government was based on the same kindness. He would never hesitate to say "yes," and as a result approved most projects, from big hospitals and small paving ventures to the Doucets' weird business enterprise.

East Coast Energy was all sizzle, and a lot of small folks, and quite a few big ones, got burned financially. Tom Kierans, president of McLeod Young Weir, and J. Alfred Doucet were both well-educated, and smart and adept at verbal persuasion; each was able to make anything he said come across with such conviction that it was almost always believed.

Dr. Doucet approached an employee of McLeod Young Weir in Halifax, Ross T. Montgomery, and asked him to try to take the energy company public and raise funds. Montgomery very properly went to Tom Kierans at McLeod's Toronto office, as Fred Doucet asked him to do. Kierans apparently looked the company over and told Montgomery that it needed equity money and instructed him to help Fred find his needed seed capital privately, on the clear promise that if the company ever went public for funds, McLeod Young Weir would be given the account. Ross explained the rules to Fred, and then Ross, Fred, and another broker, Bill Ritchie, set out to attract some pretty heavy hitters in business — including a future prime minister, Brian Mulroney.

Some big names in Canada became associated with the company, and Kierans provided advice to Montgomery, who initially worked very hard, free of charge, to get them started. Ross said that Fred was the real asset as he dealt in super-salesman fashion with prospective investors on planes, in barbershops, and even in his small home village of Grand Etang. As the deal unfolded, it appeared to be ready to go public, and Ross called Toronto to inform Kierans, who dispatched the underwriter and director of corporate finance, Peter Gillan, to Halifax. Fred and Ross had become fast friends by then; the company was very important to them, but for Peter Gillan that created a situation in which the chaff outweighed the wheat. Even with the seed money and the right to drill off Nova Scotia, the only real asset the company could boast of was hope. Gillan was conservative and was very worried about the assets and the lack of funds. He wondered out loud if there was any gas out at sea or just Fred Doucet's hot air.

The first meeting with East Coast's board of directors indicated that the structure of share capital, and some of the hopes of a few directors, were unrealistic. A series of lengthy meetings followed, held at various posh offices of some impressive Canadian business people. But Peter Gillan did not seem to share Kierans's and Montgomery's enthusiasm for the reality of the deal as he saw it. "Hopeful Fred," said Peter Gillan, who was not taken in by name-dropping. Peter's habitual diligence usually resulted in work carried out thoroughly and simply, with little resistance or interference. But Fred Doucet wanted to be involved at almost every stage, and Gillan did not want his involvement in that aspect of the promotion.

Halifax-owned Scotia Bond was entitled to be, and able to be, a lead dealer with McLeod in the proposed venture because Bill Ritchie, a large shareholder in Scotia Bond, was also a director of East Coast Energy. McLeod and Scotia Bond appointed George

Mitchell, of the Cox, Downie firm of lawyers, to represent the syndicate formed to distribute the East Coast shares to the public on a "best-efforts basis." This in itself caused a strenuous and strained argument between McLeod and Dr. Doucet, as he demanded that his deal be an underwriting. In an underwriting, the dealers involved agree to buy, at commencement, the shares of the company going public, and then go out and sell them for a profit. The risk is substantial — especially on a speculative issue like this one. So McLeod would agree only to try to sell the issue on a best-efforts basis, with no risk to McLeod and the other dealers.

George Mitchell was a model of propriety in what otherwise became an amateur farce. Dr. Doucet said that he believed that Wood Gundy, a prominent Canadian international investment dealer, was very eager to do the public offering exactly as Dr. Doucet wanted it done, and without McLeod's and Scotia Bond's conservative need to check and investigate so much. Bill Ritchie, of Scotia Bond, wanted the deal to succeed, but insisted on proper process. He felt that Dr. Doucet was bluffing to force Scotia Bond to structure the issue his way. Dr. Doucet claimed that Gundy would underwrite (buy the deal) as principals, and sell it from their own treasury. Bill Ritchie and I doubted this — and my habit is never, ever, to bluff, as I do not relish "eating crow." I listened to Dr. Doucet, who was seated in a CEO position at the large table on the top-floor board room of the Professional Building at the corner of Spring Garden Road and Robie Street. Later I stood at the multi-windowed side of this classy office, looking at the twinkling lights of the city, with Peter Gillan, my McLeod colleague, at my side, while Dr. Doucet and the others, including entrepreneur Ralph Fiske and Philip Oland of Moosehead Breweries, were huddled quietly in another room.

I whispered to Gillan that I was going to set some ground rules; he agreed, and when we returned to the table Dr. Doucet outlined his prospective deal. He wanted us to give them $10 million less a 4 or 5 per cent commission, consisting of two million $5 shares. He went on to point out that this deal was good, and that we could more or less take it or leave it. I told those assembled that, while I did not have the authority to spend $10 million of McLeod's money, I did have the authority to say no to the deal. I tried to remain calm and polite. I said that we did not agree with Dr. Doucet, and that Mr. Gillan and Mr. Ritchie would structure a presentation that was better for the public and simpler for his company. The commission would be 8 per cent — a normal fee — with no purchase or underwriting, simply a best-efforts sales agreement. Doucet reddened, blustered, and his comments were animated and disconnected. He shut his notepad holder with a snap and stood up. Then, he looked at me with a grimace of anger and said, "You understand we will have to consult other investment dealers." I was still polite and suggested that he should do just that since I felt that most, if not all the people around the table cherished their reputations too much to be involved in a failure. I added that we would drop the matter until he "canvassed the street of dealers." Then I would ask our board whether they still wanted to be involved or not. The meeting broke up on a sombre note, Gillan and Ritchie both agreeing that no "Doucet mousetrap" would be accepted.

Negotiations continued for weeks, with little progress. A meeting was called by Dr. Doucet at Ralph Fiske's board room at Historic Properties. Peter Gillan was busy, and told me to insist at the meeting that every professional condition be met. It started with Dr. Doucet vacillating between keeping us and replacing us, with dealers he had allegedly found on Bay Street. He went on to say that he was leaning toward retaining us only because Kierans had allowed Ross Montgomery to help with seed money; he added that he wanted $5 shares sold. I interrupted and said that speculative issues should be in the neighbourhood of $1 if they were to be marketed effectively, and we did not want to give false impressions and hopes. The banter and arguing were still going on at midnight. I delivered an ultimatum at 1:00 a.m. that things would be done our way or we would not be involved. My suggestion was a convertible one for ten, $15 preferred — or $1.50 a share! I left bleary-eyed, and drove 65 miles to my house in Kentville. Raspy-voiced and dead-tired, I fell asleep in mid-sentence, talking to my wife.

At 6:00 a.m., the phone rang for a dreamer's eternity. My wife answered it and gave it to me. Ralph Fiske asked politely that I come to Halifax for an 8:00 a.m. meeting. I showered; dunked my head in cold water; shaved, almost removing my chin; and chugged down a coffee. I had had three and a half hours' sleep and, as I drove to Halifax, I feared a long argument awaited me.

I arrived at Mr. Fiske's office at 7:45 a.m., and by 8:30 we were back to the 1:00 a.m. position. I told those assembled that my credentials were poor compared with theirs; I was simply a mechanic and had absolute instructions from Gillan. I told them I was going to breakfast and would phone them for an answer. As I left and walked dejectedly back to the Toronto-Dominion Bank Building, I was fearful that we might actually get the crazy deal.

I guess it's called dealer's dysentery, and it often occurs when you're doing transactions with unknowns involved. I set my office clock alarm for one hour later and fell into a sound sleep. When the alarm woke me, I phoned Kierans (at home, because it was Saturday) and told him where things stood. He instructed me to soften up a bit, as he thought the deal had potential. When I called Gillan, he did not agree with Kierans or with Doucet, and also said he did not like their pressure tactics. I was filled with apprehension when I phoned Mr. Fiske, but to my amazement, they had agreed to all of our conditions, including the fee. I thanked him, but on the way home to Kentville I had the feeling that I had first-mate's papers for the *Titanic*.

The prospectus deadline for completion of the deal was December 1982. The usual promotional travelling show-and-tell meetings, organized by McGuire Public Advertising and Fred, Peter Gillan, Ross Montgomery, a lawyer, and in some cases Tom Kierans, went out to sell the deal to dealers, institutions, and large investors. Unfortunately, small investors were flocking in numbers, which worried me, and I told everyone in the show to be careful. Ross did exercise some influence over Fred, and could keep him level and cool, forestalling his tendency to zoom into overdrive or overkill mode. McLeod's chairman, Austin Taylor, almost totally ignored the deal, asking only how much they were paying us as a fee. In retrospect, I wish that was all I had to do with it.

Meanwhile, Ross and Fred were selling the stock to pension funds, big investment management funds, and even to the Maritime Telegraph and Telephone Company pension fund, which purchased $250,000 worth. The big investors did not concern us, as they are wise and responsible and experienced in assessing risk, but the pensioners, green kids, widows, and orphans were sinking whatever they could into the shares. December arrived too slowly for me but too soon for Dr. Doucet, as the issue was low by $3 million. Fred insisted that we extend the deadline into January. After many meetings, Kierans gave in to Fred, and we were now looking for more big investors. Fred located Walter Wolfe, a somewhat mysterious European entrepreneur, in Montreal and, using his compelling spiel, sold him on the deal.

I was fearful of Wolfe's involvement as it appeared that he might be a tad aggressive, and his Canadian lawyer was Michel Cogger of Montreal. Mr. Cogger and Dr. Doucet agreed to do a half-million-dollar purchase for Mr. Wolfe, payable in U.S. funds drawn on a Bermuda bank. The Greenbergs of Ottawa, and the Quebec government energy arm, Sogepet, bought $1 million worth, and finally we reached $7 million. I absolutely refused to do more or extend the deal. It had kept us from sensible projects, clients, and work, and I was sure that some disaster or lawsuit would occur. It didn't take much of a prophet to make such a prediction.

In February 1983, the trouble started when Walter Wolfe wanted out because he needed money quickly. We told him that the market was too thin to sell that amount of speculative stock. Michel Cogger called us daily, trying to get out of the deal, and finally he asked me if I'd be offended if he went directly to McLeod president Tom Kierans. I quickly agreed in order to get rid of the hassle, even though I felt sorry for Cogger, who was caught between Wolfe and Fred Doucet, who was now ignoring them. Tom Kierans agreed to help Cogger and Wolfe out by making a stock margin loan to them of $250,000 against their shares in East Coast Energy. My notes and those of Suzanne Wilde, an assistant at McLeod, and the Ontario court record would later confirm the exact nature of Kierans's deal and Cogger's acceptance, even though Kierans hated to be reminded that he had made the loan to impress Cogger, who was close to Brian Mulroney, a man Kierans correctly judged would soon be prime minister. But then Cogger refused to pay back the money, and the word "lawsuit" was uttered.

The Ontario court record shows that Kierans flew to Montreal and met with Cogger for hours. What was said between them is a matter for conjecture, but Cogger disavowed Kierans's version, which was from notes supposedly written in a taxi on the way to the airport. Since I have a learning disability which necessitates my making notes of everyday transactions, I have extensive notetaking experience, but even I cannot write notes in a moving car.

The deal was destined for disaster. Walter Wolfe would not allow his agent, Michel Cogger, to repay McLeod the money because East Coast was already suffering a cash crunch. Kierans instructed Fraser, Beatty of Toronto, the same firm that was involved with the Buchanan blind trust, to sue Michel Cogger and Walter Wolfe. The suit came to court in Ontario in 1986. The judge found against Mr. Wolfe, and excused Cogger as his legal agent without responsibility. The decision had not resulted in payment by 1987.

The only hope for saving East Coast Energy was for the company to be the beneficiary of a second miracle. Doucet correctly saw the gas-transmission rights from the oil (and gas) patch to land for distribution as an asset with intrinsic value, and he needed it to involve more investors and lenders, or for a lever to the money pits of the western oil companies. There were many forces at work trying to acquire those same rights, which only Buchanan could ultimately bestow. Mobil, TransCanada PipeLines, and the premier's old pal Neil Nichols, along with Ralph Medjuck and Gerry Doucet, all camped in the premier's office, trying to acquire the distribution rights and attempting to thwart their opponents' chances.

A long-time pal of Buchanan's at TransCanada Pipe may have hurt his career by his role in the great Atlantic Energy bubble. The man convinced his company that he had clout with Buchanan, which he did, and through a subsidiary they invested heavily in developer Ben McCrea's real estate project called "Founders Square," and also opened an office there on Hollis Street in Halifax. They made generous contributions to the PC party through me and were generous to Nova Scotia–based charities. He wanted the gas-distribution contract (pipeline) for his firm, and based on his being an ex–Nova Scotian pal of the premier's, he had high hopes.

Meanwhile, Ralph Medjuck thought he was buying a different kind of insurance by arranging a takeover of several troubled real estate ventures of Buchanan's from trustee Robert Bruce. Bruce had named the company he used to corral Buchanan's various enterprises "Alder Holdings," an ironic allusion to the abundant wild useless bush that dominates Nova Scotia. Medjuck seemed obsessed with the idea of having the gas-distribution system for Nova Scotia, before he had a company or firm partnership. Fred Doucet did not sound like a fan of Medjuck's when he alluded to greed and allowed that the developer "had gas already."

Doucet exerted considerable pressure on me to push Buchanan for another miracle and to save East Coast Energy by granting the company the gas-distribution rights. In conversation with those three main competitors for the pipeline, it became clear that only Trans-Canada PipeLines was qualified, ready, and experienced. In the interim, a Mobil executive was quoted, or misquoted, as having uttered a threatening-type statement, saying that his firm "would have the distribution rights." In essence, all concerned felt certain that they would be selected by Buchanan. Doucet openly speculated to me about having the inside track, and only Buchanan's school chum seem worried, but still had faith that the premier would choose him. Each time they arrived at the premier's office, where almost all of them were camped during that period, each was encouraged by Buchanan's warm reception and attentive hospitality. But some of us recognized that Buchanan was using Mackenzie King's old trick of not making a decision and, by not uttering a refusal and being so civil, allowing each applicant to jump to his own self-interested conclusions.

Buchanan's delaying tactic would again succeed, allowing time to resolve the dilemma.

The Doucet company went bankrupt. Medjuck was reported to have financial problems from stock market speculation. He seemed to fade away from the table and forget the energy business. Mobil just quit and pulled out altogether. Then TransCanada PipeLines closed their Halifax office, and the aspirants for the Nova Scotia gas-distribution bubble fizzled out. TransCanada PipeLines sold their interest in Founders Square to Ben McCrea, but ended up in a legal squabble over it. Shortly after that, Buchanan's friend seemed to be the victim of a personality war with the new management of TransCanada PipeLines and was suddenly no longer a member of the executive and discussing a possible lawsuit, based on his thirty years of loyal service to that company.

18

DEVELOPER RALPH MEDJUCK

EFORE THE LAST WORKING MEETING FOR THE purpose of trying to resolve the Buchanan finances, I had knowledge that Joe MacDonald had a small trust account at the McInnes, Cooper law firm, from which he paid minor expenses for the premier. I had once received a big cheque from that account for some emergency Buchanan expenditures. Dickson spoke to me and said that Ralph Medjuck would be giving me money for that account. I had not personally known Medjuck until about 1978, when I discovered that the former Dickson law partner was providing $2,000 a month to pay research staff at PC Headquarters for Buchanan. That was very confusing to me because Medjuck was a self-proclaimed confidant and fund-raiser for Liberal leader Gerald Regan at that time.

Medjuck is a sartorially splendid clothes-horse; very successful; a director of several companies, including the later troubled Central Trust. Women found him attractive. He is very charming and gracious, and one of the most talented negotiators I've observed. He opened a substantial brokerage account with me, and then, on several occasions, presented me with whole smoked salmon, having been told it was a favourite of mine.

Dickson called me and said that a small financial crisis existed, and Joe MacDonald needed money for a survey. The party people, strapped for cash, had fits when Joe wanted to do surveys, so I handled that familiar type of crisis. Dickson said Medjuck would be in touch to make a substantial donation; before long Medjuck visited my office in person. He ordered tea, and while he made a long-distance call on my phone, he passed me a cheque for $40,000, payable to me personally. I told him I would not accept the cheque; I was afraid it might cause income tax problems, and I didn't know the law on a donation made under such circumstances. I excused myself and phoned Joe MacDonald, who told me it was legal and I should accept it. I was still not sure, so I called lawyer Harry Rhude, whom I trusted implicitly and knew well from dealings with him in his position as chairman of Central Trust. Rhude was a strong but inactive Liberal, but, other than my father, I admired and trusted no one more than Rhude. I knew he would not bend a rule, had no vested interest, and would quickly apply what I call the "smell test." Rhude told me that it was not necessary to declare political donations and that no law of which he was aware prevented people from hiding their donations, so the gift was not illegal. But he advised me that, to protect myself, I should convert the cheque to a bank draft payable, in trust, to the McInnes Cooper Robertson law firm, and to make photostats of the cheque and the draft.

I went back to Medjuck, who was still making calls on my office phone, and waited. He told me that he was considering the matter a loan on his books, but I sent someone to the T-D Bank to buy a draft, as Rhude had suggested. I still have the photostats.

In later years, after Sandy Cameron was through as Liberal leader, Cameron and I worked together and became close friends. Cameron confirmed that Medjuck was a political chameleon; Medjuck had attended the Liberal leadership convention when Sandy had run against Vince MacLean, and he had showed up with a Cameron campaign badge inside his suitcoat on one side and a MacLean badge on the other side — depending upon whom Ralph was talking to, he would judiciously show the appropriate badge, like a Western sheriff flashing a star.

Sandy Cameron and I developed a farcical skit from that story to entertain other employees of the firm. I would approach Cameron in an exaggeratedly affectionate and gushy manner, hand outstretched, and say, "Sandy!" and Cameron would reply, "Ralph!" Then I would flash my coat open, saying, "See, I'm wearing your button, Sandy." But then I'd pretend I'd flashed the MacLean button by mistake and quickly open the other side of my coat, saying, "Oops, I wonder who put that damn MacLean button in there." The staff demanded numerous encore performances, and Sandy got the best last laugh when he would say, like the Bartles and James wine cooler TV advertisement, "And thank you for your support."

Ralph Medjuck survived credit calls from banks and brokers several times when he was allegedly at the gates of a financial "Boot Hill." Bernie Vaughan, an ardent Catholic and Tory, said, "Ralphie is like Lazarus, risen from the dead-broke." Medjuck next set his sights on acquiring the development rights to a piece of government land situated on the waterfront side of Water Street, in one of the most valuable real estate areas of Halifax. He made no bones about his intended success, and was already sketching major proposals before the government board made a decision. One of his most ambitious plans included a proposed aquarium, which was not taken too seriously by some observers because of the cost and maintenance problems. I ran into Kip Brison, a stock broker, at about that time, and I told him that Mr. Medjuck's proposal for an aquarium should be impressive to the government board. Kip said, "It'll end up being a gold fish bowl in the lobby." It was obvious that there were other suitors for that same Crown land, and one was a major Canadian Insurance Company.

Their Toronto representative came to my office without an appointment. I ushered him into the small board room, expecting a PC donation cheque, as firms on the make quite often develop religion and donate generously. He sat down at the table near me and removed an 18-carat-gold Rolex President's model watch from his arm and slid it gently in my direction. I stared at him and the watch. He said, "Know what that is?" I said, "Yup." He said, "Next time I come back, if the Life Company is happy with my progress here today, I could leave it." I said, "Nope." He was embarrassed and flustered, saying, "I hope I've not offended you." I said, "'Fraid so. First, you insulted me with a stupid question; next, you indicate I'm cheap as well as stupid by offering me a fake Hong Kong Rolex." He was very red-faced by then and apologetically said, "Oh no, I offered you a real Rolex. They cost over $16,000." I said, "Aw shucks, I've already been bribed with one of those." We kicked him out and wrote it up in the daily diary.

The announcement that Ralph Medjuck's company and Joe MacDonald's firm, McInnes Cooper Robertson, would jointly be involved in the development of that government land did not receive the roaring press and opposition indignation it deserved. I would have screamed if I had been a member of the opposition. The design was also a subject open to comment. The building is green metal with large dark windows and is named "Cornwallis Place," but it looks like, and is nicknamed, the "Green Frog."

Even the NDP were silent on the "Green Frog," and speculation about that was not as it could have been, because of a stressful domestic situation. NDP leader Alexa McDonough's husband, Peter (whom she later divorced), was a partner in the law firm of McInnes Cooper Robertson; had the McDonoughs not been rumoured to be suffering marital distress, she could have been criticized for her low-key performance on the "Frog."

PART 3

BUCHANAN IN DECLINE

1984 – 1990

19

THE MANDATE

POLITICAL WINDS AND FORTUNES CHANGE QUICKLY. In 1983, when federal MP Elmer MacKay resigned his seat in Central Nova to give new leader Brian Mulroney a place to seek election, the federal Tories desperately needed Buchanan's help to elect Mulroney. MacKay had so many byways paved in Central Nova by the provincial government that Joe MacDonald joked about a man who bent over to tie his shoe in Pictou County and got paved into the street. But Elmer MacKay was very unhappy with provincial Tory finance chairman David Chipman during that by-election. MacKay approached the premier's office and wanted the more experienced provincial group to raise money for Mulroney's by-election. Rumours of tons of donations and overspending reached Chipman, and to avoid what he thought would be a potential scandal, he refused MacKay's request. But Chipman did not attempt to interfere with my being volunteered to raise money. After MacKay became the federal solicitor general, some people thought he would oppose Chipman's becoming a judge. Fortunately for Chipman, he had formed a personal relationship with Brian Mulroney during two leadership races and, when Buchanan interceded with Mulroney, any opposition MacKay had didn't matter.

In the 1983 by-election, I raised $23,000 for the federal Tories, and MacKay told me that they had so much money that he didn't know what to do with it. I reported that to Roy Busche and, after the election, he approached Elmer MacKay's riding association to borrow money. They turned us down. Chipman, Crease, and Busche were furious, as initial overtures to Ottawa to retrieve the old Nova Scotia PC party's $500,000 Stanfield loan was rebuffed by the federal Tories. Nobody raised much trouble because it was not hard to see that the Tories were going in federally.

In 1984, when John Turner, the new Liberal prime minister, called a federal election, there was little doubt that Mulroney would be elected. Suddenly a whole bunch of ambitious Tories, who had their own agenda, wanted to run the federal campaign in Nova Scotia without Buchanan's help. "Pizza Joe" Stewart; Stewart McInnes; his collector, Ross Montgomery; and a fast-running young crowd, who sometimes jet-planed to Boca Raton for weekends of golf and fun, took over. Fred Doucet was in charge of Mulroney's national campaign, and he picked his own people to run it. But Mulroney made one faux pas after another, and following the televised debate with Turner, it became apparent that the Tories were not a shoo-in. Norm Atkins, a tough, practical professional from Joe Clark's day, was resurrected quickly, and Doucet was shoved aside.

Buchanan was enlisted by the new chief, Atkins, who wanted the provincial party's assistance. Buchanan put Dickson and Macdonald in place to try to salvage the marginal seats where we were trailing the Grits. Dickson approached me on a Friday and asked me to raise $20,000 for him by Tuesday. I did it, but not without some luck, and not all of it good. Someone gave me the name of a Cape Bretoner, Dr. Alban Prossin, who ran a labour-oriented therapy organization, which he claimed was underfunded and poorly supported by government. Dr. Prossin's brother had run for the Liberals provincially in Halifax County, but the good doctor declared himself a "staunch Tory." I found Dr. Prossin to be a wonderful man, but my ass pained me whenever we spoke. He asked what kind of money we considered a good donation. I usually don't state an amount, but to shock him I said, "Oh, I don't know, let's say ten." He never flinched and wrote a cheque for $10,000, payable to the PC organization. He also instructed me as to which candidates and constituencies were to get the money, and I agreed, subject to approval by Fred Dickson. Then the money went to provincial PC treasurer Roy Busche, with instructions to send a letter to each federal candidate on the list, with a copy going to Prossin so he would know his wishes had been followed. The happy candidates would know who had assisted their campaigns. Most people who donate money have sincere motives; party believers will give to any cause within their ability. However, some people are merely favour seekers and give to the party they think will win an election to ensure that they will have clout with party people. I try not to classify people, and in Dr. Prossin's case I assumed he would go home to Sydney happy, and I could get on with business. Over the next months, however, Dr. Prossin began telling party people how much he had given and used my name as a confirming source of his loyalty. Dr. Prossin next called me from Ottawa, saying that he had done a federal research project for the Post Office and claiming that he was speaking from the prime minister's office. He asked for my help in presenting him to various elected federal Tories and I told him daily that I had no connections there. His memory must have been short, because for a period of almost a month he phoned me every day, including Sunday, asking for the same help. Finally, I got angry and stopped talking to him, only to hear later that he had received some federal appointment.

The federal election campaign of 1984 took Buchanan's mind off his own troubles as he liked campaigns. It was good therapy for him. He stopped talking about moving to Massachusetts, and his old bounce was revitalized. Dickson and MacDonald advised Buchanan to strike quickly, while the federal Tories were still on a honeymoon with the public. So Buchanan called a provincial election for November 6, 1984. I guessed that he would run, win, stall for a

149

period, and then, like 1950s boxing champ Rocky Marciano, hang up his gloves — undefeated. I was wrong. We all turned our attention, filled with thoughts of sugar-plums, to the Mulroney Tories in Ottawa. We were wrong about that too!

The federal Tories, with few experienced hands, had a massive majority and great expectations. Mulroney earned his government's first public abuse by appointing cronies to every cushy job in sight. His first move, which sparked a controversy even among party members, was his selection of a St. Francis Xavier University pal and leadership worker, Dr. J. Alfred Doucet, as his chief adviser in the Prime Minister's Office. Doucet was smooth, educated, even brilliant, but he was politically stupid about people. He came across as unapproachable and arrogant. While Doucet was top banana, the prime minister, the cabinet, and the party blundered into consistent chaotic embarrassments and public failures. Party people were furious at Doucet over many things; he was totally blamed for the PMO's stupidity.

On one occasion, the prime minister contacted a Halifax woman, Helen Gillis, about accepting a Citizenship Court judgeship. He spoke to her directly, after checking her credentials through local people and the solicitor general's facilities. Ms. Gillis told the prime minister she was pleased to be asked but had to give it some thought and discuss it with her long-time employer. She was told by the prime minister to call back when she had decided that she would accept, and she did as instructed. A person at the prime minister's office asked the nature of the call. The Halifax woman said, "I'm instructed to call about my appointment as a Citizenship Court judge." She was told that she would be called back. Days grew into weeks, and at just about the time she had mentally dropped the subject, she was phoned by Dr. Doucet. Before she said more than "Hello," Dr. Fred, whom she had known for years, began to berate her about her phone call "seeking a Citizenship Court judgeship." Doucet said, "You don't just call up the Prime Minister of Canada and ask to be made a Citizenship judge. There are many qualified, ranking people on that list, and frankly I'm appalled by your nerve." Helen Gillis said only, "Thank you, Dr. Doucet, but please tell the prime minister that I did return his call and that you have changed my mind." Embarrassed, she hung up without giving him an opportunity to further insult her. Eventually Mulroney phoned her again and, after a long talk, she reluctantly accepted, but not without telling a shocked prime minister about Dr. Doucet's rudeness.

Most of the Mulroney government's wounds were self-inflicted, and rather than affixing all the blame to Doucet, some Eastern Canadians applied the seafaring expression "As goes the Captain, so sails the ship" to the prime minister. New MPs and cabinet ministers could be excused for gaffs, but Elmer MacKay, the solicitor general, had been in Parliament for over a decade and was a minister in the short-lived government of Joe Clark. MacKay should have known better, but made an unforgivable legal mistake when his old friend Richard Hatfield, the premier of New Brunswick, got into legal troubles during a Royal Tour of the province.

The RCMP discovered marijuana in Hatfield's suitcase during a routine search of baggage about to be put on the Royal Tour aircraft. The resulting international publicity and scandal were carried in the tabloids clear to southern California. While the RCMP were on the spot, which had senior mounties wishing there was a way to sweep the incident out of sight, Hatfield panicked and called MacKay for a meeting. He travelled to Ottawa and met with MacKay in a hotel room, but professional media sleuthing had discovered the meeting. One journalist raised the question of how many ordinary citizens could, like Hatfield, arrange a meeting with the solicitor general, if they were under investigation. If the RCMP had made any headway in finding a way to sweep the Hatfield marijuana case under a rug, his meeting with MacKay killed the possibility.

The 1984 provincial Tory win saw some changes that were expected as well as a few surprises. One shocker was that NDP lawyer Bob Levy, who was to become a celebrity, was elected in Kings South (for fifty years a Tory stronghold), defeating the sitting member, Dr. Paul Kinsman, by sixteen votes. Tory Dick Weldon was defeated in Dartmouth, and PC Malcolm MacKay went down to NDP candidate John Holm in Sackville. Liberal leader Sandy Cameron lost his seat to Tory Dr. Chuck McNeil in Guysborough. Sandy's father had once held the seat, as had his grandfather, but being on the road during the campaign cost Sandy. Cameron's wife was seriously ill during the election, and he had a bad time. The electorate can be cruel and fickle, and no form of combat is so debilitating to the ego as elections and politics. Liberal MLA Bill Gillis, who complained so much that his own supporters were sure he would lose, surprised everybody and won.

The tidal power dam, which was constructed as a pilot of the proposed Fundy mega-project, was opened during the federal election campaign by Premier Buchanan. As a courtesy, he invited federal Liberal minister Gerry Regan to speak, because there was federal money in the dam. Regan gave a partisan speech, which was in poor taste at such an event. Buchanan defused it when he stood and said, "The foregoing was a non-paid political announcement."

The Liberals called a leadership contest to replace Sandy Cameron. Vincent MacLean, the combative Cape Breton MLA and former Speaker and minister in the Regan government, was the first to enter. James Cowan, a classy, academic Halifax lawyer, was the second candidate. Cowan is the son of the late Judge Gordon Cowan, who years before was himself a Liberal leadership candidate. The campaign was slow in opening, but MacLean seemed to have the jump on Cowan from day one. Unlike public elections, in political party inside elections, the party faithful are drawn to partisan speeches and rhetoric; they love it when a candidate kicks the other party or government in the pants. Vincent MacLean, a political street brawler, was better at partisan politics than Cowan. Usually Cowan appeared a little shy and tried to stick to positive ideas, which sometimes made him sound dry and academic. Objective observers, impartial people, and most Conservative party members thought that Cowan would be the tougher man for Buchanan to beat. He would have been the more able of the two to lead the Liberal party to victory because he had more public appeal than MacLean, who was widely regarded as a pit bull who couldn't overcome his own bombastic nature.

The Cowan camp seemed to be making inroads as the campaign progressed. MacLean, apparently suspecting that his support base might be eroding, intensified his campaign activities, with power speeches and even more toughness, while at the same time attempting to smile and look statesman-like. One Liberal said, "When Vince shows his teeth, you don't know if he's smiling or going to eat you." Cowan put pressure on, while maintaining his dignity, but, sadly, a faction in the party started a whispering campaign which suggested that Cowan was the "old-boy" establishment's darling, and that he was receiving financial help from vested interests in Halifax. His youthful looks and nice manners were branded as a disadvantage in going "for the Tory jugular." In one Liberal woman's words, "The fools didn't think he [Jim Cowan] could muck-rake as well as Vince MacLean."

MacLean won, as expected, and came out of the race loaded to hunt Tory elephants. He went after the government, their legislation and individual conduct. He pressed a charge with the RCMP against Tory cabinet minister Billie Joe MacLean (not a relative). Vince was in continuous combat mode. Billie Joe was accused of expense-account fraud and was in trouble when the investigation was completed. Meanwhile, Liberal party insiders tried to convince Vince to cultivate a friendlier TV image, to use a less rambunctious style, and to cultivate the loyalty of the Cowan people. Cowan's people were angry about the leadership campaign rumours and whispers, which appeared too organized to be spontaneous.

Years later, in 1988, after the Conservative party squeezed by MacLean's Liberals to a narrow win, Tory financial coordinator Suzanne Huett said, "It's a damn good thing for the Conservative party that MacLean is leader instead of Jim Cowan, because Cowan would be premier now if the Grits had been smart enough to choose him as their party leader." Buchanan said that Huett was right. Political parties often make selections that are not the most appealing to the public. Party members, armed with biases, are usually motivated by favours wanted or owed on a long ledger of political back-scratching. Cowan was to be kicked again after the leadership race by a small mistake, much amplified by the media.

Jim Cowan practised law, and his father was a judge. The pressure on any son to equal or exceed his successful father is great, but politics and public affairs had made Jim Cowan well known to the media. One of Cowan's clients in Dartmouth complained to Cowan's firm about his tardiness in settling an uncomplicated legal matter. Cowan's firm acted at once and satisfactorily concluded the client's business. The client belatedly decided to file a complaint with the Barristers' Society against Cowan. Cowan was treated poorly, and his story was leaked to the media.

In James Cowan's case, it looked like the Barristers' Society had overreacted because of his high profile. He was disciplined, and the incident was publicized, but dishonesty wasn't involved — only tardiness. It was widely believed that he got screwed; a letter of reprimand quietly tucked in his file would have been enough, but a fine or suspension was too much. Cowan went back to practise law, MacLean had clear title to the leadership of the Liberal party, and Buchanan was still premier.

20

MacLean versus MacLean

HARRY HOW ADMITS THAT HE WAS SORRY TO LEAVE politics in 1983 to become the chief Provincial Court judge. But his wife's deteriorating health, a dream of financial security, and the belief that it would be less stressful than being in the Legislature prompted him to make the change.

The new man that Buchanan chose to become attorney general was Ronald Giffin, a small-town lawyer from Truro, Nova Scotia, who was the MLA from the Colchester County seat where R.L. Stanfield and G.I. Smith had achieved automatic election endorsements by a largely Tory population.

Giffin appears studious, gives an impression of pomposity which evaporates upon coming to know him, and has a tendency to speak too quickly. He was proud of having been selected for the second-most important portfolio of government and displayed almost childish enthusiasm for the task. It was not to be a peaceful job, and his strong ideas for the office would have improved it, but some changes were resisted by elected and non-elected government people. Giffin served from November 1983 until February 1987, and was criticized by Sandy Cameron during the 1984 election campaign to such an extent that Giffin commenced a legal action against him. Both men, being nice guys at heart, quietly dropped the matter after the election. Giffin was then placed on the political hotseat by his deputy.

Giffin inherited Gordon Coles as deputy attorney general; Coles ran that department with such an iron hand that the chief of prosecutors, Gordon Gale, was later to testify to the royal commission investigation of the Marshall conviction that Mr. Coles lacked the will to seek or accept objective legal advice. Giffin was suddenly faced with another Tory cabinet minister being investigated, Billie Joe MacLean, and the Department of the Attorney General handled the case, which was later to embarrass him, even though his integrity was not questioned.

Cabinet colleague Billie Joe MacLean was distant from his opponent, Liberal Vincent MacLean, in personality and nature, as were their politics. Billie Joe was from the Huey Long of Louisiana school of ward politics: he tried to deliver jobs, roads, and prosperity for his constituency, and everything else came second. Vince MacLean was a law-and-order advocate whose give-no-quarter performance made people shiver. There was no doubt that the two MacLeans loathed each other.

Billie Joe's expense account was brought to the attention of the RCMP by the auditor general, whom several Tory MLAs said was an ardent Liberal and whose appointment by Buchanan was vigorously opposed by other Tories. An investigation took place, and Gordon Coles and the RCMP had different views about charges being laid. The royal commission would later describe the Billie Joe investigation controversy as follows:

> The case began in 1983 when the Provincial Auditor General asked the RCMP for advice on MacLean's expense claims, some of which appeared to be fraudulent. According to a letter from the Auditor General to the Deputy Attorney General, the RCMP determined that "there is justification to take the matter further."

Deputy Attorney General Coles again assumed direct charge of his department's response, and that seemed designed to protect MacLean from investigation rather than to determine whether there was substance to the allegations. Coles and the Director of Prosecutions Gordon Gale were said to provide inadequate analysis and advice to the Attorney General, dismissing the allegations against MacLean as "accounting irregularities," and arguing that no further investigation or prosecution was warranted.

Once again, Attorney General Ron Giffin properly followed a hands-off policy because of the politically sensitive nature of the issue. Giffin testified that he simply followed the advice of his deputy when he wrote to the Speaker of the House dismissing the matter. Once his involvement was requested, Giffin had an obligation to at least find out whether the RCMP had conducted a proper investigation of the matter. Later, Giffin did become directly involved — when he shouldn't have — in the discussion of the specifics of plea and sentence negotiations in the MacLean case.

Although the RCMP had concluded that the matter should be investigated further, they once again did nothing on their own until April 1985 when the Liberal Leader, Vince MacLean, directly requested them to investigate. We believed the RCMP's reluctance to proceed with politically sensitive criminal investigations without clear authorization from the Department of the Attorney General is not only a dereliction of duty, but also indicates a failure to adhere to the principle of police independence.

Again, —— although Billie Joe MacLean did not ask for any special treatment from either the RCMP or the Attorney General — the justice system's response indicated an undue and improper sensitivity to the status of the person being investigated.

Back in 1983, Vincent MacLean was not the Liberal leader and had made no bones about his belief that his leader, Sandy Cameron, had been too soft on the Billie Joe affair. When Sandy Cameron was defeated in 1984, Vince finally won the party leadership he had wanted so badly. He almost immediately labelled the Billie Joe affair a cover-up, and personally filed a complaint against Billie Joe with the RCMP, and a second investigation was implemented. Billie Joe MacLean was then charged with fraud relating to the use of various receipts for his expense account. Upon submission of his various accounts to the Speaker of the House, he had been granted approval for payment by the Speaker. MacLean was advised by his lawyer that the approval would be grounds to defend the payments. The Director of Criminal Prosecutions, Gordon Gale, had himself viewed the investigation and MacLean's documents as garbled accounting, not warranting a charge. But the RCMP, likely because of previous experiences with the attorney general's office and because Vince MacLean had laid the complaint, charged Billie Joe MacLean.

Billie Joe's world suddenly fell apart. He already had severe financial problems, and Revenue Canada was after him for back taxes. Some Tory caucus members were pushing to have him fired, with the same secret pressure they had previously applied to Buchanan regarding Rollie Thornhill. Billie Joe suffered a heart attack, and his future looked bleak. He was a victim of many forces at that time and he relates some bizarre events, which are not entirely unbelievable upon examination.

First, there was Lawrence O'Neil, a Tory lawyer who had worked in Buchanan's office as an assistant to the premier, and who was well connected to the halls of power. In 1984, Mulroney convinced O'Neil to run for the Tories in the Cape Breton seat, once held in the mighty Liberal grip of Allan J. MacEachen, who had retired. Surprisingly to some, O'Neil won the seat in the 1984 federal election. Billie Joe's provincial seat crossed the line into O'Neil's federal seat, and O'Neil also had Billie Joe's brother, Dr. Jim MacLean, as a Tory MLA on the other side of his constituency. O'Neil was concerned for his own image and well-being as the two MacLeans were popular members who had influence on the votes in his federal seat. O'Neil approached Billie Joe and gave comfort, promising to try to raise money to help him with his problems. O'Neil called me and asked me about raising $75,000 to help Billie Joe MacLean to defend himself. I told him that he would have to discuss it with Chipman, Crease, or Buchanan. Then Buchanan called and said that he wanted Billie Joe to be found not guilty and that we should help for the sake of the party's reputation. I discussed it with several people before the next Finance

Committee meeting, and there was no enthusiasm for the task, except that Bob Stappels said that he thought it could be done, and he sounded convincing. Suzanne Wilde scoffed at the idea and said it would never happen, and she was right.

I then received a call from a federal MP who told me there would be a federal job for Billie Joe MacLean if he just had the mess quickly disappear. I did not carry that message, but Billie Joe MacLean later told me he was approached by a prominent Tory lawyer who told him he would receive a federal appointment, after a reasonable period, if he pleaded guilty and avoided the long litany of evidential embarrassment for the party.

In a 1990 interview, Billie Joe MacLean, whose son was once a working associate of mine, told me that he had been misled by the PC party and double-crossed politically. He said he had only recently recovered from the heart attack and was emotionally distressed and clinically depressed when the carrot of escape was dangled before him by a federal MP. He claimed that he was misled, lied to, and taken down a garden path by several powerful Tories, to get him to plead guilty to the charges in exchange for an agreed-to legal slap on the wrist. MacLean says he had witnesses on the phone for some of the conversations and made tape-recordings of the others.

Billie Joe pleaded guilty to the charges, and was treated lightly. He soon discovered that he had another ordeal to face. Vince MacLean was not satisfied with the fact that Billie Joe was already ruined, and started pressing to have him expelled from the Nova Scotia Legislature. Suddenly Billie Joe's calls to cabinet and caucus colleagues were not being returned.

A special session of the Legislature was called as the Tory caucus reacted to Vincent MacLean's tough stance, and a wet-eyed Buchanan presided over his old friend Billie Joe MacLean's expulsion by a members' free vote at the Nova Scotia Legislature. Billie Joe said only, "Thanks, John," and departed when he was voted out.

A by-election was called for the seat vacated by Billie Joe MacLean. The Liberals, PCs, and NDP nominated candidates and, to everyone's surprise, Billie Joe was nominated as an independent candidate.

Vincent MacLean campaigned personally for the Liberal candidate, and NDP leader Alexa McDonough speculated openly that the NDP would win the seat. Buchanan knew that the Tory candidate couldn't possibly win.

The last laugh was Billie Joe MacLean's. The voters did the talking and he was re-elected as an independent MLA. The voters seemed to resent the way the three parties treated their native son. Billie Joe expressed his thanks to the voters and, turning to his son, said audibly, "That Halifax bunch can observe the mistletoe on the back of my suit-coat."

21

ELMER MACKAY ALMOST TO THE RESCUE

BUCHANAN'S FINANCIAL TROUBLES, AND THE MONTHLY expense stipend the PC party paid him, were a burden on party finances. The party was always in financial need. The burden was largely being shouldered by the Finance Committee, and I was nearing exhaustion. I grew to hate politics. My opinion, albeit a layman's, at that time was that Buchanan was verging on clinical depression.

Billie Joe MacLean's legal troubles, the publicity surrounding the Roland Thornhill affair, former PC president John Grant's attitude, and a mushrooming personal debt were consuming John Buchanan's full attention, and the provincial budget was out of control. The Halifax Board of Trade and the media harped about debt, but the causes and remedies were not clearly addressed or spelled out. The government aircraft was in the news, and Ralph Medjuck's rental activities were newsworthy, but the opposition did not exploit these issues in terms that the public would be induced to follow. Dickson said that, had he had the unused ammunition that was available to the Liberals, he could defeat the government of John Buchanan in one session of the Legislature.

Part of the blind trust Crease created for Buchanan, which was managed by the trust accountant Robert Bruce, was a holding company that managed all Buchanan's troubled business assets. Crease reported to Bruce regularly. Some of the trust money he raised was first paid to the trust's lawyers, Fraser, Beatty in Toronto, and then dispersed by Bruce out of Halifax. But efforts to keep up with Buchanan's banks were taking a toll. Party finances couldn't continue to pay Buchanan a monthly cheque and cover party expenses too.

The windfall that Crease and Roy Busche had anticipated from the federal Tories paying back the Stanfield loan had been eradicated when the federal PCs refused to acknowledge the debt. Crease and Bruce spoke to Buchanan about it, and he was disturbed that the federal Tories were so arrogant in refusing to pay back what they had originally come for with hat in hand. At Crease's suggestion, Buchanan called Elmer MacKay, and Elmer said that he thought he could help. MacKay called me and told me to bring Buchanan and meet him at the airport on the following Saturday. He also told me that he had apprised the prime minister of the details of Buchanan's debt and the financial troubles of the PC party; he also asked about the blind-trust solution to Buchanan's financial plight.

I picked Buchanan up early on the appointed Saturday in February because the highways were treacherous; freezing rain had coated everything, including the trees, with a shiny, slippery, silver coat of ice. On the way to the airport, we came upon emergency vehicles and police near a highway overpass. An unfortunate man had crashed his car through the heavy steel guard rail of the upper bridge and had been killed on the road below. The sun was starting to shine, and everything was wet and sparkling as we left the scene of the accident, but I noticed that it had a bizarre effect on Buchanan. He seemed lost in thought and then he said, "Imagine. He got up this morning, likely didn't kiss his wife goodbye or was even a little grumpy to her, and took off as usual; now he's dead." I tried to lighten things up by saying, "You should write Harlequin novels."

Buchanan continued, as though I hadn't spoken, "I hope his bills were paid." It was then that I understood the extent of his preoccupation with his debts.

At the airport, MacKay sat at the runway level in front of the big windows in the waiting area. As Buchanan and I approached, an RCMP officer who knew John stopped him and they carried on a conversation which lasted too long; I was eager to deal with business. About a dozen people spoke to him or tried to get his attention, and I thought what a stupid place it was for such a sensitive meeting.

We moved to a quiet corner and sat huddled together like players at an alley crap game, trying to figure how the PC party could get their money back from Ottawa. The conversation was constantly diverted by political matters as MacKay tried to remember provincial problems he needed Buchanan to correct. They wouldn't allow me to take notes, and I didn't see how Buchanan could remember all of the requests. I also had trouble keeping them on the subject of money, as they almost ignored me and talked politics, like old athletes talk about past victories and old game scores. We talked for over an hour, and MacKay clearly understood the problems we faced. MacKay said he had talked to Mulroney, and then I was asked to phone the prime minister that afternoon to discuss a solution. I knew what a hassle it was to call the prime minister, and I absolutely refused to spend Saturday afternoon dancing on a phone wire with experts trained to avoid people like me. MacKay assured me the call was expected, and I said that I'd first try to palm the task off to Ken Matthews, and they both laughed.

That afternoon, at MacKay and Buchanan's insistence, I called the prime minister's weekend phone number, and the operator went through the usual polite drill used to fend off nuisance calls. I told her the prime minister was expecting my call, and she said they would call me back if the prime minister was available. About five minutes passed, and Dr. Fred Doucet, the prime minister's right arm, phoned me, saying in his famous low, clear, precise voice, "Ahaa, Rip. What was it you wanted of the PM?" I said, "Fred, it's a private matter, and it's a job I was asked to undertake by the premier, and

Elmer, who has already briefed Mr. Mulroney." Doucet then asked me to brief him. I said, "I really apologize, Fred, but it's not my decision to make, as I'm the errand boy, nothing more." Doucet made a funny animated clucking sound and said, "That's unfortunate because, unless I'm informed, he won't be calling you back." I said, "Fine, thank you," and hung up. I never spoke to Doucet again.

I then phoned Ken Matthews, who like Crease, had a lot of service marks and was a well-known Tory who had been involved in Buchanan's personal mess from the start. He knew of the meeting and had talked to MacKay. I told Ken what happened when I had called Mulroney. He was puzzled, as he had understood that the call was Mulroney's idea. I told Matthews I wouldn't ever call the prime minister again and insisted he make the next attempt. Ken Matthews was no party lightweight. He knew Mulroney personally and was a lifetime close associate and adviser to Bob Stanfield. I figured if he couldn't get Mulroney, I wasn't going to try. Several hours passed before Matthews phoned me back. He said that he had received the same rude reception from Doucet as I had, and his anger showed as he added, "That fucking, pompous little turd Doucet will rot in hell before I'll deal with him again." We both called MacKay and expressed our disappointment and anger. Elmer told me that Fred Doucet was even in charge of toilet paper and went so far as to offer advice to the prime minister's residence. I said, "Well, it's your baby, Elmer. I won't kiss anyone's foot, or Doucet's ass, even if he were prime minister."

MacKay called me back immediately and said I was invited to Ottawa to meet Tory bagman David Angus, of the law firm Stikeman, Elliot, and likely the prime minister too. I cleared it with Matthews, and I paid my own way to Ottawa, where MacKay's Nova Scotian chauffeur picked me up at the airport. On the way to MacKay's office, I had to stop at a drug store for Tylenol as I had developed a headache. It was a sign of things to come.

At Elmer's office, the staff made me coffee, and we talked baseball while we waited for David Angus. He arrived on time, and we went into the boardroom. MacKay and Angus sat on one side of the table, and I sat on the other. Angus was serious, unsmiling, and as officious as a Crown prosecutor while he asked me questions about Buchanan and made notes of my answers. When that was complete, Angus told me that he would let me know what could be done and acted as if I was a constituent looking for a job with the government. He did not admit that the federal Tories owed us any money, nor did he smile.

Later, Elmer and I went to the House of Commons, and I had a thirty-second brush with Mulroney in the lobby. I was seen on TV by some friends who teased me that my grey carriage coat with the black collar looked like a 1910 undertaker's coat.

Back at the Ottawa airport, en route to Halifax, I bumped into Joe Stewart, who told me he had been in Ottawa, at the request of the prime minister, to go over names for federal appointments from Atlantic Canada. Before Stewart could explain his important task, he had some sort of attack with breathing problems, and I rushed to get him a Seven-Up and gave him two of my remaining Tylenol. I also carried his bag onto the aircraft, an act which I later told Buchanan cleared me to say that I was Joe Stewart's redcap, to roars of laughter by Ted Crease.

MacKay phoned me the next weekend, and I could tell by his manner and preparatory preamble that we would not be getting help from the federal Tories. MacKay spelled out how hard David Angus worked raising money and said Mulroney didn't want to lose him, so they couldn't give us the $500,000 as doing so would discourage all the federal fund-raisers. I reminded Elmer that it was our own money we sought, and he said that we must remember that that loan was made to the Stanfield bunch and not to Mulroney's people. I said, "Elmer, it's one federal party, the same one that borrowed our money." Elmer then made a surprising suggestion. He told me that I should meet Mel Shea, a former St. Francis Xavier University classmate of Mulroney's, at the Halifax airport, and that Shea was prepared to help us bail out Buchanan. Shea, known in his home section of Boston by the Irish nickname Bob, was well known to Crease, who sat on the board of Halifax-Dartmouth Industries with him. Crease despised him.

I drove out to meet Shea and, on the way back to Halifax, he pumped me for information. I told him nothing and, as I deposited him at the Sheraton Hotel, I said, "I hear that you will make a sizable donation." Shea smiled and said only that he'd talk to Ted Crease. Crease told me later that Shea gave him a few thousand dollars, and I said, "Well, Elmer certainly solved the problem for us," and Crease chuckled.

Joe Stewart was suddenly very friendly toward me, apparently because I had shown some concern when he was ill at the Ottawa airport. Stewart visited me at my office and said that he knew we had some troubles and implied that he knew the whole story. I soon found that he did not, but he patronized me and asked our employee, Ross Montgomery, to arrange for me to allow the federal Patronage Advisory Committee, known as the PAC Committee, to meet in our boardroom. Later Stewart and the Honourable Stewart McInnes arranged an appointment for Ross Montgomery to the Investment Advisory Board of the Canada Council, and McInnes offered me an appointment to the board of Canada Post, which I declined.

David Chipman did not like what he termed the "oinkie" nature of the feds running to the trough, and made no bones about it. Joe Stewart called Chipman the "ice-man" behind his back, as the jealousy between the federal and provincial Tories reached sandbox or playground levels of pettiness.

Stewart claimed to me that he would have a say, even in the appointment of judges; Chipman doubted that, but I didn't. According to MacKay, there were to be judicial appointments, and the three names were: lawyer Lorne Clarke, a closet Stanfield Tory of Truro, Nova Scotia; Ken Matthews; and David Chipman. Stewart told me he disliked all three. He said Elmer MacKay did not want Chipman, as he was supposedly still angry over David's position on fund-raising during the 1983 federal (Mulroney) by-election in Central Nova. More surprising was Elmer's alleged support for a Pictou County lawyer, ahead of Ken Matthews, who was a long-time political friend of MacKay's. In the end, Lorne Clarke was the compromise appointment as Chief Justice of the Appeal Court of Nova Scotia. But there were still two openings, and Buchanan lobbied for both Chipman and Ken Matthews. At first Elmer didn't respond, but finally he made it into a deal. Elmer MacKay is a baseball nut, and he proposed to me, in all seriousness, a list of trades and appointments he needed from Buchanan in exchange for appointing Chipman and Matthews. As in baseball deals, "a player to be named later" in Elmer and Buchanan's trade was a sought-after provincial appointment for "Big Joe" Stewart. Yet, MacKay seemed to dislike Stewart. I assumed he wanted to get rid of Stewart with a favour.

First, David Chipman and Ken Matthews became judges of the Appeal Court. For Chipman, it was a lifetime dream-come-true. It was my feeling that Elmer's dream of a provincial appointment for Joe Stewart came from a book MacKay had sent me, William Kinsella's *Shoeless Joe Jackson Comes to Iowa* (a story from that collection would later be the basis for *Field of Dreams*, a movie starring Kevin Costner). The main character in the story is told by a ball-player ghost that if he "builds a baseball diamond in a corn field, they will come," meaning that his dream of meeting former major league baseball players will come true. Elmer MacKay liked the story so much he read it twice.

In Joe Stewart's case, Elmer may have arranged for the diamond to be built, but Buchanan apparently didn't believe in ghosts.

22

THE GREAT NOVA SCOTIA LIQUOR COMMISSION CAPER

AVING THE GOVERNMENT IN THE BUSINESS OF selling alcoholic beverages is a mixed blessing. On the one hand, they exercise some control over the distribution of liquor and receive the benefit of tax revenue and profit. But, on the other, according to some people, it's wrong for the government to be selling a damaging narcotic, the results of which drive up health-care costs.

Regardless of the moral question, the Nova Scotia government liquor business has grown. The provincial Liquor Commission was in need of better facilities for warehousing and control, so the provincial government planned to call for proposals, on a cost-effective basis, for the development of a Nova Scotia Liquor Commission head office and storage depot in rural Halifax County, at the Bayers Lake Industrial Park. That news spread quickly, with greedy business people scrambling for position among the pols, causing my mother to comment, "It's like dropping a sugar cube into an ant hill and watching the ants run themselves into a frenzy." Later John Grant went to Ted Crease and told him that he had been approached by the agent for a group of business people who had offered to pay $250,000 - in $50,000 instalments over a five-year period — for an assurance of getting the government Liquor Commission deal.

Crease went nuts. I had heard of only one other occasion on which he had lost his usual low-key professional mellowness; he was, in all regards, a real gentleman. When Crease spoke to me, it was clear he was appalled by Grant's suggestion. He said, "The damn fool! Doesn't he know that John Lindsay [a developer and contractor] and I plan to tender for that project ourselves, and if I won't bribe to get it for me, why the fuck would I risk going to jail for someone else's deal?" Crease predicted that Grant's poor judgement would create future problems, and although Crease would not live to see it, his prediction would come true, and to a degree he had not dreamed of.

Crease was not awarded the tender, and he never complained, nor did he reduce his considerable effort to assist Buchanan, the blind trust, and the PC Nova Scotia Fund. The Nova Scotia Liquor Commission deal was not a dead issue, however; later, the media, the opposition, and the RCMP would dig into it. Meanwhile, we continued to be preoccupied with PC finances. It cost a lot of time and energy, and meetings, which I hated.

At one of them, Ted Crease paced the floor of the executive-office waiting area at the Royal Bank's regional office on George Street in Halifax. Since he had given up smoking those awful riverboat gambler's cigars, his tobacco craving made him impatient. While I read an outdated *Time* magazine, I was amused by Crease's monologue, delivered in a low, raspy, tobacco-starved voice, as he complained about PC money problems taking all his free time.

George Buckrill, the Atlantic vice-president of the Royal Bank, had invited us to lunch at his office. We knew that he was nervous about the PC party's loan, Buchanan's debt, or some other Tory who was behind in payments on a note. The bank obviously wanted no more Thornhill-type publicity.

Buckrill is a tall, imposing figure, but is soft-spoken and has an infectious sense of humour; in fact, he seems almost disappointed if you don't tease or harass him. He was so successful for the bank in Halifax that it was widely believed that he would have had all the city's best business accounts if he hadn't worked himself into a promotion to head office. Upon entering his inner office, we made joking remarks about wealth, referring to the decadent opulence of the surroundings, and we said it was the profit from the Tory loan that had made it all possible.

The purpose of the meeting was what we expected. Buckrill said Roy Busche wanted us to meet him to give a report on cash flow by projected collections, and David Chipman had been too busy to attend. We told him what we thought we could raise to keep our party's loan in good form, and Buckrill then discussed the premier's loans, and mentioned another Tory MLA, who had a loan which was outstanding for too long and was being repaid too slowly. I had had very little to say until that point, but upon hearing about the new tardy loan, I said, "George, in the Marine Corp, they have an expression which says, of secret things, that they are on a 'need to know basis' — and about some other slow-paying Tory I don't need to know." Buckrill roared his approval. He then asked if Ralph Medjuck was likely to win the Nova Scotia Liquor Commission warehouse development tender from the government. The commission was calling for proposals, and the deal was in the $10-million range, which is a fair-sized golden egg by Halifax standards, especially if the government is the long-term tenant of the building. I immediately suspected that Ralph Medjuck was applying for new credit, since the Royal was one of his banks, and I thought Buckrill was checking to see what was potential cash flow and what was Ralph's window-dressing. Crease and I exchanged glances, and Crease said, "I have a strong interest in Medjuck's not being the successful applicant." Buckrill nodded, and before he could speak again, Crease said, "The most active lobby is from Bob Stappels's group, and I imagine he is an account of yours too, but perhaps his group banks elsewhere." Buckrill made no comment, but it was obvious he had at least one financial application on his agenda as he tried to see how much we knew. Crease told him the liquor deal was a small gold mine to anyone who landed it, and said openly that he and a contractor had an interest in landing the deal too. The rest of the meal was laced with good local gossip, with George teasing us about a line of election credit, which in the end I would be asked to organize with a multi-signature Tory note.

On the way down in the elevator, Crease said, "That liquor deal is haunted. Grant has already mentioned the $250,000 pay-off and I have a bad feeling that someone's trying to do something wrong on this deal." He added, "It could be a political cesspool if the deal crosses any lines." He decided to walk around the corner to Hollis Street and go to see Buchanan. The last words he said to me as he went through the iron gates of Province House were: "If Medjuck gets that fuckin' deal, it'll stink up the province," meaning the opposition would latch on to Medjuck's old relationship with Buchanan. The other interested applicant for the warehouse deal, Bob Stappels, had a lawyer, Walter Thompson, as one of his partners. Walter is a brother of Stephen Thompson, who was one of Ted Crease's partners at Bell and Grant, the insurance broker, so there were conflicting and connecting applicants for the deal.

The auditor general's report about the Nova Scotia Liquor Commission distribution centre and head office, issued in 1989, said that the facility was completed in 1986 on the advice of commission management, an outside consultant, and the commissioners. The selection was to do a lease/purchase option over an outright purchase, although an outright purchase would have cost $1.3 million less if financed directly by the province at 12.4 per cent.

The commission originally received eleven submissions, from which a short list of six was compiled. Five submissions were received from that group of six (two groups, Canterbury and Corkum, combined their applications). Ralph Medjuck's Centennial Group was one of the applicants. The choice was subsequently narrowed to Stappels (Canterbury/Corkum) and Eastport Properties Limited.

Stappels's proposal was evaluated as $3.7 million more expensive than the Eastport proposal, but according to the auditor general's 1989 report, it was decided by the commission that Stappels's group, on criteria other than price, was the best proposal. The other comparisons of total costs were made on the basis of whether the building was: (a) purchased from developers, on land purchased by the developer; (b) purchased from the developer, but built on Nova Scotia Liquor Commission land; and (c) a lease/purchase arrangement calculated two ways.

The Nova Scotia Liquor Commission staff then prepared a schedule, which compared the undiscounted payments of one candidate (Eastport) over thirty years with payments for a similar deal by Canterbury/Corkum over twenty-five years. The auditor's report states that comparison results in a total cash outflow to lease/purchase of the Eastport property of $39,542,310, and a figure of $39,071,139 for Canterbury/Corkum. (The Nova Scotia Liquor Commission payments were made to Uniacke Properties Limited, a company established, after the project selection, by the principals of the Canterbury/Corkum Group.) The auditor general's report suggests that, from a cash-flow perspective, it would have been cheaper for the Nova Scotia Liquor Commission to purchase the facility outright.

Stappels was a Tory Horatio Alger, flamboyant, larger than life, slightly overweight, with sort of a bull-in-a-china-shop personality. He is kind-hearted and overconfident, and to say he is not a character would be like suggesting that hockey's Don Cherry is shy. His pal told me that, once, on a trip to Bermuda with his entourage of noisy business pals, Stappels had himself pushed into a crowded bar in a wheelchair, slouched low with a blanket wrapped around him, like an invalid. He made a big production of them spoon-feeding him several drinks, as if he was disabled and couldn't serve himself. As the liquid was increased, his mobility and noise level rose until, finally, with every eye in the bar on him, he jumped from the chair and did a violent solo twist dance, yelling, "Oh Jesus, I'm cured!"

Some time after the Liquor Commission contract was awarded, Stappels arrived at a PC Finance Committee luncheon at Tory Headquarters on Hollis Street, and announced that the Uniacke

Group should be given to him as an account, as he was going to deliver big bucks. Suzanne Huett, the finance coordinator, assigned him the account, although she didn't want to, and tried to get me to take it. Fortunately I did not, and history would prove it a lucky decision for me, as trouble lay ahead.

That same night I received a phone call from Stappels, asking for a meeting to discuss Uniacke's account. He missed several dates, which was typical of Bob, but eventually came to my office, with Walter Thompson. They said that they had decided to make big donations, but were worried that some might draw an inaccurate inference that the donation was connected with the award of the contract (which had been made by an open and fair tender). I said I couldn't see why it would look bad, but they should seek advice from another lawyer if they had doubts. Walter Thompson said he knew a donation was legal, but he didn't want the world to know they were giving so much money. Stappels then asked me if I could call Crease, who was on holidays in Bermuda, and find out when Stappels and Walter could meet with him to discuss ways of making their donation secret. I agreed to make the call.

When Crease returned, they met in my office, and Stappels again made it clear that he was representing his shareholders on one side and the PC party on the other, and used the term "wearing two hats." Crease made it clear that he harboured no disappointment, even though his own application for the liquor warehouse had not been successful.

One coincidence that emerged from the meeting was the fact that Walter Thompson's firm had been successful in bidding against Crease, and yet one of Crease's partners in the Bell and Grant insurance brokerage firm was Walter's brother, Stephen. Not much was made of it, though, and by the time the meeting ended, Crease and Stappels had agreed to work out the mechanics of the Uniacke Group's donation.

That meeting was to become a focal point for an RCMP investigation into the financial affairs of John Buchanan.

23

THE HON. STEWART
McINNES'S BLIND
TRUST DÉBÂCLE

PAUL VAUGHAN WALSH WAS ONCE REGARDED AS A media whiz kid, holding, at a young age, responsible positions in radio and television. He was widely considered to be a great writer and investigator. However, his addiction to alcohol, pills, cocaine, and gambling reduced his sober working time to brief periods between detox attempts. Walsh had hoodwinked, cheated, or lied to so many associates and media people that, no matter how good his news sounded, he was ignored.

During the time that Gerald Regan was premier, it was a young, keen Paul Walsh who uncovered much of the embarrassing information surrounding the fiasco of the cruise ship Regan's government had promoted. Then, for a period, he moved to New Brunswick and became involved in a public relations firm with a brother of John O'Brien, Buchanan's press secretary. Walsh claimed to be a personal close friend of New Brunswick premier Richard Hatfield. When one of his drinking companions expressed scepticism, in rather pointed terms, about Walsh's claim, Walsh walked to the telephone, dialled a direct number, talked briefly, and summoned the doubtful companion to the phone. It was said to be Premier Hatfield on the line. Occasionally during that period, Walsh would breeze into Halifax and hit the high spots with the few media people who would associate with him — almost always on borrowed money. One of those who stuck by Walsh was free-lance journalist Harry Flemming, who does a weekly CBC-TV talk show. He wrote in 1992 that Walsh was a liar who never ceased to disappoint him, although Flemming sometimes let Walsh stay at his apartment, according to his own account.

Walsh was obsessed with what he called the "Grant story," and claimed that he had uncovered misconduct, including kick-backs, political pay-offs, and offshore deposits. He tried to sell the story to the media and to Al Hollingsworth, who was later Liberal leader Vincent MacLean's adviser. They all refused because he couldn't be trusted. Walsh saw his failure to sell to the CBC as the fault of newsman Jim Nunn, who would almost certainly have nothing to do with that side of the operation. Walsh was, by that time, vengeful and dangerous and, according to John Grant, planned to get even with Nunn by planting cocaine on him and then calling the police. Nunn, who is considered to be perfectly proper in his conduct, even by people who do not like him, was warned to be careful. Paul Walsh's deadly nature became totally reliant on mind-altering chemicals. This dependence resulted in a disaster for Richard Hatfield, a mystery involving John Grant, and Walsh's own weird death.

Just after the MacKay–Hatfield meeting in Ottawa, and despite the publicity that seemed to ensure that the authorities would charge Hatfield, Paul Walsh, whom I had not seen for four or five years, phoned me and said that he was at a New Brunswick radio station and had to find out from Elmer MacKay if the premier would be charged. I had no idea why he was so persistent, but he had obviously been drinking. He said he knew I could get MacKay on the phone, and told me he was calling from a radio station where he worked. After several polite calls, he got quite animated, and I became angry over his rude behaviour. I told him if he called again I would report him to the radio station. He then told me that he had to find out for Richard Hatfield, who didn't dare call MacKay himself. I hung up on him. The same afternoon, Walsh called again and, after telling me that a reporter was on the line, asked, "Can you confirm that Hatfield will not be charged?" I said, with tongue in cheek, "Yes, now will you stop calling me?" and they hung up. Several days later, I heard that a New Brunswick radio station had run a hot-news bulletin stating that an unidentified Ottawa source had revealed that Mr. Hatfield would not be charged. Hatfield was charged the next day, and I understand that Mr. Walsh was not welcome at the station after that.

Richard Hatfield was tried and acquitted, but his reputation and his government were ruined. How it happened would later become known to me by accident.

Stewart McInnes is a lawyer in one of the most respected and prestigious old Halifax law firms: McInnes Cooper Robertson. His father, Donald McInnes, a prominent founding partner of that firm, was, until a mandatory-retirement rule forced him out, a longtime director of the Bank of Nova Scotia. Stewart has earned his own credits as a good citizen and lawyer who is active in the community and the Progressive Conservative party.

It was natural that Brian Mulroney would seek the support of people like McInnes when he ran for the leadership of the PC party. After Mulroney won, Stewart McInnes decided to seek the Tory nomination in Halifax to run against incumbent Liberal MP and cabinet minister Gerald Regan. Unopposed for the nomination, he defeated Regan, and the new prime minister selected him for cabinet as Minister of Public Works.

McInnes was a brokerage client of salesman Ross T. Montgomery of the Halifax branch of McLeod Young Weir (Scotia McLeod), where I had my office as a director of the same firm. Montgomery was a federal Tory fund-raiser, and I was a collector for the PC party of Nova Scotia. In February 1987, Ross Montgomery left McLeod's employ and went to work for Nesbitt, Thomson, another major investment dealer. Most of his clients, including Stewart McInnes, moved with Montgomery and became clients of his new employer.

The new government of Brian Mulroney had implemented new rules requiring members of government, especially cabinet ministers, to place their investments in a blind trust, managed by an "arm's-length" trustee, so that personal investments would not conflict with government decisions. McInnes chose his fund-raiser and close associate Ross Montgomery as his trustee. McInnes is a corporate lawyer and should have realized that his selection of Montgomery might subject him to criticism or difficulties in future. But, in fairness to McInnes, neither the federal government nor the Investment Dealers Association had issued clear instructions for brokers and ministers to use in setting up the newly required blind trusts.

To further cloud the connection between McInnes and trustee, Montgomery was also given a federal appointment to the Investment Committee of the Canada Council. That appointment almost choked a young employee in our Halifax office who was jealous of the older, more sophisticated Montgomery. Previously, when Montgomery had still worked at our offices, the young man had spent a lot of time annoying Ross. He used to hide small containers of milk in Ross's office; the milk would sour and produce a rotten smell, disturbing Ross and amusing the perpetrator. It was funny but childish.

It was because Montgomery had eventually grown unhappy with the atmosphere at McLeod's offices that he had left us to go to Nesbitt, Thomson. What happened next was clearly designed to hurt Ross, but it also embarrassed Stewart McInnes and damaged my career beyond repair.

The opportunity to hurt Montgomery arose from the fact that his mail — including the personal blind trust documents of the Hon. Stewart McInnes — continued to reach our office after he left our employ. All mail to an investment dealer's office is usually handled by one key employee to ensure that clients' cheques and securities are in safe hands. At McLeod's Halifax office, that employee sat just outside the office of Montgomery's erstwhile tormentor, who had free access to the mail early in the day.

I was aware neither that Montgomery's mail was still reaching our office nor that Montgomery was Stewart McInnes's sole trustee as well as his stockbroker. I found out in a strange way. My wife and I returned to our Halifax residence after a trip to the country in May 1987. I found, in the front mailbox of the house, an envelope containing account information of the McInnes's blind trust, with Ross Montgomery's name on it. The documents were McLeod Young Weir account summaries, so I took them to our office and called a meeting of the accounting people to ascertain where the documents originated, or if any of them had left the papers at my house. Everyone was as mystified as I was, so I placed the papers under the corner of my desk blotter and temporarily forgot about them.

That mystery was to bother me again, but another, no less bizarre event was about to place Montgomery and McInnes far out of my thoughts.

After attending a PC Finance Committee meeting, and just before 6:00 p.m., I returned to our offices at Purdy's Wharf, a beautiful office complex built on pillars sunk into the rock bed of Halifax Harbour, to get my tattered briefcase prior to going home for the weekend. I left the elevator at the eighteenth floor and walked down the tunnel-like hall, past the abandoned reception desk and the board room, heading toward my own office. The latch and lock on my door were defective, and I seldom closed it, except when a client visited, so I was mildly surprised to find it closed, but assumed that a secretary must have shut the door for some reason. I put my arm straight out, football-style, and the flat of my hand contacted the door. As the door swung open, it was impeded by a chair, which fell over as my weight pushed forward. My mild surprise quickly changed to gaping disbelief and shock as I discovered the well-known drunk journalist, Paul Vaughan Walsh, kneeling on the floor in front of a young male employee, performing oral sex on him. The young man was sitting on my sofa with his trousers down and, when the door opened and the chair crashed over, their shock was as great as mine. Walsh, obviously stoned, tried to stagger to his feet, while the young man attempted to pull up his pants in a sitting position and avoid the stumbling Walsh at the same time.

An animated, unbelievably bad scene followed. The young man blubbered and cried in embarrassment, blurting out that he was already having troubles with his wife who suspected he had a girl-friend, but he kept crying that he was not gay. He was totally out of control with humiliation and fear of exposure.

Walsh, on the contrary, was arrogant, aggressive, and angry. He stood so close I could smell his awful alcohol breath, partially masked by mouthwash, and lashed out with a verbal assault. He yelled, "You shouldn't be so fucking sanctimonious." He said that he could tell me a thing or two about who some of his sexual partners were, including the Premier of New Brunswick, Richard Hatfield.

I put both of them out of the office, collected my bag, and departed, knowing that Walsh couldn't get back in past security at the elevator after 6:00 p.m. After a deadly weekend, during which I replayed the scene in my mind a hundred times, I phoned a close relative of mine and told him the story. He told me to cool it for a week or so and we would talk again. I asked a friend of the young man if the guy had a widespread reputation as sort of a bisexual athlete. The man laughed and said, "I don't know about that, but I'll tell you, he's as horny as a two-peckered goat."

That incident, and the direction our company was headed, caused me to ponder my future. I seriously considered quitting. Stress hummed in me like a high tension wire, and discussions with super-visors or compliance people in Toronto were usually unproductive, inconclusive, or at least frustrating, as their decisions were based on abstract political and social considerations, like "family connections." Once I tried to fire a saleswoman in Halifax who was holding wild parties in her apartment and showing porno films to an assortment of transient male visitors — activities that had caused negative gos-sip. The woman was acting like a lovesick moose and our reputa-tion was suffering accordingly. I called the assistant compliance officer and he said he'd let me know what to do. When he finally called back, I was informed that her home conduct was none of our business. Her family was well connected, so she was not fired. On another occasion, when I reported the incident with Paul Walsh, I was told by the senior compliance officer, D.T.C. Moore, that it was just Maritime weirdness and to forget it.

Politics was no longer fun either. We were so deeply in debt at the PC party that the constant calls for more money were exactly like the harassment one associates with the activities of a consumer finance company. I made up my mind early in June 1987 to retire from politics and the investment business.

First, I wrote Finance director David Chipman a letter, tendering my resignation from the PC Finance Committee, citing personal reasons, and then I drafted a letter of retirement to my company. I delayed my resignation from the firm for the poorest of reasons: greed. A head-office rumour suggested we were about to sell the firm for an exaggerated price to a chartered bank. I owned about 41,000 shares of company stock worth over $1 million, so any big sale could double my potential take.

Then the decision was moved out of my hands. My wife and I spent a weekend in the Annapolis Valley and, late on Sunday night, we drove back to our home in Halifax. We had timed the VCR to record "CBC News," as we always watch the news before retiring for the night. I put the tape in the play mode and saw Mike Duffy, a broadcaster who was then with the CBC, holding up account papers from my company and announcing that the Hon. Stewart McInnes's blind trust appeared to be in conflict: first, because he had a close associate as trustee, giving supposed access to the transactions in his account; and second, because he personally was receiving mail from us that showed him what securities he owned. It was a sleepless night, as I correctly guessed that Monday morning would see us under attack.

On Monday, Liberal MP Sheila Copps raised the matter of McInnes's account in Parliament, and the national publicity that followed was constant and cruel, as media people swarmed to the attack like a pack of hyenas.

The events that followed would have had the slapstick qualities of a 1920s silent movie starring the Keystone Kops or Charlie Chaplin, except that they were tragic and debilitating.

McLeod's chairman, Austin G.E. Taylor, whom I had regarded with respect and great admiration, suddenly found himself on what he perceived to be a public hot seat, which demanded decisive action. Company compliance people, lawyers, and the Investment Dealers Association of Canada suddenly descended on our Halifax office, and we were accused of being lax or of leaking the confidential documents of Stewart McInnes to Duffy and Sheila Copps.

Meanwhile, former Toronto journalist George Bain called me and said he had been solicited in a bar by a person who offered to sell him McInnes documents. Bain wrote a column about it in a local paper. I recognized Paul Walsh from his description and from the widespread rumours and street sources. I couldn't find Walsh, but I engaged lawyer George MacDonald, of McInnes Cooper Robertson, to warn the media that the documents were stolen, and I set out to find where Walsh lived. At about sundown on a warm June night, I drove to where I'd been told he lived and banged on the door. The house was surprisingly nice and located next to one of Dartmouth's many lakes. It was more surprising that he could find someone to rent to him — according to other reporters, he was always in arrears. Walsh came to the door, loaded out of his mind. I physically dragged him outside and accused him of having stolen documents from our office. He said that he and his pal had "fixed my fuckin' wagon." I lost my temper, slapped him and tore his shirt, and told him that I'd call the police. He had been in jail previously on bad-cheques charges and begged me not to call the police, promising that he would return our papers. We entered the house, where his wife, Maureen, was, and he gave me one document. I warned him again (for his wife's benefit) that I would call the police, and left. Meanwhile, a McLeod employee flew to Toronto and confessed that he had been part of the leak with Walsh, but claimed that I had instructed him to do it.

On July 7, 1987, Austin Taylor and company president Tom Kierans hired a private aircraft and were flown to Halifax, with other company officers. They suspended me by inviting me to meet them at a hotel and then changing the locks on the office doors. I couldn't return for my raincoat or personal mail. On the next day, Taylor and

Kierans visited my house, after I had asked them not to, and made the suggestion that I needed to see a psychiatrist. After they left, my son gave me detailed notes of what he had overheard them offer me in exchange for seeing a shrink. If I said that I was mentally ill and accepted the blame for the leak, I would be retained as an officer of the firm. On July 9, they phoned me with a similar offer, which I recorded. I flew to Toronto, on July 11, to meet Taylor privately at the Marriott Hotel. I have a record of the meeting, and I suspect that he recorded the conversation, but he later claimed that I confessed, which I did not. I was fired on July 22 — by phone. When Taylor notified the press of my firing, Paul Walsh wrote a letter to my wife, expressing remorse and saying that he had been used by a former employee to get even with me. I have that letter.

The Investment Dealers Association of Canada informed me that, if I signed a confession, I would be fined only $17,000, including costs. I refused. Over the next three years, a lengthy IDA hearing was conducted and I was found guilty; suspended for two years; and fined $115,000, including costs. Walsh had disappeared and could not be located to testify. We later discovered that he was in hospital, suffering from injuries received in a car accident.

The letter of resignation that I had written David Chipman just before those tragic events had not been acted upon, because Chipman was expecting an appointment to the bench and never got around to replacing me. But the firing and the IDA charges prompted me to resign at once, to save the party and the government embarrassment. Buchanan not only refused my resignation, but appointed me finance chairman to replace Chipman, who, according to Dickson's description of appointments, "had gone to Glory" as a judge of the Appeal Court.

After I had been subjected to constant media attention about the IDA charges, I went to the PC party annual public meeting at the Sheraton Hotel in Halifax, in the winter of 1990, and publicly resigned without forewarning, as I felt Buchanan's appointing me was to his own detriment. I was out of work and out of politics.

The next time that I saw Walsh was on a Saturday in the spring of

1990 at the Halifax Shopping Centre. My wife was with me, and surprisingly Walsh appeared to be cold sober, but I wouldn't talk to him. He pleaded for absolution from my wife, making much of his remorse and guilt and telling her that he had arranged a confession to clear me and he intended to commit suicide. My wife, who is normally a kind, placid person, said only, "Go for it."

Walsh sent a message, in June 1990, to my house. I recall the exact time, because my mother was there awaiting surgery for cancer, and my daughter-in-law and our new grandson were also there awaiting medical treatment. I made notes of the message and turned it over to police. The message was an obvious request for money, and Walsh mentioned negotiations with McLeod's lawyer. Walsh was next heard of when the police fished his body out of Halifax Harbour in June 1990. The official ruling was suicide; in light of his comments to us, it is consistent, but I still consider the decision suspect in light of his many vicious activities.

A bizarre series of events began on a cold Sunday in April 1991 when my wife and I were walking down Tower Road in Halifax, toward Point Pleasant Park. A man on a bicycle stopped and identified himself as Walsh's brother. In the course of a long discussion, we got the distinct impression that he had information that would help us, but seemed reluctant to make a decision to act. As we left him, I asked, "If you can help me, why not do it?" He said, "I don't know anything," and drove off. But, barely a month later, a lengthy sworn statement by Paul Walsh was given to me in the lobby of Founders Square in Halifax by a woman in a green raincoat; she had a very bad cold, and would not give me her name. There were eight legal-sized pages containing extensive details of Paul Walsh's life, the leaking of McInnes's papers, and how he and the McLeod employee had done it. It was dated April 1988, and by the time I received it Walsh was dead and the IDA hearing was over. *The Globe and Mail* carried the confession in April 1992, but the IDA ruled that I had had my trial and wouldn't reopen the case. When I appealed to the courts, it was ruled that I was tried fairly, because I had voluntarily subjected myself to IDA justice.

One strong source of evidence that would have assisted me was my exclusive daily dairies. I kept hardcover, bound diaries in which every important detail of each day's events was recorded. When I was suspended by McLeod Young Weir, those diaries disappeared, and my employers consistently claimed that they never saw them. However, a letter from McLeod's lawyer, Brian Grasmuck of Davies Ward Beck in Toronto, to my Halifax lawyers in September 1987 admits that they have the diaries, but says they consider them McLeod's property. I never could convince the IDA that McLeod had the diaries.

Then a unique event happened when it was too late to help me. Barry Morse left the employ of McLeod Young Weir and came to visit me in 1991. He gave me a sworn Canada Evidence Act statement disclosing that the same troublesome Scotia McLeod employee had taken some of my diaries and had destroyed others. It was too little too late.

24

John Ramsay Grant: Capital Punishment

A T ABOUT THE SAME TIME AS THE BUCHANAN TRUST fund was established, former PC party president John Grant became disillusioned, bitter, and unhappy with what he considered too little legal work from the Nova Scotia Power Corporation. Grant was openly complaining about party people whom he thought received more government business than he did. He was especially critical about lawyers David Chipman, Fred Dickson, and Joe MacDonald, whom he called "the gang of three," after a term used in Chinese politics. Grant appeared to be travelling a lot outside the province in an attempt to develop new contacts for legal work; he said that he had made connections in Hong Kong and Taiwan. His open comments about the Buchanan debt were causing us to fear that the opposition would pick it up. Dickson asked me to talk to Grant, to try to placate him. I had hardly started the conversation with Grant when he became furious and accused me of being Chipman's errand boy. He went on to complain about the "gang of three" and Buchanan's finances, and became so animated that I withdrew.

Grant then phoned Chipman, saying that I had pressed him for bigger political donations. Chipman phoned me, recited the complaint, and gave me a lecture about pressure, even though he admitted Grant's firm was not generous in its political giving. I exploded; I had not put pressure on Grant for money, nor did I condone his criticism of Chipman and Buchanan. I admitted I had told Grant that his firm was a political tightwad, after he called me an errand boy. I was so angry with the call, and with politics in general, that I resigned, and hung up on David. We had worked together, sometimes under pressure, for over a decade, and this tiff, precipitated by Grant, was our only one. Crease, Chipman, and the premier asked me to reconsider; when I returned, I apologized for being childish, and the incident was never mentioned again. Ted Crease, whom David Chipman had nicknamed "Daddy Warbucks," was a peacemaker and sincere friend to all of us.

Lawyer John Ramsay Grant was high on the ladder of success and still in his mid-forties. He was tall, impressive, and slender, with reddish-blond hair and piercing, hazel eyes he said had come from his Scottish ancestors. He had everything: looks, a good income, a cultured and attractive wife, great kids, and a large expensive home in ritzy south-end Halifax. He had practised law with one of the big four legal firms of Nova Scotia, Cox, Downie, since early 1971. Previously, he had practised in Toronto, with McMillan Binch, before deciding to return to his native Nova Scotia. Grant was a "successaholic" who planned everything with the precision of a bomber pilot, including his decision to become president of the Progressive Conservative Party of Nova Scotia in 1977. Grant said that he knew there would be little competition for the thankless job of president while the party was in opposition. His plan was to grab the presidency before the party won, pre-empting the many people who would want the powerful position afterward. He openly said he wanted the job to better his social and business position.

Grant was perceived to be cocky and arrogant, and he appeared to ooze confidence, but in private conversation, when he relaxed, he displayed insecurity, and sought constant assurance that he was performing his duties. Frequently he would compare his clout with that of other people around Buchanan; after the PC party was elected to government, Grant repeatedly said, "I've got no clout like that fuckin' Dickson — he's got real power." He also made no bones about using his power in selecting people, organizations, and social contacts that would further his personal goals. In contrast, his wife, Debbie, displayed no similar motives, even though she was an asset to Grant's social climbing. The Grants were among the most gracious hosts in the social circles of old Halifax, but John never seemed satisfied.

Grant lobbied hard for legal work, but craved power and influence, and the prestige associated with being an insider; that need led him to lobby for many people and causes. Special interests flocked to him with various proposals, and he frequented the halls of power.

As the provincial Tories rode the crest of the power wave, the lawyers were the most active seekers of favour, patronage, and appointments. Some openly campaigned to be judges, or had advocates do it for them. Martin Chernin, a Sydney, Nova Scotia, developer who was a long-time friend of Buchanan's, may have taken up the lobby of lawyer Alan Stern, with whom he had some family connection, on his own, but he lobbied me for Stern. Stern was slight, walked with a sort of a slouching amble, and had eyes similar to those of former Tory leader R.L. Stanfield's in that he appeared to be constantly squinting as though he had been caught in the sun without dark glasses. Stern did some administrative law for the Barristers' Society and had a general practise, but was considered well down the line in experience.

Grant heard Chernin speaking of Stern at a Finance Committee meeting. Grant said, "He looks like a judge; he looks cogitative, or even sleepy, like they all do because they read cases late every night." Then somebody at the meeting said that he knew a lawyer who fell asleep at the Halifax Club almost every day, and suggested that, if looking sleepy were the test, then Buchanan should be given that man's name as well. Grant was, at first, not aware that the guys were pulling his leg, as he was sincerely interested in who was made a judge.

I said, "Certainly a lot of lawyers I know look like Sleepy of the

'Seven Dwarfs,'" and somebody added, "I knew a lady who could play 'Snow White.'" Grant became miffed, and his face reddened. I sensed his feelings were bruised when he told us that we were not taking the subject seriously. So I asked if he had ever thought of becoming a judge, because he had a diverse practice and almost twenty years' experience. Grant's reply was very serious, and it was obvious he had a plan: "First, I must have a long list of accomplishments, some directorships which have prestige, and then I want the Order of Canada; and of course you have to be rich to be a judge, because not many can live in style on those incomes." Then Grant amazed me as he turned and asked, "Do you think I look — well, sleepy? Or is my countenance one like Stern's, which suggests that I'm cogitative?" I couldn't resist; the devil seized my tongue and I answered, "John, excessive masturbation will also make you look sleepy."

Maybe that's why Grant and I were not really close friends. We were only civil to each other, after he complained to David Chipman about my saying that his law firm was a frugal donor to the PC party. But Grant was a gracious man, and surprised me by inviting my wife and me to a pre-Christmas cocktail party at his home in December 1986. The parties at the Grants' were a "Who's Who," of Tory and business wheels in Halifax. Because it was an olive branch of reconciliation, I felt that we had to attend, even though I hate cocktail parties.

During that party an incident was brought to my attention which meant little to me at the time, but would later mean a lot. Jane Dexter, who was then married to lawyer Robert Dexter, the mighty Sobey Stores' main legal counsel, approached my wife and me and said that she had heard the Hon. Stewart McInnes, and broker Ross Montgomery, who worked for me, discussing the minister's blind-trust account in the hall. She said Montgomery mentioned several stocks, including National Sea Products, which they had bought or sold. Jane Dexter had lived with a lawyer long enough to realize that an elected politician's blind trust was not blind if the owner was informed of its contents at a cocktail party. I was not smart enough then to understand Mrs. Dexter's charge, but I did approach Montgomery that night, and asked him about the McInnes conversation. He admitted that they had talked, but said it was only in a general way. My wife heard him say it. I cautioned him about being indiscreet. But John Grant, who was a personal friend of Stewart McInnes, later told me that the public discussion of that blind trust — by Montgomery, who was a trustee; McInnes, who was the owner; and Jane Dexter — put the facts "on the wind," breeching confidentiality. I also did not fully realize the significance of Grant's caution to me.

John Grant's disappointment over provincial politics grew after he left the provincial presidency in 1983. He paid more attention to federal politics, was active in the Mulroney camp, and worked for the 1983 Mulroney by-election in Elmer MacKay's old Central Nova parliamentary constituency. He was a real force in the 1984 federal election, and suddenly he was travelling to Ottawa more often. Then he received the appointment from the prime minister as director of the Canadian Investment Development Corporation. Grant was making contacts for business and became the head of the federal party's $1,000-a-head PC 500 Club. He was appointed a director of Care Canada, and later he was an officer of the Nova Scotia branch of the Hong Kong Business Association.

Some of those appointments apparently produced opportunities for Grant to do private legal work, lobbying, and consultations, for which he billed the client under his own name rather than through his law firm. He was embarrassed when *Canadian Lawyer* magazine published a list of law firms doing legal work for the various departments of the federal government. Listed among them, for just under $300,000 in fees, was Grant's firm, Cox, Downie. Apparently that news came as a surprise and shock to the firm's partners. Grant had a lot of explaining to do.

The seemingly perfect life of John Grant then began to fall apart. He resigned from Cox, Downie, and a cloud of unpleasant rumours hung over his head like a swarm of bees. Some of the stories were way off base, but a dipsomaniac lawyer from another firm leaked a fairly accurate story. The cadaverous lawyer was temporarily confined to bed for excessive drinking when an old pal of his visited him on a stopover in Halifax from England. Propped up in bed, with a partially full bottle of liquor in his hand, he revealed to his visitor a long story about Grant's conduct, which he apparently had heard at work. Grant was alleged to have been moonlighting — running his own legal and consulting business outside his firm's affairs. In addition, he was said to be improperly charging travel expenses from some of those transactions to other clients' accounts at Cox, Downie. Grant was alleged to have been depositing his improper earnings in offshore bank accounts, which clearly suggested intent to mislead his partners and/or the tax people. Grant was making contacts at his many meetings with business people who needed government red tape cut, and he was using those contacts for his personal benefit.

The federal government's immigrant investor program, which was to cause a major problem about unethical conduct in a big Toronto law firm, was also an area into which John Grant had made some inroads. Grant had Hong Kong social connections and was representing some business people there who needed help with government in Canada. That connection broke the story of John Grant's private business ventures and contributed to his undoing.

During that period, I was being investigated, and later prosecuted, by the Investment Dealers Association of Canada about the leaking of the Stewart McInnes blind-trust information to Liberal MP Sheila Copps. Grant and his wife had shown sympathy for me while I suffered adverse publicity. Then, Grant surprised me by phoning for what he termed a long appointment. That was unusual, because political acquaintances often just showed up at my office and took a chance on catching me in. I cleared the time Grant asked for, but I dreaded the meeting because I felt I wouldn't be able to cope with his depressed state. Grant never showed up for the appointment. Normally that fact would have caused mild frustration or vexation, but, in light of Grant's condition, I was worried about him. I phoned his house and summer cottage, trying to locate him, and got no answer. Next I phoned his father, Donald Grant, and, while I tried to be low key, I did say that John had stood me up, and that I couldn't reach his wife. His father was obviously worried, thanked me, and said he'd be in touch. That night he phoned my house and told me be in the next day, if I had time. I agreed.

On Friday, August 19, 1988, Grant arrived, dressed in fashionable summer attire; he was smoking a small cigar, although he had claimed to have quit. His face was flushed, and he was very depressed. He sat in the big chair near the window with the commanding view of Halifax Harbour. From our eleventh-floor vantage point, he stared at Dartmouth, the water, and George's Island. Steepling his hands over his midsection, he sat, stretched out in the chair, and spoke as if he were talking to himself. He asked, "How the fuck do you stand it? Are you taking anything — tranquillizers? I mean the crazy bunch of bastards are trying to put you out of the business over a fucking trust-fund leak. You're in the paper all the time. How the hell do you function?" I said, "John, my investment dealer's problems make me sick, but there's nothing I can do about them but fight." I asked, "How about your troubles?" I could see his eyes were getting wet, and I was sorry I had asked. Before he could answer, I tried to shift the subject to the upcoming provincial election. I told him we were going to have to borrow a lot of money, and that the election was going to be tough, with little hope of winning. Grant silently took out a cheque and made it payable to the PC party for $500 on one of his holding companies, Inglis Investments. He said that money is the ammunition of political wars, as he handed it to me. Then he fixed those piercing eyes on me, and asked, "Do you know what I've done?" I shook my head. He said, "I've done some stupid things, but I've offered to undo them, and I know I'm wrong and have to pay, but some people want to put me out forever. There's even talk of jail." I was stunned.

He said, "Do you know that Paul Walsh ruined you, and he's made my life miserable?" I listened in silence. Grant leaned forward and placed his hands palms down on my desk and looked directly at me, as if he were about to address a jury. He said that the previous year, in the spring of 1987, before I was fired (in July), he was watching TV on a cold, wet night when Walsh showed up at the front door. Grant said that Walsh usually reminded him slightly of Quebec politician Lucien Bouchard, and I agreed. He said that Walsh was wearing an old suitcoat with its collar up and smelled strongly of Listerine mouthwash, which he either was using to cover the smell of alcohol or drinking for its alcohol content. Walsh was loaded, he said, and unsteady on his feet. When he finally spoke, Walsh didn't mince words. He said, "I'm in a game and need $200 now." Grant, who had a caustic tongue and could be really obnoxious, told Walsh to fuck off. Walsh said, "You should give me $200,000, but for today $200 will do." Grant again told him to get lost. Walsh became vicious and said, "You big-feeling prick — I'm serious, and if you doubt me ask your pal Dick Hatfield. He ignored me and I fixed him at the Fredericton Airport." Grant said Walsh told him that Hatfield and he had a sexual relationship, and then Hatfield got sick of him and avoided him, so Walsh punished him by putting marijuana in his suitcase for the police to find.

Grant still couldn't see why he should give Walsh anything, but Walsh had an ace. He told Grant that a male lawyer with whom Walsh had had a sexual relationship had informed him that a mutual Chinese client of his and Grant's had claimed that Grant had charged him $80,000 for a political favour and representation, and that the cheque was cashed outside Canada.

Grant was then terrified. Walsh's story about the Chinese client was true. Grant admitted to me that he had been doing consultations and charging for them, and that other lawyers in the PC party were doing the same. He mentioned some mining company dealing for a government loan and said two lawyers were helping them. I suspected that he was rationalizing his own conduct, but he really sounded convincing. He went on to tell me about the immigrant investor business, and also admitted that the contacts he made at board meetings were turned to his own advantage.

Grant first claimed that he did not give cash to Walsh, but, as his story unfolded, it became obvious that Walsh was paid. He said Walsh showed up repeatedly, at all hours, and several times, before Grant left Cox, Downie, Walsh came there looking for him. The Walsh pressure reached a peak in late 1987, when Walsh was in very bad shape. Suddenly, in early 1988, Walsh stopped coming, and Grant hoped that he had moved away. He didn't see Walsh from January 1988 until midsummer. At that time, Walsh told Grant he had been in a New Brunswick detox program, and that Richard Hatfield was HIV positive. Grant said, "If Hatfield's positive, and you had sex with him, you must be positive too." He said Walsh told him that his relationship with Hatfield was over four years ago, and that he wasn't worried. Walsh wasn't long getting back into alcohol, and tried to pressure Grant by telling him how he leaked the McInnes documents and ruined me. Grant didn't believe the Walsh claim about Hatfield, but he knew Walsh was trouble.

Grant said that it was a relief when he was discovered, as at least he got rid of Walsh. Grant said that, in one drunken stupor, Walsh had told him that he intended to plant cocaine on CBC-TV Halifax broadcaster Jim Nunn, as Walsh blamed Nunn for some slight by the CBC. I told Grant that I intended to warn Nunn, and I later did warn him in person.

John Grant said he had tried desperately to satisfy Cox, Downie; he had offered to repay the money, and had said that he'd move away. However, somebody there had insisted that Cox, Downie consult with a lawyer from another firm, and that counsel advised a report to the Barristers' Society. Grant said that advice was politically motivated; because it came from Ted Wickwire's big Liberal law firm, it granted him no leeway. (Wickwire has since died, and that legal firm no longer exists after changes and a reorganization.)

Grant made me feel very bad when he said how sorry he was that we had never been close friends and that he regretted causing a ruckus about me with David Chipman. He recited his troubles like a confession. He spoke with kindness about the moral support he received from Donald M. Smith, our old political pal, who was Nova Scotia's agent general in London. Smith was a former cabinet minister in the provincial government of R.L. Stanfield, and had helped us in the 1978 provincial election. Recently, he had been in Halifax and had visited Grant, and me too.

When John stood to leave, he told me that he would be called before the Barristers' Society before long, and that he had no hope. We shook hands, and I almost lost control as I realized how desperate and alone Grant obviously felt. I phoned Donald "Porky" Smith and told him of the visit, and said that I thought Grant was severely depressed and a potential suicide. On the following Sunday, I wrote in my notes that "a year from now, John Grant won't be alive." I did not see Grant again as I was preoccupied with the provincial election and the big loan we arranged at the Royal Bank for the PC campaign.

The PC party surprised everybody, including themselves, in the fall election. However, any good feelings about the election were erased by what happened next. On Monday, September 19, 1988, I answered the phone to hear Buchanan's voice. He said, "I have some very upsetting news. Are you ready?" I said, "Shoot." He said, "They just found poor John Grant dead in a Dartmouth hotel. He committed suicide." We both cried. I feel guilty that I hadn't been much of a help to John Grant, and hadn't done anything to forestall the inevitable.

Buchanan said that Grant had received bad news from the Barristers' Society on the previous Friday, and had disappeared on Saturday, after learning that he could be disbarred and that a report would be made to the Department of the Attorney General for a possible prosecution. The media were hard and cruel, offering speculation on every aspect of the story surrounding Grant. It was rumoured, first, that Grant was murdered to silence him on the subject of political embarrassments. But the medical examiner's report seems to erase foul play as a possibility. The report, signed by Dr. R.A. Perry, concluded:

> *Mr. Grant was a prominent lawyer in the city who had recently had some problems apparently relating to money. He had been before the Bar Society on Friday, September 16, 1988, and the matter had apparently been referred to the Attorney General's Department.*
>
> *Opinion: A 47-year-old male who died by suicide on or about September 18, 1988, as a result of multiple cuts and stab wounds.*

John Grant obviously needed approval more than life itself. He sentenced himself to death.

My mother offered a thought-provoking comment: "They no longer sentence people to death for murder. Why would John Grant feel his conduct warranted capital punishment?"

25

HERE COMES THE JUDGE

T HE SUPPOSEDLY DEAD, AND ADMITTEDLY DISCOURAGED, PC party faced a provincial election in 1988 with faded hopes and no money. Every single seat would be important. Party regulars felt that an election writ would signal a sure loss, and the Liberal party was so confident that rumours of who would be in the new Liberal cabinet were circulating.

But, once again, Buchanan was to prove that his political opponents, as well as some of his supporters, underestimated his political skill. Without warning, the premier appointed Robert Levy, an NDP MLA from Kings South, and a lawyer, to a judgeship, and virtually assured the Tories of winning back that traditionally Conservative seat. The appointment preceded the campaign, and it instilled confidence in the PC party machine, clouded the real opposition issues by creating a straw-man factor, and allowed Buchanan to open the PC campaign with a bang.

NDP leader Alexa McDonough didn't see the appointment so much as a bang but as a stink. She appeared before the media cameras and could hardly control the emotionally motivated quiver of her lip, as she labelled Levy's accepting the appointment as a sell-out. Levy had caught his leader flat-footed and unprepared when he gave her notice of his intentions.

Robert Levy was the son of a former Stanfield Tory MLA, Clifford Levy, who also became a judge. Bob Levy had a natural inclination to politics, and ran for the Tories in the 1970 provincial election. But he left the PC party in anger, stating as his reason that the party was a pork barrel of patronage. Levy ran unsuccessfully for the NDP, twice federally and twice provincially; however, losing seemed only to strengthen his drive. Motivated by his anger at the Tories and the strength of his political conversion, Levy became a credible NDP candidate. But changing political allegiance in Nova Scotia is not a simple task. In fact, even in England, switching parties was called "ratting" by Prime Minister Winston Churchill, who once changed parties himself. About Levy, reporter Parker Barss Donham wrote that he had left the Tories by ratting, and when he accepted the Tory government appointment to the bench, Churchillian coinage was again borrowed and it was said that "Levy re-ratted."

Parker Barss Donham, a free-lance journalist who also writes for *Readers' Digest* and does a CBC-TV commentary, was one of those who said that, "Levy was a rat in teddy bear's clothes." Barss Donham was generally not popular with Tories, but he wrote about Donald Marshall Jr.'s case with such compassion that people who had once despised his work became less critical afterward.

Levy had gone to western Nova Scotia to practise law for Nova Scotia legal aid in Kentville. He built a good client base from that practice, and then opened his own law practice in Wolfville, which is in Kings South — Harry How territory. When How left to accept an appointment as chief judge in 1983, Kings South was vacant. A by-election was called for early 1984, and the Tories nominated Paul Kinsman, a physician, who had a large family practice in Kings South. The NDP chose Bob Levy. It was a wise choice.

Dr. Kinsman was opposite in nature to hand-pumping former MLA Harry How, and a contrast to the street-wise Bob Levy. Kinsman is naturally reserved, almost shy; excessively neat, and less gregarious than the late emperor of Japan, Hirohito. Kinsman's intelligence, character, and ability were highly visible assets, but some voters felt he lacked personal warmth and charisma.

Levy campaigned so hard in that by-election that he physically exhausted himself, but he cut the Tory majority, even though Dr. Kinsman won by more than 800 votes. But, in the fall of 1984, when Buchanan called a provincial general election, Bob Levy was ready. Dr. Kinsman again won the Tory nod, and even Levy confessed his battle was uphill against a sitting Tory member in Kings South. Another factor, which he hadn't considered, was to help Levy in that election. Paul Kinsman did not like to campaign or to go hand-pumping, and to his credit he did not ignore his busy medical practice. While Levy pounded the streets and by-ways, Kinsman stayed home. As the campaign entered the home stretch, there were warnings of trouble for Kinsman. Buchanan sent me to Kings County to find out what was happening, and if Kinsman was falling behind. I reported to him that Levy had a chance of upsetting Kinsman, and suggested that Buchanan personally go into the constituency to help. But the premier's schedule was not merely very busy, according to Dickson, but overbooked. I said only that without Buchanan we would lose. Dickson was not happy with me, but with a great deal of rearranging and compromise, he set up a quick visit by Buchanan for the last Saturday before polling day, to help the slipping Kinsman. Buchanan went to the busy New Minas shopping area on that Saturday to meet with Kinsman for several hours of campaigning. Kinsman arrived late, barely shook hands with Buchanan, and departed for the hospital. Dickson said he considered beating me first, with a bat, and then Kinsman, because the trip was for naught. Robert Levy defeated Dr. Kinsman by eighteen votes, and it was the first time in anyone's memory that there was not a Tory majority in that section of Kings County. The local Tories asked for a recount, and it changed Levy's edge to twenty-one votes. Buchanan ignored Dickson's pressure to forget it, and called for a judicial action to overthrow the election on the grounds that twenty-one ineligible Acadia University students had voted.

Judge Doane Hallet presided over the case, and found for Levy. Dickson was unhappy with Buchanan and said, "What the fuck did you expect? All those guys are Liberal party hacks or appointments," and I asked, with tongue in cheek, "Do you mean that the judges are Liberals and wouldn't find for the Tories?" Buchanan was not amused.

Buchanan's elephant-like memory was honed from 1984 until 1988 by the direct, unrelenting questions and attacks by Levy in the Legislature. Levy was easily the most effective researcher and MLA in the House, and his opposition tactics made him the darling of the media. So when Buchanan appointed Levy a judge, the press was angry about the alleged sell-out. Bitterness expressed by such writers as Barss Donham and Harry Flemming was typical, and their open unhappiness caused Buchanan to laugh with uncharacteristic joy as he named those two men "Heckle and Jeckle" after the 1950s cartoon characters who were stuffy crows.

But Levy's accepting a judgeship, despite Buchanan's political motives, was based on strong personal reasons. His personal life was in a shambles, and he was going through a severe domestic disruption and was concerned about his kids' well-being. He had become unhappy about being away from home. A friend whom Levy admired said, "Take stock of your life now that you are forty-one, and ask yourself if you want to be a successful politician, ten years from now, at fifty-one, or a successful father." Levy's signal to Buchanan had been in the form of a complaint.

The committees of the Nova Scotia Legislature have members from all political parties, and at one time MLAs were paid extra for attending meetings. But Alexa McDonough, the NDP leader, had made a big public issue of the extra pay, saying that the provincial budget was out of control, and thus MLAs should not get extra pay, as they were salaried by the government already. Buchanan yielded to that argument and cut out the extra pay. The financially strained among the MLAs included Bob Levy, who complained bitterly to Buchanan about the loss of committee pay. Buchanan was less than diplomatic to Bob Levy in reminding him that his NDP party and Mrs. McDonough caused the change. But Buchanan presently backed off a bit. That is how Buchanan got the idea of putting Levy on the bench.

Former NDP party leader Jeremy Akerman provided another insight into Levy's departure. Akerman, who had left the party because he had felt disappointed about the factionalism within it, said, "Levy is suffering from Shaw's syndrome." He likely was referring to Alexa McDonough's father, Lloyd Shaw, the wealthy industrialist brick manufacturer, who was patron of the NDP in Nova Scotia. Akerman had once been more popular, in public polls, as NDP leader than the Liberal and Tory leaders, but claimed that Shaw and the intellectual wing of the party interfered so much that Akerman resigned. Akerman claimed that Levy had suffered the jealousy of the NDP party's "red-wing" intelligentsia in silence for four years, and could no longer stand it. (Levy denied this!)

Harry How said that Buchanan had political instincts second to no other elected person. Buchanan's boldness in suggesting directly to Bob Levy that he leave public life and accept a judgeship, on the occasion of Levy's complaining about committee pay, was further proof of the soundness of his judgement, as Levy accepted gladly and without delay.

There is no question that Buchanan acted out of political motives; he wanted the Kings South seat back, as he realized in 1988 that the party would need every possible seat to keep a majority. As the gong sounded for the 1988 election, it was Buchanan, outright luck, and a lot of political screaming about the wrong issues by the opposition that allowed the Tories to win, almost by accident. After the Levy appointment, Pictou's Joe Stewart claimed to journalist Al Hollingsworth that he and MLA Donald Cameron, who was later to become Premier of Nova Scotia, had engineered the Levy coup. But Mr. Cameron was not anxious to have the credit when the media started the front-page charges of a "sell-out."

Before Buchanan called the 1988 election, the spring sitting of the Legislature was a hotbed of rhetoric, because everybody could smell an election in the air. Liberal MLA Guy Brown was the most effective member of the opposition, and he raised a subject that could have run the Tory government out of office if it had been pursued. Brown's detective work had uncovered documents that called into question developer Ralph Medjuck's profitable rentals to the government.

Medjuck had briefly been one of Buchanan's law partners, and after that a partner of Dickson's, but the opposition never seemed to get around to marrying up the facts to embarrass the government. However, the Brown questions were well researched and provided enough facts to cause a public stir. The name of Government Services deputy minister Michael Zareski showed up in the press in August 1988, in response to Brown's query. Mr. Zareski was to become a famous civil servant in the future. Brown was on the Government–Medjuck lease like a Georgia prison bloodhound. On August 25, 1988, the media reported that Guy Brown had acquired, and made public, a copy of Medjuck's lease document with the Nova Scotia government. He said the lease showed that $4.3 million would be paid to Medjuck's company as a management fee, in addition to the $60 million in rent. Deputy minister Zareski was one of the government people who was quoted in a Halifax *Chronicle-Herald* article on August 25, 1988, by writer Alan Jeffers; in that article, Zareski publicly defended the operating cost of the building, including the Medjuck management fee. Mr. Zareski is the same man who lunched with developer Medjuck, was aware of negotiations for the building lease with Medjuck, and was quoted explaining it. Mr. Zareski was obviously not angry with the Buchanan government then, but he would later destroy the Buchanan premiership.

That spring, as the Legislature session closed, the possibility of an election being called dimmed slightly in the face of obvious opposition gains, Brown's persistence in exploiting the Medjuck deal, and slipping Tory popularity. Polls showed the Grits and NDP doing very well, and the Conservative party losing ground. The cartoonist at the *Chronicle-Herald* seized on the Medjuck lease of the Joseph Howe Building to the government, drawing the Howe statue in the Nova Scotia Legislature garden holding its nose! If Buchanan had quit, the continued reign of the PC party would be in doubt, as a number of spin-off conclusions by the opposition could be linked to his departure.

Fred Dickson knew exactly how tired the public perceived the government to be; his first thought was to rally the Conservative Finance Committee together to convince Buchanan to go for it! Committee members were canvassed to see if we could raise the needed money, and, with a lump in my throat, I gave the assurance that we could deliver. We had a poor poll position, unenthusiastic campaign people, financial pressure unequalled since 1973, and a premier who wanted to enjoy what was left of his life while helping his wife overcome cardiovascular problems; it was not an auspicious start. Getting John Buchanan to run was one important consideration, but reshaping and refurbishing the tired public appearance of the party was in Dickson's and Joe MacDonald's laps, and they knew the problems.

Buchanan's team made few promises, stressed the "new PCs" and John Buchanan making very few mistakes, and ran a middle-of-the-road campaign. But Vince MacLean was ahead, money was very slow coming in, and corporate donors were flocking to the Grits. Information came to us that the Grits had $1 million available for the election.

In our camp, we had difficulty raising money for the budget, and a mild but discernible panic was visible on Dickson's and MacDonald's faces; I was fried several times and told once more to "stand and deliver." My committee was working at an unbelievable pace. When the advertising and campaign people demanded their next cheque, the treasurer informed them that we didn't have it. I anticipated a riot, so I organized a $200,000 loan from a chartered bank. To secure it, however, I had to have guarantees; I was no longer in a position to do it alone. I canvassed with the party's finance coordinator, Suzanne Huett, and twenty co-signers were arranged for, with difficulty. One Cape Breton party stalwart, Bill Manson, son of former Stanfield cabinet minister E.A. Manson, created a chuckle over the money-borrowing and note-signing. A campaign meeting was held at the Lord Nelson Hotel in Halifax for workers from all over the province. At that meeting, I was concerned only with getting my twenty co-signers for the $200,000 bank loan. I stalked various prospects, and sometimes had to ambush people, but the signatures were acquired. I saw Bill Manson talking to some of the Cape Breton Tories across the hotel ballroom. I sent Suzanne Huett over to entice Bill to walk near the big pillar where I sat, half-hidden, waiting to trap innocent passers-by. She led the faithful Bill right to me, and before he said much more than "hello," I launched into a flag-waving, tear-jerking speech about our need for the money, the loan, and his very important endorsement. The affable Manson, obviously deep in thought, said, "Okay, I'll sign, but it will cause me a lot of trouble in Cape Breton." Concerned, I asked, "Trouble from your wife?" And Bill replied, "Oh hell, no, but the Cape Breton bunch sent me down here to borrow from you, and when they find out I lent to you instead, they'll either think that I'm stupid or shoot me."

Another Cape Breton lady, whom I call Ms. Tory, and her husband were approached by party president Irene Swindells, after I asked her to make the request. The dear lady from "western Cape Breton" preached a sermon about not signing notes, hating loans, and her age causing potential difficulties to her estate. Irene figured it had not been a good idea to ask. Just as the senior lady's tirade ended, she said, "No, I'll not sign a note for $10,000 because loans are bad, but I'll give you the $10,000." Amen!

We still had $400,000 less than the Liberal party, which had a large pool of money invested from bequests and from the trust pools of the money raised by charging commissions to people who received government business during the 1970s.

At first we thought our campaign hopes were overshadowing our judgement, but we started to sense a change in public attitude occurring, albeit slowly. The committee kept the people in the political trenches inspired and informed, and the Dickson image concept was working miracles. Likely the peak for us came during the televised debates by the three party leaders. Buchanan was upbeat and his usual self, a fact which often provoked MacLean. Privately, MacLean dubbed the premier, "Teflon John," but publicly he spent too much time on the attack. McDonough of the NDP was considered tops by the media, and of course the Liberals thought all the media were NDP or Tory. Vince was not always embraced by the media. Dickson figured that if Alexa came out best, it was Liberal votes she'd be taking away, and that wouldn't hurt us. A very bad piece of luck for the Liberals was one of the most decisive factors for the Tories. The killer schedule that Vince MacLean was stuck with by his coaches produced a nervous look to his left eyelid. Coupled with his animated new style, it did not improve his appearance on television, or in person. At times he gestured incorrectly for his verbally expressed mood, and appeared a little sinister, even when he smiled. In the end, Vince blew it on TV, and was received poorly by viewers.

Our strategists felt that we came out of the TV debate at least even with the Grits, and possibly a tad in the lead. The Liberals must have thought the same, as they got on the campaign horse and ran off in all the wrong directions. Another factor, like a lucky bounce in baseball, was the Angus Reid political poll. The pollster publicly released the results of his last poll just at the key campaign time, announcing that the Buchanan Tories would win.

How much influence, if any, that poll had on voters has not been substantiated by any scientific study. But we did know that it had a great effect on fund-raising and inspired party workers to new heights. Vince MacLean reacted with justifiable anger, claiming that Reid published the poll for the Tories' benefit. There was no evidence to support that opinion, but none of this endeared Reid to the Grits.

The Liberals made an impressive election showing; they improved their numbers by winning fifteen seats back from the Tories. Their popular vote soared to within three percentage points of the PCs, with all of the Cape Breton seats, except one, going to the Grits. Without our good luck and fortunate breaks, Vince MacLean would have won. He at least silenced the critics within the new buoyant Liberal party.

Billie Joe MacLean, the former Tory who was expelled from the Legislature and who kept his seat in a by-election (as an independent), was finally defeated by a Liberal. Cape Breton rejected the

Tories, although, as usual, most mainlanders still thought the government had catered too much to Cape Breton. Winning the election was not to be a good thing for Buchanan personally. If he'd lost, he would probably have been left alone to enjoy life. But there was trouble brewing. The public report by the royal commission studying the events surrounding the wrongful conviction of Donald Marshall Jr., and the condition of the justice system in Nova Scotia, was publicized. That report would cause shame for both the Liberals and the Tories. It would also be the beginning of the last phase of the premiership of John M. Buchanan.

26

CONTROL

AFTER BEING TOTALLY IN CONTROL WHEN THE Tories took power in 1978, John Buchanan moved through various stages of problems and government scandals, to the point where I felt he had lost effective control. During the height of his personal problems, his worry and stress allowed decision making on some daily matters to pass to his adviser Fred Dickson, more by default than by intent.

From about 1984 until 1988, the premier longed for personal freedom and peace of mind but continued to enjoy the social or state side of government. In that period, some MLAs were jealous or overambitious, and Buchanan's power was eroded to the point where he could no longer hurry things through cabinet. After 1988, he seemed to have little influence or power over the members, and while some were loyal, many sat on their hands. Cabinet upset him terribly at that stage, and the federal government would rarely give direct, quick answers to related political problems, and, when they did, often never followed up with action.

But Buchanan couldn't get much done at any level after the 1988 election. One example was the spiralling costs of health care in Nova

Scotia. The premier formed the Royal Commission on Health Care; there were many people interested in serving on it, but almost all the aggressive applicants had an axe to grind or were not qualified. The premier wanted Halifax doctor Earle Reid to head the royal commission. Reid, who made more than $500,000 a year in his special practice, was not eager to have the job, which he viewed as a thankless task. Some members of cabinet opposed Reid because he is direct, blunt, honest, and known to have the view that the Nova Scotia health-care system is fat and wasteful. One member of cabinet, according to Buchanan, even tried to dissuade the premier from appointing Reid, by saying that Reid frequently had run-ins with the agency who paid doctors' fees. Reid was furious about that charge, and turned the job down; however, finally Buchanan conscripted Dr. Reid.

Reid dived into the study with the other members of the commission, and over an extensive period they prepared a sensible, money-saving, cost-efficient system of health care that improved and streamlined that currently in place. The report was no sooner printed than some ministers made it clear that it would never be implemented. Reid, in the meantime, had been recognized by other Canadian provinces, and several foreign countries, as an authority on the subject of health-care efficiency and was invited to share his knowledge with them. John Buchanan could not convince his cabinet to implement any of the recommendations of a study which cost a lot of public money — generally said to be just under $2 million. Buchanan was bitter about that, and remorseful that he had appointed some of the cabinet, and admitted he could no longer get much done. The end was near, but the premier did not yet realize that some members of his own cabinet wanted him out.

Buchanan was to suffer other rebuffs by cabinet, and finally, in disgust, he told me we should mimic the U.S. system and have the federal and provincial premiership limited to eight years, as is the presidency of the United States. The event that made the premier most angry involved an old friend, former Stanfield cabinet minister Donald (Porky) Smith, whom Buchanan had appointed to be

Nova Scotia's agent general in London, England. Smith was mentioned in the press as being involved in a dispute with cabinet minister Donald Cameron. Buchanan couldn't seem to find the handle to end the dispute, which mushroomed into "much ado about nothing" at the government's expense.

It was secretly reported to the media that Donald Smith had a dispute with the Department of Development. Smith would not comment, but the media championed the issue and sought clarification from Donald Cameron. A number of the press boasted privately that they could always provoke Mr. Cameron into saying "too much." Some media people viewed his manner as refreshing, but party people often would have preferred his silence. In the case of the agent general, Mr. Cameron found himself caught between pressure from his department, who felt Mr. Smith was too independent, and pressure from the media, who put Cameron in a position, he thought, of having to defend his integrity. Pushed by the various factions and his conscience, Cameron criticized the expenses and operation of the London office of Nova Scotia's agent general, Donald M. Smith. The agent general's office had been opened for the promotion of Nova Scotia industry, trade, and tourism with Europeans; it existed long before the government of John Buchanan took office. Donald Smith was appointed to the position by order-in-council, and he had a contract with the provincial government for over ten years. When Mr. Smith had been approached by Premier Buchanan in 1979, it was because Smith had a good history of high-level government business and community-service experience. Smith was also a member of the prestigious Duke of Edinburgh Awards Organization. He agreed to accept the appointment but, being knowledgeable about how governments operated, insisted on a contract to protect both parties. Smith also insisted that he report directly to the premier's office. He wanted to avoid working for a variety of ministers, deputies, and senior civil servants, and to lessen the confusion that often occurs in cabinet shuffles. He understood the problems of such changes, and wisely chose to avoid that prospective grief. Some civil servants at the Department of Development did not like that arrangement, and, in protest, were often slow or unresponsive to his needs, logistical problems, and requests for support for his operation. On Smith's side, he carried out his functions with a dedication above what was required of him. He provided embassy-level service, assistance, and hospitality to visitors from Nova Scotia of all social, business, and political backgrounds. The relationship with the Department of Development certainly created a misunderstanding that cast the London operation in a poor light, in Mr. Cameron's view. When the problem festered, Cameron was pushed out on a limb. He spoke out, and the media loved it. Finally, Cameron was reported publicly to say, "I caught Smith's attention when I stopped his pay for three months." What Smith said of Cameron privately was kept quiet, but was probably most appropriate. Donald Smith followed the age-old British parliamentary custom that non-elected "government employees are not supposed to comment publicly." A long-time friend of his noted that Mr. Smith's personal wealth is great enough that holding back his salary would have little effect.

Smith visited me in Halifax during that controversy and revealed that he would quit the minute his term, which was an extension of his original appointment, was complete. Smith is a blunt, strong-willed, experienced politician; he is armed with a good intellect and his debating ability would have mangled Cameron in a normal parliamentary forum. But Smith maintained silence out of respect for the tradition that servants of the Crown do not criticize the government in public. The fact that Cameron did not honour the reciprocal tradition that elected people do not publicly criticize public servants angered Smith. After Cameron repeatedly broke that rule, Smith said, "Cameron is a horse's ass who can't even speak the Queen's English; he mispronounces the word 'government' as *guv-ment*, so how could you expect him to understand its traditions?"

The Public Accounts Committee of the Nova Scotia Legislature has members from all three political parties. However, the governing party, because its members organize or select that committee, traditionally has the most members, and the majority of the votes. Some meetings, where discussion is mostly about the provincial budget, spending, and business, are not stimulating or exciting to some MLAS; as a result, attendance is treated cavalierly by some. In 1989, the Tory members of that committee were either bored or asleep at the switch because one Tory MLA was not present when the meeting convened. There may have been a legitimate reason for his absence, but it looked bad, especially since NDP leader Alexa McDonough claimed that attendance at committee meetings was less compelling to government MLAs after extra payments to members were discontinued, at her suggestion, to save money.

Vincent MacLean, the Liberal leader, and his other member of that body made a motion to table the contract that had been signed between the government-controlled Nova Scotia Power Corporation and a new mining company that the provincial government had enticed to Nova Scotia; it was Westray Mines, a division of a larger Canadian mining company known as Curragh Resources. MLA Billie Gillis, the other Liberal member of the Public Accounts Committee, was chairman of the meeting when the vote was called. The vote was a tie because of the absent Tory. That allowed Chairman Gillis to vote a second time, and he voted to table the contract so that any inducements that had been made to Westray by the government would be revealed.

Notice by letter was sent to President Louis Comeau, the former federal Tory MP, who Buchanan had made president of the Nova Scotia Power Corporation. Comeau is a capable and experienced political animal and, while he is said to play every issue cosy and close to the vest, his own appearance at the committee had precipitated the vote. When Comeau had been asked to reveal the Westray agreement, he said, "There is no reason to make the Westray contract more available than the DEVCO [Cape Breton Development Corporation] contract or any other contract."

After the vote, Comeau stalled. Then he had the Power Corp. solicitor, Richard J. Smith, write to public accounts chairman Billie Gillis and refuse to deliver the agreement. Smith said in a letter, dated May 24, 1989, "that the publication of the details of their contract could place the competitiveness of their product at risk."

The news that the Public Accounts Committee had passed the motion demanding the Westray contract was not received with pleasure by Buchanan. On political matters he was without equal and he could not understand the government members being outmanoeuvred by what he perceived to be a lax strategy. He issued firm instructions for his members to make a motion reconsidering the proposal about the Westray contract. At the next meeting, the Tories moved it be reconsidered and then, with their majority in place, voted the first motion down.

Buchanan felt the attitude of the Tory MLAs was poor because it was not the only time that they had been outperformed by the opposition. The opposition members of the Public Accounts Committee had shrewdly managed to get before the committee former federal auditor general Kenneth Dye, who was a hard-rock critic of government waste. Mr. Dye embarrassed the provincial Tories when he revealed the waste and misuse of federal funding that the provincial government had received from Ottawa. On that occasion, Buchanan correctly read the public's opinion about an aggressive-sounding federal civil servant coming to Nova Scotia to tell us how to spend our federal funding. Buchanan's public response was to put Mr. Dye in his place, and the public loved his response. But Buchanan was angry that Dye was sneaked in to testify because our MLAs didn't seem to have political sense or instincts.

As the crisis with Buchanan evolved, Fred Dickson was consulted about the bigger decisions, working a marathon schedule, running between various ministries and government departments. He had become the invisible premier. Dickson had considerable influence on Buchanan, and sometimes could move the premier to act when it seemed impossible that he would. But not always.

In the past, two appointments that some ministers opposed were made by Buchanan. One was while Dickson was still principal assistant, and the other after Fred had gone back to his law firm. Both would came back to haunt the premier, who ignored the advice. The first of these appointments was the selection of a new auditor general, and Buchanan chose to make a simple political path and appoint the second in command to the retiring auditor general. Dickson made a list of competent, independent, and apolitical senior chartered accountants whom he felt would be more suited to the task. Buchanan wouldn't change his mind, even for Dickson. The antagonism toward Buchanan's choice was based on a widespread political opinion that the person selected, although competent and honest, was often influenced by a former Liberal civil servant. By the time the next election was over, Buchanan admitted that he should have listened to Dickson.

Later, Buchanan would make a second appointment mistake. Despite political party people's attempts to change his mind and one or two cabinet ministers' opposition to his choice, Buchanan would stick to his guns; ironically, it would lead to his own undoing. The Deputy Minister of Public Works, Donald Power, was planning to retire. Buchanan intended to appoint a young man from that department to be deputy minister when Mr. Power left. In the meantime, Buchanan made an effort to convince Don Power not to leave the government, and to accept a new position as manager of the construction of the multimillion-dollar Camp Hill Hospital project. Power's decision was to bring him an embarrassing legal problem in the twilight of his career!

Buchanan's choice of a replacement for the tough, penny-pinching Power was a young man brought into government service by a former Liberal cabinet minister — Michael Zareski, whose brother had once been an assistant in Regan's political employ. Michael Zareski was considered unique and eccentric. And, while perception is not always fact, Mr. Zareski and Buchanan would be the centre of a media storm, and Zareski would eventually end John Buchanan's premiership. The Tory members of the Public Accounts Committee were lax by allowing Liberal MLA Bob Gillis to outmanoeuvre them on the Westray contract with Nova Scotia Power Corporation. They should have learned a lesson but they didn't.

That same complacency of Tory MLAs was to create what Joe MacDonald would call a "Royal shit storm." The Liberals on the committee proposed that Michael Zareski, the former Deputy

Minister of Government Services, be called to testify at the June 1990 meeting. If the Tories had been awake, they could have stopped Zareski from appearing. Almost every MLA knew Mr. Zareski's background. Aside from the fact that many of them were angry that Buchanan had appointed him against their wishes, Zareski was supposedly angry at the government. Michael Zareski and his wife were embroiled in a personal dispute and Mr. Zareski believed the government and some of his own family members had acted in consort to discredit him, first by sending him to a mental hospital in Ontario, and then by directing his salary to his wife. On June 13, 1990, the sleepy Public Works Committee heard Zareski's name called, and the government people had no idea what was about to happen. Joe MacDonald said later that Zareski's testimony was like putting an outboard motor into a barrel of manure.

Zareski is an articulate, pleasant-appearing young man whose presentation is cool, clever, and low key. His performance was professional and deadly, but his features were placid and displayed no anger, even though he was about to wipe out the Buchanan premiership.

Michael Zareski publicly accused the Premier of Nova Scotia, John Buchanan, of (as published in the *Chronicle-Herald*):

- giving certain bidders on government work his blessing;

- reprimanding Zareski for awarding a tender to a low-bid Newfoundland firm instead of a higher-bid Nova Scotia firm;

- instructing Zareski to hire a specific firm to manage the Cape Breton Regional Hospital Project;

- telling Zareski to lease office space from developer Ralph Medjuck instead of Trizec Corp., which had the lowest bid;

- refusing to deal with Confederation Life for their Joseph Howe Building but agreeing to pay millions more for the same building to Medjuck after he bought it;

- appointing a friend of the premier's, Mark Cleary, as the

"Paper President" of a company restoring Government House with the result that the man received a percentage of all contracts awarded to that firm. [He further alleged that "The Paper President" of the firm demanded $30,000 to step down as President of the company, some of which money *he suspected* was for the premier's pocket. It was not, but Mark Cleary was convicted of influence-peddling in 1992 and fined $4,000.];

• exercising influence over Government Services hiring "right down to the janitors" and insisting a former Tory area Vice President, Lloyd McQueen, be hired as Director of Publishing for the Province; and

• having his house painted and his children chauffeured by Government Services employees. [That was proved untrue by the RCMP.]

In the weeks which followed, Zareski added public fuel to that controversy by claiming that government staff, paint, and lumber were used to repair John Buchanan's personal summer cottage at a nearby lake. The actual testimony was followed by cabinet minister David Nantes questioning the pale, sartorially perfect Mr. Zareski, who sat, saint-like, obviously pleased at the attention his allegations were receiving.

Nantes referred to Zareski's having been in a mental institution, and suggested that his release was against professional advice given by the Guelph, Ontario, institution where he had been sent for treatment. Zareski claimed that he was forced into that institution against his will, and accused the government of complicity with his wife and brothers. He said that the medical person supervising his case would confirm that the release was made because he was no longer ill. Zareski stated that he had been fired by the Government of Nova Scotia on October 8, 1989, and said that he intended to sue for wrongful dismissal; he eventually lodged that suit.

Nantes, the minister of health, was attacked by opposition leader Vincent MacLean and accused of using information obtained from confidential government sources in an attempt to discredit Zareski's allegations. Vincent MacLean complained formally about Nantes.

NDP leader Alexa McDonough wrote to the RCMP to complain about the Zareski charges, and called for an investigation.

Lawyers claimed that statements made at the Public Accounts Committee hearing enjoy "limited privilege," meaning that neither Zareski nor the media could have actions brought against them for slander or liable. Nantes appeared to be safe because he had spoken at the hearing, and the Halifax City Police came to a similar conclusion and said that no charge would be laid. That was not the end of the Nantes matter. City alderman Walter Fitzgerald, a former Liberal cabinet minister in the government of Gerald Regan, and Liberal fund-raiser Lonnie Holland, both publicly criticized the city police and suggested the matter should be looked at again. Holland criticized Chief of Police Blair Jackson in the last week of that respected policeman's active working career before retirement.

The Nantes controversy was complicated by Tory attorney general Tom McInnes, who appeared to be leaning over backwards to be impartial and fair, so as not to favour his cabinet colleague Nantes.

McInnes not only was fair, but was viewed by me as causing a problem for Nantes. McInnes was seen as Minister of Vacillation by some Tories. He was called "Cowboy Tom" since, like federal Tory MP Elmer MacKay, he ran around in trousers so tight that the initials on his drawers showed through, and he wore cowboy boots with a business suit, which the premier felt was more suited to Calgary than to Halifax.

My own uncle, Tory George Brison, was a critic of Tom McInnes from the time, early in 1979, when McInnes was Minister of Transportation (Highways). McInnes was indecisive and hid out on important issues. Brison said, "Tom McInnes was the poorest Minister of Highways in the province's history." My wife, who liked Tom and was particularly fond of his former wife, Bernadette, was upset by those remarks, and she said so. Then my uncle said, "You're right. He wasn't the worst Minister of Highways. His assistant was."

Perhaps McInnes shouldn't be blamed for the charges against Nantes, and David Chipman privately conceded that it was a silly charge with little hope of a conviction. He was right: Nantes got off.

Meanwhile, Zareski was on a roll with the press. Reg Fendick of the Truro *Daily News* said, "Zareski believes Buchanan personally took kickbacks." I was angry, but amused by that allegation as I had personal knowledge of Buchanan's finances; clearly, he not only never stole a dime, but never had one. I had never known a man less interested in money. But the public believed the charge. The damage could not be undone, and no matter what the RCMP proved or disproved, the public was left with the impression of corruption.

Dickson said of Fendick's article, "He crossed the line without being subtle, and it will never be undone, and he'll [Fendick] get away with it."

Dean Jobb, a reporter, is alleged to have based some of his reports on information from a "secret source" in accusing Premier Buchanan of fixing his cottage with government lumber, paint, and labour. Possibly one secret media source was a man who had been fired by the provincial government for stealing. The person involved has a strange reputation. When he was caught stealing from the government, he admitted to his crime and was fired; he was then charged, and got off in court only because Mr. Zareski's people failed to warn him that any statement he made could be used against him. If Buchanan had overruled Mr. Zareski's department and put the man back to work, as he had petitioned Buchanan to do, he would not have been whispering into phones about the premier. Some media were notified of the background of the person who was their secret source. The information on him is in government departmental and court records, which were a matter of public record. But no public notice of that was reported.

Mr. Buchanan subsequently provided the invoices for paint and other products used on his cottage, and the names of the workmen who did the job. Both the store where the purchases were made and the workers confirmed Buchanan's version. All of which proved Zareski and the press were wrong - except in the public's opinion.

In a black-bordered, itemized list of alleged Buchanan improprieties, the *Chronicle-Herald*, of June 14, 1990, said that "Mr. Buchanan told him (Zareski) to choose a bid by *law partner* Ralph Medjuck."

217

Mr. Medjuck had not been a Buchanan law partner since the early 1960s, but Dickson had been a partner after that time.

Another reporter said, on December 30, 1990, "through the summer of 1990 Buchanan appeared to be lost in a fog, a desperate man running from a scandal like a man set upon by dogs."

Buchanan was good at dealing with criticism but frustrated by the ongoing media trial to which his family was subjected. No action was available to him until after the authorities had looked into the matter and given their report, and that would take a long time. In addition to Buchanan's defence being limited to denial, Zareski was always available for additions to the public "musings," no matter how bizarre they became. In one paper, a picture was displayed of Mr. Zareski standing on his head to amuse the reporter. Mr. Zareski started to publicly postulate about becoming Premier of Nova Scotia, and taking Mr. Buchanan's place as head of the PC party.

Meanwhile, Mrs. Patricia Zareski produced the file numbers of sworn documents filed before the court protonotary in October 1989, at the Halifax Court House, by lawyer Janet M. Chisholm. Michael Zareski was to denounce and deny the statements, but they were sworn by Patricia Zareski and suggested that Michael Zareski was not an average civil servant.

She outlined Michael Zareski's behaviour, including a two-day disappearance, and his pronouncements that he was an apostle of Jesus, and said she discovered that he was keeping company with a female psychic. She told of how she and Mr. Zareski's family had convinced him to seek treatment for his alleged mental condition. But it would do no good to kill the messenger. Zareski had already mortally wounded the premier.

Buchanan came to my house in August 1990 unexpectedly, late in the afternoon, at an hour that rural Nova Scotians call supper time. As was his custom, he removed his shoes and coat, then sat in my big, shabby chair. While he talked to my wife and made phone calls at the same time, I almost saw a flash of the old Buchanan, who could carry on three conversations and talk on the phone all at once. My wife served him food on a footstool, but even Annapolis Valley apple pie did not excite him, as it usually did. Buchanan was known to be a healthy eater, yet he hardly touched the meal and only picked at the pie. He told us that he was almost broke financially. He was not blue about that, but he was sorry that he could not help his son, who was in a business slump and needed money. He talked of how long we all had been together and how sorry he was about my own health, which had deteriorated. I knew he was finished with being an elected politician, but I didn't like to ask for more information. Suddenly, he put his shoes on and walked outside; as we looked at the fading daylight and his old station wagon, I saw a side of him I had never seen before. He said, "It's over and I did my best." I said, "What about Ottawa?" and he said, "I likely have little choice because I won't put up with this guff any more." He had come to tell us he was giving up, without spelling out the details. I thought of his years of hard work; and blinded by my personal affection for him, I could only think of a tired political joke about a first-class elected person who discovered at election time that a voter he had repeatedly helped was voting against him. When the constituent was confronted and reminded of all that had been done for him, he replied, "Yeah, but what have ya done for me lately?"

The RCMP investigated Mr. Zareski's allegations over a period of about fourteen months, and Buchanan was cleared of the accusations in September 1991; but the media and the public had already done their worst.

27

GHOSTLY RUINS

THE ANNOUNCEMENT CAUGHT POLITICIANS, THE PUB-
lic, and the media unprepared. It was a relief that
Halifax reporter Reg Fendick did not use his overworked word "embattled" and create the expected
and antiquated 1940s Walter Winchell cliché
"Embattled Premier Bombshell Resignation." The
Government of Canada's announcement said it all in a few words:
"Prime Minister Brian Mulroney today announced that his Excellency
the Governor General has agreed to summon the following individuals to the Senate of Canada." Buchanan's name was first, and a New
Brunswicker's second. Fred Dickson, visibly moved, said, "Buchanan
deserves better than the publicity and pain he's getting."

Political life goes on. The Zareski mess was not just local news,
as the national GST Senate fight spotlighted the background of each
new Senate appointment. In Nova Scotia, the people of the province
were treated to the first announced aspirant for John M. Buchanan's
job as party leader and premier. First off the mark with his decla-
ration was Michael Zareski. Unbelievably, he was reported to be a
candidate, and sounded as if he fully intended to go through with

his newly declared crusade. Reporters questioned Zareski and treated him seriously, granting him space and air time, despite the fact that he was not a member of the Progressive Conservative party. Zareski, uttering political-sounding statements, appeared to be for real, at least in his own mind. What he was doing was answering a call from a secret voice, silent to all but himself, which suggested that he should be the next premier of Nova Scotia. Buchanan's wife said, "Ashes to ashes, dust to dust: for the campaign of St. Michael, I give, I must — a Loonie."

In the fall of 1990, the fickle winds of political irony were not confined to the Conservative party. The common street opinion was that Vince MacLean of the Liberal party was doing so well on his road to the premier's office that he could hardly look sad at the war memorial. His dreams of being a shoo-in took a detour in short order. First, the public opinion polls showed that NDP leader Alexa McDonough and her party were in first place in the public's view. Then the subject of Liberal party money and fund-raising, which had kept the party on the front pages periodically since 1983, was raised again by a member of MacLean's own party. George Hawkins, the son of a former Liberal senator, blurted out publicly that the Liberal Party of Nova Scotia had several secret funds that were administered by people other than the democratically elected party executive. Hawkins's public statements led to an admission by Vincent MacLean that he was accepting a salary, in addition to his government income, from the secret trust funds. Liberals believed that Hawkins was getting revenge for the suffering of James Cowan, who had been the other candidate in the contest MacLean had won to lead the party. But Hawkins and his supporters claimed a sincere concern for an open process, and said they disliked undemocratic rule in the party. Following Mr. Hawkins's revelations, party leader Vincent MacLean gave up his party income, which had been paid by the party trust funds.

The news had lost its impact and settled into yesterday's trash when Hawkins struck again. At the Liberal party's annual meeting, with hot television prop lights blazing amid rolling TV cameras, George Hawkins stood and made a motion to have all party funds handled by the executive of the party, taking them away from the back-room boys who were suspected of running the party. Former premier Gerald Regan, looking troubled and as stern as a "hanging judge," turned a penetrating stare on George Hawkins as they passed each other at the meeting in full view of public television.

Some people in the Conservative party were temporarily amused by the Liberal party trust-fund controversy. When Liberal leader Vince MacLean decided to stop accepting the fund payments, even though the payments did not bother everybody, media attention and public interest in the trust funds seemed to wane. However, the issues of trust funds was not over, and was to return to haunt the Tories too.

Meanwhile, the Conservative party readied itself for a leadership convention to choose a successor to John Buchanan. Three Tory cabinet ministers — Donald Cameron, Tom McInnes, and Roland Thornhill — and a defeated PC candidate — Clair Callaghan — declared themselves to be candidates. The public hardly seemed to notice the race, which was about as interesting to many Nova Scotians as the mayor's race in Flin Flon, Manitoba.

No one candidate seemed to have attracted a majority of any one specific age group, economic sector, or gender to his or her camp, although Donald Cameron had the support of most caucus and cabinet ministers. Cameron always seemed to be ahead during the race, so his every move was microscopically examined by political pundits throughout the campaign. The first vote did not prove that Cameron was a sure thing, even though he led when the ballots were counted. The second vote was so close that the officials of the well-organized convention decided a recount was necessary to ensure accuracy. The waiting and closeness of the count bred nail-biting tension.

Despite ballot "floor-dealing," pressure, and trade-offs, personal bitterness was almost non-existent. The delegates seemed to have made their decisions on each ballot and carried out the vote with precision and good humour. Cameron boasted that he was a new and different political broom, and appeared credible when he promised to change customs and political practices in Nova Scotia while opposing patronage. He had expounded reasonable and believable political plans, and he was elected leader and premier on the third ballot.

Donald Cameron, often appearing to react too quickly, especially to media people, suddenly found that being premier was not a cakewalk. The new premier had hardly moved into his office when he was faced with defeat because of the erosion of his slim legislative majority. The new government was also deprived of a vote because of the vacancy that had occurred in Halifax Atlantic when John Buchanan was appointed to the Senate. The voters in that riding, once safe Tory territory, were reported to be very angry with Cameron and the government.

The opposition cried foul when the new premier delayed opening the Legislature in midwinter, as had been the custom in Nova Scotia. Cameron compounded their anger when he called a by-election for August 1991 in the vacant Halifax Atlantic seat. Midsummer elections were viewed as unusual and had the potential for a small voter turnout, due to holidays. Claims of manipulating the democratic process abounded.

Just as the opposition were spreading the impression that the new premier was avoiding a vote, opposition Liberal MLA Guy Brown suddenly accused the Cameron government of being about to call a snap election. Cameron defused the issue with a smile, saying that the opposition was criticizing him for not holding a vote and also for planning a vote. The potential of a popular cry for the opposition again fizzled out because of their own contradictions.

In his first month as premier, Donald Cameron was faced with a slipping majority, post-election confusion, and media accusations that he was continuing patronage in the awarding of government business. The patronage charge arose from a contractor's claim that his bid to build a bridge was cheaper than that of the Cameron supporter who won the contract. Cameron, obviously angry, explained the contractor's claims away, and the furore subsided. It looked like things were settling down, and then Cameron made his first moves to cut government spending.

Citing wastefulness, the government discharged various political appointees of the Buchanan government, including long-time chauffeur Jack Wheatly, who had driven six premiers during his tenure. That was followed by the announced sale of the two expensive autos kept for use by the premier's office. Donald Cameron, hoping to demonstrate good management by frugal example, said that he would drive his own car. He asked the media and public to allow him the chance to show them he meant what he said about good government.

Just as it appeared that Cameron might get a chance without the ghost of John Buchanan haunting him, *Frank* magazine broke the story of Buchanan's financial difficulties and the monthly payments to him by the PC party. Cameron was again on a political hot seat. It was a stern and angry Cameron who called a press conference after the *Frank* magazine exposé. Cameron announced that a blind trust in the former premier's favour had been discovered, and added that he had turned the matter over to the RCMP for investigation.

Cameron's dislike of Buchanan was no secret. Mrs. Buchanan allegedly despised Cameron too. But the new premier's call for an RCMP investigation made enemies for him when it could have been avoided. The reactions would cause a rift which would not soon be forgotten or forgiven. Common rumours were that Mr. Cameron's self-proclaimed adviser, "Pizza Joe" Stewart, engineered the Buchanan revelations by gossip. Stewart has denied it. But it backfired on the new premier, whoever did it.

A by-election was called in Buchanan's old seat, Halifax Atlantic, in August 1991. The voters spoke decisively by rejecting the publicly squabbling Tories in favour of a Kennedy-like NDP candidate named Robert Chisholm. Liberal leader Vince MacLean, mortally wounded by that by-election, used an old business custom according to which a victim is always called for; MacLean fired his affable, talented assistant, Al Hollingsworth, an act which would lead to his own undoing. Neither Cameron nor MacLean was out of the swamp of troubles from the Buchanan years — yet.

28

THE I-KNOW-NOTHING SCANDAL

THE NIGHT-TIME TV RERUNS USED TO FEATURE A SERIES called *Hogan's Heroes* about a Second World War prisoner-of-war camp operated by the Germans, but dominated by shrewd allied POWs. One particularly likeable German guard, Sergeant Hans Schultz, had a penchant for not knowing or seeing very much. When he wanted to avoid self-incrimination or deny knowledge of an event, he used his favourite expression: "I—knoow nothiinngk!"

After Premier Cameron called the RCMP in to investigate the Buchanan blind trust, Buchanan's power, prestige, influence, and popularity declined. Buchanan was severely distressed, and lost twenty-two pounds. Tories who had once been trying to jump over each other to curry his friendship avoided him and assumed the Sergeant Schultz position. Even close associates tried to distance themselves from him, and people who used to claim they were in the know suddenly developed political amnesia. As news and rumours circulated, the Nova Scotia Liquor Commission warehouse, which was developed by the

Uniacke Properties Group, was featured in the media as a source of police attention. A part-time ATV news reader named Rick Grant tried to lead the media charge. Mr. Grant was liked by Buchanan. At one stage, in response to a request, Buchanan was going to give Rick Grant an appointment to a job. When that fact surfaced, a powerful Tory named Bob Stappels was very unhappy, and for some reason the subject of Grant's job never came up again.

But Stappels was involved in the Uniacke Properties Group, which may have been Rick Grant's motive. Virtually all the people involved in a real estate deal with the Nova Scotia Liquor Commission were interviewed by reporters and police, so it was obvious that there was some connection to John Buchanan's blind trust. (The facts of the Nova Scotia liquor deal are available in the 1989 Auditor General's Report.)

Bob Stappels was one of the main shareholders of Uniacke Properties, which had developed the Nova Scotia Liquor Commission property for the government. During the RCMP investigation, in April 1991, I met him on Tower Road when my wife and I were out for a walk. He said that he was not making any statements to police, and that one of his business associates had already received legal advice on the subject of such statements. I told Stappels that one of my main memories was John Grant's unprovable contention that an agent for some developer had offered a $250,000 bribe, payable over five years, to obtain the contract on the project. Stappels said words to the effect that that kind of nonsensical talk only fires up speculation and should not be broadcast. My wife said, "Certainly John Grant and Ted Crease, both of whom are deceased, won't be telling the story." Stappels initially knew nothing of Buchanan's blind trust. Later he did know.

Bob Bruce, who helped Crease organize the blind trust, was interviewed several times by police, which seemed routine. But he was very concerned about his wife's distress over the constant media harassment at weird hours of the night. Also, the fact that Bruce's firm, Coopers and Lybrand, was being mentioned in the same stories, which seemed to link their business with the government to the blind trust, was disturbing to him. A rumour circulated that the police were using wiretaps to collect information. One media person who was active in the political story had a distinctive, almost effeminate, voice over the phone. One night after I heard the wire-tap rumour, I phoned Bruce's South Shore home. I changed my voice to a falsetto whisper and said, "Oh Bobbie, I think you should let us show the world your blind truss." Then I added, "Truss, not trust, you big silly." I fooled him at first, but then he realized it was me. He said, "You bastard, now they think I'm hiding something else."

Then Buchanan phoned me and said that he was very disturbed that the reports were so poor and lacked fairness. He felt very bad that two men who acted with Bob Bruce as trustees, Dr. Earle Reid and the Rev. Monsignor Murphy, were being dragged through the TV publicity when they were only well-intentioned participants. Buchanan asked me to try to get Bob Bruce to have a press conference to correct the terrible allegations being circulated. The media were missing facts, and distorting the story. I doubted that Mrs. Bruce would want Bob to speak publicly, but, when I asked, Bob said "yes." I called Dan O'Connell of the CBC to outline my proposal, and he seemed interested, subject to the approval of his TV news editor. Bob Bruce later did a show with O'Connell, who presented both sides of the story in a fair manner. In the meantime, I called Dean Jobb of the *Chronicle-Herald*, hoping to make a similar arrangement with him; in exchange, I asked that a correcting story about me be run too. My lawyer, Dale Dunlop, confirms his knowledge of Jobb's dealing with me.

Jobb came to my office about the proposal, and agreed to the conditions. To be sure, I asked him to consult his paper's editor, and I made notes of his agreement. I then cleared what I would tell Mr. Jobb with Bob Bruce. I consulted lawyer Dale Dunlop, of Walker, Dunlop, in Halifax, who agreed to make the final exchange with Dean Jobb. I lent Dunlop a draft chapter from this book, which detailed accurately the facts about the blind trust, for him to convey to Jobb. Dean Jobb met at least twice with Mr. Dunlop and was given the facts.

The *Chronicle-Herald* then ran a fair and comprehensive story about the Buchanan blind trust and presented the information correctly. But Jobb never did the correcting story on me, even though I gave him documents, including a sworn statement by a witness. When my lawyer, Dale Dunlop, asked Jobb why it had not been run, he said that he had been away on holidays. I could not believe that the paper would agree to something, and then not do it, as their reputation was good, even among people who despised them. Jobb gave me the same excuse he had given Dunlop.

We consulted a well-placed person on the condition his/her identity be held secret and we were reliably informed that senior management at the paper knew nothing of the Jobb agreement, and I believe that. We were advised to report the matter to the Press Council, but I wouldn't bother. Months later, I was taking a course at Dalhousie University and told that story to a senior lawyer. He said, "People who play games with media power usually end up in hot water."

I believed that there was a genuine mystery connected to the Nova Scotia Liquor Commission deal, and that thought was reinforced when I saw Fred Greene, a shareholder of Uniacke Properties, being interviewed on television. Mr. Greene said he was pressured to give money to the PC party and was "touched-up," pushed, and harassed for a donation. I did not cover any of those accounts for the PC party, but I couldn't believe Mr. Greene would tell a story like that on television during an RCMP investigation, unless it was true.

In the meantime, as rumours about police wire taps circulated, a Micmac Indian friend of mine called me and first spoke in English, and then suddenly switched to Micmac, knowing full well that my entire vocabulary in that language consists of about three cusswords. It was a joke, of course, at the expense of anyone who might be listening. When I saw him in person, I said, "You SOB! What did you say on the telephone in Micmac?" He replied, "I believe the approximate English translation would be: 'Stop peeking at women's buoyancy compensators.' I wanted them to think you're a peeper." Bob Bruce liked the story and said it was fitting revenge for the phone joke I had pulled on him.

Finally, it was my turn with the RCMP. When Corporal David Manthorne of the RCMP Commercial Crime Branch called and asked if I would agree to be interviewed, I said I would cooperate. Corporal Manthorne opened the interview by saying the following words to me, which I acquired from a tape recording of the interview:

MANTHORNE: *The date is the 28th of November, 1991. I am speaking to Mr. Donald Ripley. My name is Corporal David Manthorne of the RCMP Commercial Crime Branch stationed here in Halifax, Nova Scotia. We are presently at Suite 305, 6080 Young Street, Halifax, which is the office of the Commercial Crime Branch of the RCMP for this province.*

Mr. Ripley, as I indicated earlier, I am conducting an investigation into the circumstances surrounding the solicitation of several individuals for potential contributions or donations for the PC Party of Nova Scotia, beginning back in 1985. Those donors, in particular the Corkum and Canterbury Group members (which became Uniacke Group), claim that they were solicited for donations which were supposedly for the PC Party of Nova Scotia, and were ultimately told by the fund-raisers that the PC Party was badly in need of financial assistance following the 1984 provincial election. It is now believed that all of the donations solicited from those Corkum and Canterbury Group members actually went to the John Buchanan Family trust fund which had been established to assist then premier John Buchanan with his personal financial problems, and that the donors were unaware that their contributions were being used for purposes other than what they were originally told. Enquiries to date have indicated that you were involved in the initial solicitation of donations from these Corkum and Canterbury Group members, along with the late Ted Crease. I have also been advised that several, if not all, of the donation cheques obtained from the Corkum and Canterbury Group members were turned over to you and that those donations ultimately went to the Buchanan Family trust rather than to the PC Party of Nova Scotia. I would like to ask you a number of questions concerning your involvement or knowledge of the John Buchanan Family trust fund, as well as the normal fund-raising procedures followed by the PC Party of Nova Scotia, which I understand you were personally involved with for many years. Because

I am a peace officer conducting a criminal investigation with respect to the above-mentioned solicitation, I would like to read you the standard police warning. Do you have a question?

The interview with Corporal Manthorne lasted for more than three hours and, when transcribed, filled 120 pages. It covered the matters of fund-raising, but mostly it dwelt on the meeting that Bob Stappels requested me to arrange with Ted Crease to discuss the large donation that the Uniacke shareholders wished to make. I told Corporal Manthorne that I did not solicit the Canterbury (Uniacke) Group, and in the discussion of their political giving, I pointed out Mr. Greene's claim that he had been pressured. I also felt that there was also a mystery in the case, and the person covering the account was a shareholder in the same company as Mr. Greene, so why would he pressure anybody?

I explained the visit to my office by Bob Stappels with his company lawyer and shareholder Walter Thompson. I also explained that Walter Thompson was a brother of Stephen Thompson, who was a close business associate of Ted Crease, so I did not believe that Crease pressured the Uniacke Group.

Manthorne told me that the Canterbury (Uniacke) Group had informed him that they did not know that they were giving money to the Buchanan blind trust, but thought that they were donating to the PC party. I laughed at that assertion because that company had been written a thank-you letter by the Toronto lawyer at Fraser Beatty who had set up the blind trust. While initially Bob Stappels did not know of the blind trust for Buchanan, it was Stappels who showed me a copy of the letter and instructed me to ask Crease and Bruce to stop the letters being sent out, because they increased the chance of Buchanan's troubles being leaked to the press.

I asked Manthorne two questions: "Did the shareholders of Uniacke admit they got such a letter?" and "Had they continued to donate after they got it?" Manthorne seemed to grasp my points as he said that an RCMP inspector asked the same questions. Then he said that one of that group claimed that he had left a cheque with me for the blind trust. I said, "That's possible, but I don't recall it, and besides, everybody left cheques at my office for the PC party."

Later I phoned Bob Stappels and asked him if he collected cheques from his associates, and he said "yes." I asked if he ever gave any to me and he admitted that he didn't know. Then he said, "Maybe I gave them to Suzanne Huett [the PC fund-raising coordinator]." I said, "Impossible, she was living in northern Ontario at that time." Stappels couldn't remember to whom he had given the cheque, but he did remember the Crease meeting in my office.

Next, Corporal Manthorne phoned, and asked me more about that meeting in my office with Crease, Thompson, and Stappels, and I not only recalled it, but remembered that they wanted to hide their donation. I had known Crease for twenty years, and he was one of the most honest people I had ever met. I told Manthorne that it would be unkind and unfair to suggest that Crease could have done anything to mislead the Uniacke Group, especially as he was dead and couldn't defend himself. Manthorne seemed satisfied. Later I was told that guilty people try to pass the buck to associates, and I had not only not done that, but defended Crease.

I decided to phone Stephen Thompson. I wanted to hear the other version of the Uniacke claims in more detail, as the RCMP had provided little information. Stephen told me that some of the shareholders of Uniacke had been led to believe that the deal was a political decision and they had to give. He would only say: "They know it was not you, and it was not Crease." I was mystified, but he would not elaborate. I reported this to Corporal Manthorne during a phone call, and I believe he interviewed Stephen Thompson.

The next time I heard from Manthorne was in early 1992. I was wrong about the purpose of the call, as I expected more questions about the blind trust, a subject I was sick and tired of and bored by, especially the press coverage. I was not particularly fair with him, asking if he had interviewed the three Appeal Court judges involved, or if I was the only small fry left in the matter of the blind-trust public gossip. I was miffed, and went on an unnecessary verbal attack, saying that I was sick of questions and couldn't afford a lawyer.

Corporal Manthorne said, "The police do not give advice, but I don't believe you need a lawyer." I believe I recorded the call.

Shortly after that, the RCMP announced publicly that there would be no criminal charges arising from the Buchanan blind trust.

29

THE THUMB ON THE
SCALE

A N OLDER ACQUAINTANCE OF MINE GRADUATED from Harvard University with a law degree during the Depression. Realizing that he came from humble roots, I asked him how he paid the outrageous tuition at Harvard during those lean years. He said, with a chuckle, "My father owned a small meat market. He sold every customer seven-eighths of a pound of meat and one-eighth of a pound of his thumb gently and discreetly pressed down on the scale."

In December 1989, the Nova Scotia royal commission on the Donald Marshall Jr. prosecution publicly reported their findings. It proved that there was a thumb on the scale of justice. The digest of that report stated:

The criminal justice system failed Donald Marshall, Jr. at virtually every turn; from his arrest and wrongful conviction for murder, in 1971, up to, and even beyond his acquittal by the Court of Appeal in 1983. The tragedy of that failure is compounded by evidence that this miscarriage of justice could and should have been prevented, or at least corrected quickly, if those involved in the system had carried out their duties in a professional and/or competent manner. That they did not is due, in part at least, to the fact that Donald Marshal, Jr. is a Native.

One of my burning desires in politics was to change the way judges were selected and to improve the justice system. Harold Gloade, a Micmac Indian, said after reading the commission report on the Marshall prosecution, "It was ever thus in Nova Scotia, which is Alabama North if you are not white or are socially disadvantaged." Racial prejudice is not subtle in Nova Scotia. Some people found humour or satisfaction in the reported statement by the murderer, Ebsary: "This is for you, Black man." I overheard a lawyer, who is now a judge, repeatedly use that sentence as a sick joke and substitute the word "boy" for "man." Some judges are far from being free of bias in Nova Scotia. I know of one judge who was said to be fair, even to the accused in the worst circumstances of a murder case, unless there was sex outside marriage involved, or somebody had his pants off, or the colour of his skin was not white!

The report of the royal commission into the wrongful conviction of Donald Marshall Jr. is now history. His father, Donald Marshall Sr., lived to see his son's long struggle end with freedom, compensation, and vindication; the fight, in all likelihood, contributed to the father's untimely death.

The royal commission's report caused the Nova Scotia government to complain to the body responsible for examining the conduct of judges in Canada. The report of that body might be considered colourless by some observers. Not one of the people involved in the prosecution of Donald Marshall Jr. was disciplined, despite the royal commission's exposé, including those who made the decisions.

Does "colourless" mean white, as in whitewash? Many people would likely answer in the affirmative.

Donald Marshall Jr. was eventually financially compensated, but even that process (originally) lent itself to pettiness by an employee in the Department of the Attorney General.

One of the best articles produced about the Donald Marshall Jr. matter was written by Parker Barss Donham, a journalist of strong opinions. He also wrote about the other system in Nova Scotia, that of the Nova Scotia Barristers' Society, the body responsible for the regulation and discipline of lawyers in Nova Scotia.

Donham called it "the Barristers' Protective Society."

Based on personal experience, I can take no issue with Donham's opinion on the subject of self-disciplining bodies of any so-called professional body. I was once threatened by a lawyer who now holds a responsible position. When I told him I would file a complaint with the Barristers' Society, he told me that, if I did, he'd look after a relative of mine who was an aspiring lawyer. I didn't push my luck, but I think I can prove my statement.

The Law Society of Upper Canada is also a unique organization. I once complained about a Toronto lawyer opening and reading my mail, my daughter's mail, my daughter-in-law's mail, and my income tax return. A witness gave a tape-recorded statement proving it. In almost two years of waiting, the only satisfaction I got was a letter saying his conduct was not *unacceptable*. Go figure.

Kids tell it like it is. When I related that story to a youngster I know, the response was: "They ingest with a straw."

30

AFTERGLOW

LIBERAL LEADER VINCENT MACLEAN WAS BURDENED BY his party's tainted trust funds and, after a painful review of his leadership, resigned as leader in 1992. The new leader of the Liberal party, Dr. John Savage, asked his party to review the origin and quality of the trust funds; that was done. In 1992, Dr. Savage announced that the Liberal party would donate more than $1 million to the Treasury of the Province of Nova Scotia because, in the "old days," upwards of $1.3 million may have been raised by questionable practices.

The press is still not happy that the Liberals retained some of the trust money, which they say all originated through the illegal charging of commissions by fund-raisers on companies doing business in Nova Scotia. Next, Tory premier Donald Cameron gave his opinion, which is basically that the money is tainted and should all be donated to Nova Scotia.

Then a weird journalist, who is not considered to rate a Christmas card, but perhaps a sympathy card from most Tories, said, "The Tory fund should also become the property of the Province of Nova Scotia." In response to that statement, a Tory fund-raiser, who wishes to remain anonymous, said to me, "If we turned our fund over to the province and they accepted, it would be great for us because we're $200,000 in the hole."

It seems that, in these times, gifts to political causes do not rate high on people's lists of things to do — and no wonder. In 1992, David Hensbee, an executive assistant to Tory cabinet minister Tom McInnes, was forced to resign when it was revealed that he had acquired a confidential Provincial Health Services hospital tax list of citizens and companies doing business in Nova Scotia from a civil servant, and had delivered it to PC party fund-raisers, who had then used it to solicit donations. Over $40,000 was raised, and when the story broke in the press, Premier Cameron instructed the Finance Committee to return the gifts to the contributors, despite the fact that some people didn't want the money back.

David Hensbee was not charged, but had to resign, and the civil servant was charged, tried, and convicted of releasing the confidential information and fined $200. Hensbee next surprised and angered Premier Cameron by announcing that he would seek the Tory nomination in a new provincial constituency. Premier Cameron is supposed to have said of Hensbee becoming an accredited Tory candidate, "Over my dead body!"

Some of the survivors of the politics of Nova Scotia and Ottawa are worth mentioning:

Suzanne Huett, PC fund-raising coordinator, said recently, "Personally, I'd sooner be in Philadelphia than go through another scandal."

John Buchanan does not like Ottawa, where he is now a member of the Senate. He told me he hears from Joe MacDonald periodically; from my mother, who is a pal of his; and from me. He has not heard from many others, including Fred Dickson. Buchanan still owes a massive amount of money and cannot choose bankruptcy as an option because he is a senator. Mavis Buchanan, his wife, is not very well, and is deeply wounded that people believe he profited from public life.

Joe MacDonald was appointed chairman of the Nova Scotia Power Corporation by Buchanan in 1979. In 1992, the Nova Scotia Power Corporation was privatized, in the largest public-equity deal in Canadian history. RBC Dominion Securities managed the transaction.

Fred Dickson has pretty much dropped out of sight. His firm, Patterson, Kitz, did legal work for Westray Mines, assisting them in making a deal with loan guarantees from the Province of Nova Scotia. Since twenty-six miners were killed in an accident at the Westray mine, they have engaged other legal counsel. But Patterson, Kitz did not suffer a lack of legal work in the privatization of the Nova Scotia Power Corporation.

Elmer MacKay phoned me on the morning of the Westray disaster. I had not heard from him for four years. He wanted to discuss the 1987 blind-trust problems with his own account, which *The Globe and Mail* of Toronto was pursuing (and later published). Mr. MacKay says that he is again contemplating leaving public life and has another personal relationship with a lady, following his second divorce.

Robert Bruce, CA, has left Nova Scotia for employment reasons. He phones regularly and says he enjoys walking down the street in the province where he now resides without being recognized. I constantly threaten to reveal his location to the press.

Dr. Ernest Johnson was a medical adviser at the Nova Scotia Workers Compensation Board. Recently he went bankrupt. He is luckier than Buchanan.

Michael Zareski is reportedly still not employed. He lives in Cape Breton with a psychic, and he periodically writes public letters to newspapers.

Robert Stappels has placed some of his business affairs in the hands of a receiver. He, too, is suffering from the recession.

Mark Cleary, Buchanan's friend of whom Mr. Zareski spoke, was fined $4,000 for influence peddling. So far no appeal has been lodged.

Donald Power, former Deputy Minister of Public Works,

Government Services, whom Buchanan asked to stay on as manager of construction at the government Camp Hill Hospital, has troubles. Because he wrote his own new contract with the government, the RCMP charged him with breach of trust; even though the Provincial Management Board approved the contract, he was found guilty and fined $5,000 by Judge Nancy Bateman (formerly of Patterson, Kitz). He appealed and won.

A.M. (Sandy) Cameron claims that he has no intention of running again in his old riding of Guysborough, where he and his wife are enjoying life. He thanked me for asking, and said to tell Mr. Medjuck, "Thank you for your support."

Vincent MacLean has resigned as an MLA and is slowly revising his image and his views so that it will appear as if he is not interested in a federal government appointment.

Billie Joe MacLean owns and operates a successful night spot in northern Nova Scotia. He is likely to resurface as a federal political candidate, with mistletoe on the back of his suitcoat.

Gerald A. Regan has returned to the practise of law in Halifax, Nova Scotia. He is with Patterson, Kitz (of course).

Patrick Nowlan has left the Tory caucus and ran as an independent for his old federal seat. He still does not answer his mail or return his phone calls. He may be wasting his efforts.

Harry How managed Pat Nowlan's campaign as an independent because he did not approve of Brian Mulroney. Harry won the Tory nomination in Kings South for the provincial election against the sitting Tory MLA, Derek Kimball. So Kimball ran as an independent. The result was that the Liberals won that section of King's County for the first time since 1949.

Billie Gillis, Liberal MLA, provided some statistical data for this book in the name of accuracy.

Ralph Medjuck, developer, offered many times to lend me money when I was a PC fund-raiser. *I refused.* After I was unemployed, I asked him for a loan. *He refused.*

"Pizza Joe" Stewart, a former director of the federal Atlantic Canada Opportunity Agency (a lending agency), is frequently mentioned in *Frank* magazine.

Al Hollingsworth, journalist, broadcaster, former executive director to Liberal leader Vincent MacLean, has threatened to publish my actual lifetime batting average if I reveal that he assisted me in writing this book. Thus, I publicly deny — categorically — that information he supplied was of any help to me.

Frank Nichols, a broker, complained to me for fourteen years that he should get business from the government of Nova Scotia. I hope he is (still) making the same progress.

Parker Barss Donham, like former Quebec and federal Liberal cabinet minister Eric Kierans, was against the Charlottetown Accord. Unlike Mr. Kierans, he did not first get paid by the government to work on the hearings, and announce his "no" vote later.

Harry Flemming has not joined the PC party; he writes a first-class trivia column in the Halifax *Sunday Daily News*.

Donald Cameron became premier of Nova Scotia by winning his party's leadership at a convention. Two years and three months later, on May 25, 1993, his party was annihilated in a general election. One angry Tory, among those who blamed Cameron for causing much of Buchanan's grief, said, "King Donnie turfed Buchanan's clan, and still thought he could win. Up his kilt and he should quit now!"

Dr. Alfred Doucet is, or was, before an unfortunate illness, a paid federal employee; he and his brother are now federal lobbyists.

Austin G.E. Taylor, former political force and chairman of Scotia McLeod, is reportedly suffering health discomfort. His firm did not lead the privatization of the Nova Scotia Power Corporation, a fact which likely contributed to his discomfort. I didn't help.

Thomas E. Kierans, former president of Scotia McLeod, helped engineer the Doucet Company. He is head of the research institute named after the late C.D. Howe and is equally active and almost as effective as his father, Eric Kierans, in most public utterances.

Dr. Earle Reid is practising medicine again full time, after heading a health-care study for the Province of Nova Scotia. He is consulted the world over, except in Nova Scotia, where the study was mothballed. He is one of the finest human beings I have ever met.

Donald F. Ripley I am disgraced by the findings of the Investment Dealers Association of Canada. I was found guilty of leaking the information of the Hon. Stewart McInnes to Liberal MP Sheila Copps and of allowing employees to privately raise funds for small businesses in Nova Scotia. I was fined $115,000, including costs, and was suspended for two years. However, I am indefinitely suspended, as I cannot, nor would I if I could, pay the fine.

Mindful of the fact that every accused and convicted person claims "innocence," or "I was screwed," or some similarly weak excuse, I will only say this: "If you believe I did those things, that is your privilege."

However, if you compare the punishment given me with the paltry fines of $1,500 to $10,000 handed out to more than a hundred other brokers in the last ten years — brokers who committed offences involving *actual damage or misconduct* with clients' funds — you may wish to consider my treatment a tad excessive. My Indian friend calls it "a white-wash." Michael Milken only got two years, and it's claimed he collected $500 million. Oh well!

I am still John Buchanan's friend, and I know many people who benefited from his friendship in material ways. I did not, and I still admire him. To the rest who ignore him (now), I offer John Diefenbaker's words: "I wish them well and if that rhymes with anything they're welcome to it."

INDEX

Akerman, Jeremy, 201
Allen, Reginald, 41
Ames, A. E. and Company, 51
Angus, David, 164-65
Arenberg, Earl, 23
Atkins, Norman, 148
Atlantic Securities, 115-16

Bain, George, 182
Balcom, Eric, 26, 104
Bank of Nova Scotia, 115-16
Barkhouse, Ronald, 73
Barrow, A. I. (Irv) 20, 23, 30, 45, 125-26
Bayart, Kevin, 65-67
Bishop, Corporal, 124, 126
Brison, George, 8, 216
Brison, Kip, 143
Brown, Garnet, 20, 23, 27, 30
Brown, Guy, 201-02, 224
Brown, John, 6-7
Bruce, Robert, 114, 117-21, 139, 162, 228-29, 241
Buchanan, John M., 8, 31-36, 53, 54, 62, 98, 148, 158, 159, 183, 196, 221, 225, 240; as party leader, 37-41; as premier, 79-82, 86-91, 94, 101-08, 131-32; energy company, 129-40; financial problems, 109-21, 161-63; judgeship for Levy, 200-01; lost effective control of government after 1988, 207-19; 1978 election, 70-72; 1984 election, 149, 152, 198; 1988 election, 197, 201-06; RCMP investigation into blind trust, 227-34; Smith's appointment as agent general in London, 208-10; Thornhill's debt settlement, 94-96; Zareski's alle-

gations, 213-19
Buchanan, Mavis Forsyth, 32-33, 37, 62, 108, 117-18, 222, 225, 240-41
Buckrill, George, 170-71
Burns Fry, 29, 47
Busche, Roy, 70, 107, 110-1, 116, 119, 148, 171

Callaghan, Clair, 223
Cameron, Donald, 8, 98-99, 108, 201, 209-10, 223-27, 239-40, 243
Cameron, A. M. (Sandy), 94, 96, 102-06, 127, 130, 142-43, 151-52, 156, 157, 242
Canada Cement, 15
Canadian Lawyer, 191
Carroll, James, 4
Chase, "Goat", 6-7
Chernin, Martin, 189
Cherry, Douglas, 117, 118
Chipman, David R., 39, 57-58, 60, 72, 88, 110, 112-13, 119, 124, 147, 166-67, 183, 187-88, 216
Chisholm, Robert, 225
Chretien, Jean, 4
Clairtone Sound, 15
Clark, Joe, 89-90
Clarke, Joseph (Pugwash Joe), 25-26, 55, 61
Clarke, Lorne, 166
Cleary, Mark, 214-15, 241
Cleyle, Victor, 21-22, 28
Cogger, Michel, 137
Coles, Gordon, 97-98, 156-57
Comeau, Louis, 211
Connolly, Harold, 14-15
Cooper, Austin, 125-26
Cooper, George, 93

·